Raise the Roof

Books by Pat Summitt with Sally Jenkins

REACH FOR THE SUMMIT

➤Raise
the Roof

The Inspiring Inside Story
of the Tennessee Lady Vols'
Undefeated 1997–98 Season

Pat Summitt

with Sally Jenkins

BROADWAY BOOKS ➤ NEW YORK

BROADWAY

A hardcover edition of this book was published in 1998 by Broadway Books.

RAISE THE ROOF. Copyright © 1998 by Pat Summitt. All rights reserved. Printed in the United States of America. No part of this book may be reproduced or transmitted in any form or by any means, electronic or mechanical, including photocopying, recording, or by any information storage and retrieval system, without written permission from the publisher. For information, address Broadway Books, a division of Random House, Inc., 1540 Broadway, New York, NY 10036.

Broadway Books titles may be purchased for business or promotional use or for special sales. For information, please write to: Special Markets Department, Random House, Inc., 1540 Broadway, New York, NY 10036.

BROADWAY BOOKS and its logo, a letter B bisected on the diagonal, are trademarks of Broadway Books, a division of Random House, Inc.

First trade paperback edition published 1999.

The Library of Congress has catalogued the hardcover edition as:
Summitt, Pat Head, 1953–
    Raise the roof : the inspiring inside story of the Tennessee Lady
Vols' undefeated 1997–98 season / Pat Summitt with Sally Jenkins.—
1st ed.
      p. cm.
   ISBN 0-7679-0328-5 (hardcover)
    1. University of Tennessee, Knoxville—Basketball. 2. Lady
Volunteers (Basketball team) 3. Summitt, Pat Head, 1953– .
I. Jenkins, Sally. II. Title.
GV885.43.U58S86 1998
796.323'63'0976885—dc21   98-36854
                                        CIP

ISBN 0-7679-0329-3 (paperback)

09 13 12

> To the players, their parents,

and the Tennessee staff,

all of whom are an

irreplaceable part of the

Lady Vols family.

Pat Summitt

AUTHOR'S NOTE

THE REAL AUTHORS of this book were the players. They ran the court. They raised the banners. Most importantly, they permitted their personal stories to be told.

Unfortunately, NCAA rules prohibit the use of their photographs. Otherwise they would have been on the cover.

This account of Tennessee's 1997–98 season was based in part on journals kept by Pat Summitt and by Sally Jenkins, who traveled with the team throughout the NCAA tournament. However, a great deal more of what's recorded here was related by the Tennessee Lady Vols themselves, all of whom agreed to participate in this project and sat for a series of interviews after the season was concluded.

Family members also contributed. June Holdsclaw, Robert Geter, Joanne Geter, Ken and Peggy Jolly, Wanda Catchings, Harvey Catchings, Bertha Randall, Sue Carney, and Sheryl Elzy gave of their time, their family histories, and their insights.

PART ONE

➤➤➤ Playground
Lullabies

Q & A with Semeka Randall (Freshman guard)

What made you go to Tennessee?

Pat's been with me since the ninth grade. She's just always been there. I had some second thoughts after I visited Connecticut, because it could have worked out for me there. But she called me up and started yelling at me. She said, "Look here. I'm only going to tell you this one time. I've wanted to be your coach since you were in the ninth grade. Since day one. And you know that. So you make your decision." I was like, wow, Pat's yelling at me.

She recruited you by yelling at you?

I thought that was cool.

CHAPTER ONE

No Girls Allowed

I'M A FORTY-FIVE-YEAR-OLD woman with a controlling nature and crow's feet from squinting into the country sun, and it's just not like me to act the way I did. To be so free with my feelings, and to wear blue jeans, of all things. Ordinarily, I'm in charge. I wear a suit and a perpetual glare. I'm a coach, so I take the issue of control personally. I've always seen the movements of players on a basketball court as an extension of myself, like puppets on a string. Their failures were my fault, their successes my responsibility. I demanded that they act like Pat, and think like Pat. A row of little Patlings. So when, exactly, did I let go? When did I decide to let this team run? And when did they start running me?

The truth is, I loved them. Of course, all coaches say they love their teams. When really, you love some of them more than others, and some of them you don't like at all. But love or like, I've *always* yelled at them. I yell, because I'm a yeller. I'm a yeller, and so I yell. My voice gets so hoarse it sounds like tires crunching over gravel. During the season, I go through economy-sized packages of throat lozenges.

With this team, though, I was different.

My top assistant coach, Mickie DeMoss, was the first person to suggest I should go softer on them. As our recruiting coordinator, she knew the strengths and sympathized with the flaws of the 1997–98 Tennessee Lady Volunteers more deeply than any of us. Something in them got to her, early. Maybe it was the fact that they were so young and unguarded, or that they had such large eyes, begging to be taught. "Pat, don't yell at this team," Mickie said, back in the summertime. "They *want* to play for you."

We were driving through a desolate strip of Texas on a recruiting trip. I said, "What do you mean?" I'd been shouting for twenty-three years, as long as I had been the head coach at Tennessee. It had always worked before. We had been to the NCAA Final Four fourteen times, and won five national championships in ten years. But Mickie said I ought to consider something new. For once, I should try not raising my voice.

Mickie said, "They're different. They're spirited, and I don't want to see that spirit broken."

I thought about it for a minute.

I said, "Well, I can't promise you.

Mickie said, warningly, "Pat . . ."

I said, "All right, I'll *try*."

I'm not saying I didn't have my snappish moments. It wasn't like I underwent a complete personality transplant. But *something* happened to me. In the 1997–98 Lady Vols I finally met a group of players more driven than I am. They were harder on themselves than I ever could have been. That was clear from the moment they stepped on campus.

The funny thing was, what turned out to be the toughest game of the year may have been played before the season ever started. And I wasn't even there for it. I should have known right then that this team was out of the ordinary.

It was a sweltering night in the dregs of summer, August 23, 1997, a Saturday, their first day on the University of Tennessee grounds. What's the first thing they did? They went looking for a basketball. Long before anyone put on a Tennessee uniform, the whole team, a dozen young women clad in baggy, mismatching rayon shorts and raggedy T-shirts, gathered to play pickup. It was a contest of us against ourselves. A showdown. The Tennessee Lady Vols against the Tennessee Lady Vols.

There were no scoreboards, no officials, no crowds, no coaches. It was just pure game, a strictly private affair. I didn't even know about it until after the fact—and I probably still don't know the half of it. You could ask one of our players for the full story, but I doubt they would tell you because, like most great teams, they're a secretive bunch. And even if they did tell you, you probably wouldn't understand much of what they said. As someone remarked not long ago, the Lady Vols aren't a team, they're a cult. They have a tendency to speak in code. For instance, a ball is not a ball, it's "the rock," and you don't shoot it, you "throw it down." Your best friend is "your dog." If something is great, it's "tight," or if it's silly, it's "sadiddy." And this isn't a beginning, it's "the jump."

So it's up to me to tell the story.

The thing about that pickup game is that right from "the jump," it was no everyday contest. It was more than that. It was an initiation. Earlier in the day, four new freshmen had arrived, a quartet of high school All-Americans with big games and even bigger reputations. They were being called the single best recruiting class in history. And maybe they were.

But each one of them came to Tennessee with a host of private insecurities.

One by one, the freshmen parked in back of Humes Hall on the Tennessee campus and began unloading their bags and carrying them to the suite they would occupy together for the next year. They drove in from various points of the compass, from Ohio, Texas, Pennsylvania, and South Carolina. The 1997–98 Lady Vols were about to arrive.

> > >

KRISTEN "ACE" CLEMENT had one thought in her mind as she pulled up to the dorm. "Please God, don't let it be like high school." She was a glamorous left-handed point guard from Broomall, Pennsylvania, with a floppy ponytail and an almost illusory passing ability, a sleight-of-hand artist who could make the ball seem to flicker around the court. And she had a remarkable record to her credit—she had broken Wilt

Chamberlain's all-time city high school scoring mark in Philadelphia. But Ace was to prove fragile, as I would discover.

Ace was the youngest of six children, the daughter of a fifty-five-year-old divorcee named Sue Carney. I knew Ace wasn't the only one starting a new life that day. So was Sue. When Ace went south, Sue simply decided to go with her. Sue had reared her six kids largely on her own, despite the fact that she had struggled to work ever since complications from back surgery had left her with a long-term disability. She was scraping by on savings and a military pension.

Sue wanted to get out of the cold northeast, having spent her whole adult life moving from job to job in Pennsylvania, Massachusetts, and New Hampshire. Sue imagined that the south represented an easier kind of living. So when Ace was recruited by Tennessee, Sue made up her mind. She visited Knoxville with Ace and found that the pace was slow and the people friendly. It was perfect—this way she could change her life, and follow Ace's career at the same time.

Ace and Sue were wracked by nerves the day they left Philadelphia. Sue was a fast-talking, enthusiastic woman under any circumstances, but as they packed up she was going one hundred miles an hour. "Come on, come on, we're going to be late," Sue told Ace, in her staccato Philly accent, as she hustled Ace out the front door of their Broomall condo for the last time. It was 11 P.M., and they had a ten-hour drive ahead. Sue intended to make Knoxville by early morning. She wanted Ace to be on time, to get off on the right foot in the program. They had heard that I was exacting on the subject of punctuality.

When they pulled up to Humes Hall, it was only a little after 9 A.M. The doors were just being unlocked. Ace rolled her eyes. They were the first ones there. There wasn't another car or student in sight.

One thing about Sue, she didn't intend to baby Ace, even if she was her youngest. She loved her daughter enough to follow her to Tennessee, but she wanted this day to be a genuine leave-taking. Ace should feel like she was going away to college, not like she was crossing the street. That meant living in the dorm, not running home at the earliest opportunity, and not calling her mother every time she felt a stab of insecurity.

Ace was feeling plenty insecure, all right. Already, she missed Philadelphia. She was city bred. Her whole life, all of her friends, her dates, her sisters and brothers, were back in Philadelphia and New Hampshire.

Together, Ace and Sue unpacked the car. Sue hung pictures and helped Ace put her belongings away, and then she lingered in the dorm, making sure Ace was settled in. For all of her determination to let Ace go, Sue needed to feel comfortable and sure her daughter was okay before she could leave. But it was time. Sue had to apartment hunt and find what would be her own home for at least the next four years. Sue kissed Ace and was gone.

Ace was alone. She surveyed the two-bedroom suite that she was to share with the other three freshmen. Ace hoped fervently that they would get along. In high school, it seemed there was always someone who hated her. They hated her for being good. They hated her for being beautiful. It wasn't her fault she looked like a Miss Hawaiian Tropic beauty contest winner (which she was). "It's your cross to bear," Sue would tell her. This time around, Ace was determined to be liked for who she was, not hated for how she looked.

She finished unpacking. She wondered how long it would be until the first vacation. She wondered how quickly she could get back to Philadelphia.

➤ ➤ ➤

BY NOON, Semeka Randall and her mother, Bertha, were exhausted. They had driven all night from Cleveland, Ohio, eight straight hours on no sleep. They should have gone to bed early on Semeka's last night at home, but they just couldn't make themselves do it. They stayed up, sitting on the front porch of their house, or hanging out in the middle of the street. There were so many neighbors and cousins and well-wishers who wanted to say good-bye. Semeka was the toast and triumph of Farringdon Avenue; from the time she was tiny everyone on the street had watched her play ball, first in her driveway, and then later when she braved the public playgrounds playing with the guys. Now she was the *USA Today* high school player of the year, a 5-feet-10 guard built like a stick of dynamite, and with the temperament of one, too.

Semeka's last night at home had been like a spontaneous block party, with Bertha as the hostess. Bertha was ordinarily not one for hanging out in the street. She worked too hard, holding two jobs as a guidance counselor to disturbed kids, to waste time sitting on the stoop. But that night she was right there in the middle of it all. Semeka had never seen her mother so carefree. Every once in a while Bertha would jump on Semeka and hug her, saying, "Let's go, girl!" Or she would stop and look concerned and say, "We'd better go to sleep." But they never did. Finally, when the crowd had thinned out, they sat on the porch together, side by side like a couple of girlfriends, telling stories and reminiscing and whooping with laughter. Then, at about 2 A.M., they got into a car and they drove straight through the night, crossing from Ohio into Kentucky, and into Tennessee.

Almost before the car stopped in back of Humes Hall, Semeka bounded out. She was always springing around, no matter where she was going. She moved like there were steel coils in her limbs, a cache of constricted energy in her arms and legs that was ready at any moment to release. She got it from Bertha, who herself was like a can of soda that had been shaken, in a constant state of fizziness.

Without an ounce of regret, Bertha began to unpack Semeka's things. All around her, there were sad, tearful mothers. But there wasn't a sad bone in Bertha's body, at least, not one that she would show Semeka. Semeka going off to college was cause for *celebration*. Sad? Sad was the violence she saw in children she dealt with back in Cleveland. Sad was having no God to pray to. Sad were all the teenagers having babies—and, in fact, two of Semeka's best high school friends would be pregnant before the year was out. This day was not sad. This was a joyful day. "Girl, you just go on and do your thing," Bertha said, waving good-bye, blithely. "Do what you got to do."

> > >

Teresa Geter was the sleeper in the group, literally. For a start, she slept all the way to Tennessee. A center-forward with a stalk-like build, she was the best player in the state of South Carolina, and that's exactly where she would have stayed, if it had been up to her. Fortunately, it was up to her daddy, Robert Sr.

Teresa wondered what she had gotten herself into. Tennessee was a famously rigorous program, and I was widely known for my less-than-sympathetic demeanor towards people of her laid-back temperament. Teresa wasn't sure she was up to any of it. She had been named Miss Basketball in the state of South Carolina, but she was somewhat lesser known compared to the other big name freshmen. Still, Teresa was only beginning to explore her potential. Robert was convinced that playing for the Lady Vols would be the making of her, and so was I.

What her father knew, what I suspected, and what few other recruiters realized, was that Teresa was a big occasion player. She would nap through most of a game, and then explode when it was on the line. Something different came out of Teresa when it really mattered. She had practically carried Columbia High School to a state championship on her intermittently somnolent back.

But Teresa had never really been out of her neighborhood, much less out of the state of South Carolina, and she wasn't nearly ready to leave home yet. She was nervous and blue the whole trip up from Columbia. She just didn't know if she could handle Tennessee. Her way of dealing with it was to sleep. When she woke up they were on the outskirts of Knoxville and it was quiet in the car. Her younger brother, Robert, 15, didn't say much of anything, and neither did her stepmother, Faye.

But quietest of all was Teresa's father. Robert Sr. was a lanky former semipro basketball player turned schoolteacher, who had raised Teresa from the age of thirteen after her mother, Joanne, could no longer afford to keep her. Robert had taken over rearing his daughter as carefully as he coached her. He had taught Teresa everything he knew about the game on the courts of the Valley Park recreation center, where he was the activities director. Valley Park was a playground haven in the center of what was, for a time, one of the worst neighborhoods in Columbia. Robert was determined to see that his kids didn't get lost in what he called "the new world," even if it meant, as he phrased it, "putting 'em in lock down." So Teresa was *going* to Tennessee.

Robert Sr. didn't want this to be a sad day. He kept saying that coming to Tennessee was "the best thing in the world for her," and there was no reason to mope. But he couldn't sustain it. He adored his daughter, and he knew what a sensitive young woman lurked in that long body. He would talk for a minute, and lapse into silence again. Robert Sr. was just like Teresa. When he was quiet, that's when you knew he was feeling the most.

➤ ➤ ➤

TAMIKA CATCHINGS and her mother, Wanda, had driven for fourteen and a half hours straight from Duncanville, Texas. Along the way, Tamika went through a slow revolution. Thoughts swirled through her mind like the leaves spinning under their tires. First, she was scared. Then, before she was even out of the state, she got homesick. Her mother was sitting right there next to her, but she already missed her.

Tamika was the last recruit to arrive on campus, and perhaps the most highly prized. A 6-feet-1 prospect with cobra-like athleticism, as a senior in Duncanville she had won the most prestigious honor in the country, the Naismith Award for player of the year. Her talent was at least partly inherited; she was the daughter of Harvey Catchings, who had played as a center in the NBA for eleven seasons and who was now a mortgage broker living in Chicago.

Wanda and Tamika were closer than most mothers and daughters, the result of a complicated family breakup. Wanda and Harvey Catchings had divorced when Tamika was in the seventh grade. Tamika had chosen to live with her mother while her older sister, Tauja, had moved in with her father. Tamika had been a source of comfort for Wanda, a good friend and partner as she struggled to find work and support herself as a newly single mother.

As they crossed the Texas state line, Wanda noticed Tamika's eyes tearing up.

Finally, Tamika burst out, "I hope I'm making the right decision."

Tamika was thinking about the distance. It seemed like such a long way from Texas to Tennessee. There would be no casual weekend visits, no dropping in to see how the other was doing. There would only be long distance phone calls. But if Wanda felt the same way behind the steering wheel, she didn't show it. She reasoned with Tamika calmly. "This is a new chapter," Wanda said. "You know, sometimes the only way to grow up is with distance."

But as they got closer to Tennessee, something turned in Tamika. Her fear and sickness receded. She wouldn't miss Texas all that much, she realized. There had been a pettiness in high school she would be glad to leave behind. There had been jealousy, pressure to fit in, and punishment for being different. She knew some of her peers talked behind her back. They talked about her because she had a hearing problem and her speech was somewhat labored. They talked about her for daring to be good at something. *Who does she think she is?* they seemed to imply. Tamika had never known quite how to please them. What was she supposed to do? Fail? Just so others could feel better?

Tamika decided she was ready to go to college.

➤ ➤ ➤

IT WAS FIVE O'CLOCK in the afternoon when Tamika and Wanda finally arrived up in front of the dorm. Tamika discovered that everyone was waiting for her, including Chamique Holdsclaw and Kellie Jolly, the Lady Vols' juniors and most established returning stars. Throughout the afternoon, Tennessee's upperclassmen had been dropping by Humes Hall to size up the new arrivals and to see how they were getting along.

As a group portrait, the impression Catchings, Randall, Clement, and Geter made was one of extreme youth. There was something about them that seemed fresh out of the box. They huddled together, as if for protection.

They might have come in with outsized reputations, but they were walking into a team that was already larger than life. Only the previous spring, Tennessee had won its second straight national championship. Holdsclaw, a two-time All-American, was already thought to be the greatest collegian ever. Some even said she was the Michael Jordan of the women's game.

But everyone seemed friendly enough. Holdsclaw and Jolly chatted graciously and Kellie even helped Tamika carry some of her stuff in. The freshmen felt perhaps most comfortable with Kyra Elzy, a sophomore guard still young enough to remember what it was like to be a freshman.

Finally, at the end of the afternoon, the upperclassmen left them alone. "But we'll be back to get you tonight," they promised. It sounded innocent enough.

It was well after eight o'clock at night when Jolly, Holdsclaw, and Elzy showed up again. This time, they had virtually the entire Tennessee team in tow. "Okay, let's go play," somebody said. The four freshmen looked at each other, and smiled. They pulled on their sneakers. So the upperclassmen wanted to see what they had. Fine. It seemed the same question was on everyone's mind.

They walked across campus to Stokely Athletics Center. Someone flipped on the lights and a shootaround began. From a distance, they could have been mistaken for guys. They were skinny, and their oversized shorts rode low around their hips. Most of them wore shirts with the sleeves cut out, to show their biceps. An occasional work of body art peeked out.

At first they just jogged up and down the court, freshmen mixing with the veterans. Everyone watched admiringly as Holdsclaw pumped in a few of her signature fall-away jumpers, an effortless stroke learned in the projects of Astoria, Queens. Feeding the ball to Holdsclaw was Jolly, the point guard from Sparta, Tennessee, whose workmanlike style and girlish blond braid could be deceptive; underneath it all she was bitterly competitive and determined to prove she could run this group. Circling around Holdsclaw and Jolly was Elzy, the shooting guard from LaGrange, Kentucky, with a rail-thin build and arms so long they appeared triple jointed. To the freshmen, the three upperclassmen seemed to have a telepathic relationship.

Then, the inevitable happened. Why didn't they split up, freshmen against the upperclassmen? This was what they had been waiting for. Wasn't it what they all wanted, deep down? The four incoming recruits were, collectively, an all-star team in their own right. On the other side, Holdsclaw, Jolly, and Elzy formed the core of a Tennessee squad that had just won consecutive national championships. It was a natural contest. The best-ever freshmen against the two-time defending national champions—who didn't want to see that matchup?

The pace quickened. The four freshmen took a couple of loaners from the veteran side, Brynae Laxton and Misty Greene. Holdsclaw, Jolly, and Elzy were joined by two sophomores: LaShonda Stephens, a center everybody called Wilt, and Niya Butts, a reserve guard. The ball flew up and down the court. The tempo got faster, and faster again. The freshmen, so quiet and unsure of themselves all day, began to run in earnest. And they began to talk.

Randall penetrated the middle and spun in a layup.

"How you going to let freshmen come in here and do this to you?" Randall said, to no one in particular.

The game gravitated into natural matchups, starter against freshman. Catchings against Holdsclaw. Jolly against Clement. Elzy against Randall. Geter against Stephens.

It wasn't just a pickup game any more. Now, it had a point.

Playing time was on the line, and they all knew it. The freshmen were determined to prove they would be immediate factors at Tennessee and the upperclassmen were just as intent on defending their seniority. Take Catchings and Holdsclaw. Ever since Catchings had signed her letter of intent to play for Tennessee, there had been talk that this team wasn't big enough for both her and Holdsclaw. Everyone told Catchings she was crazy to go to Tennessee, that she would waste a lot of her career sitting on the bench behind Holdsclaw. Worse, some even said she was the *next* Holdsclaw. She didn't want to be the next Holdsclaw. She wanted to be Catchings.

And Holdsclaw wasn't exactly thrilled with the idea of a little imitator running around, either.

The two of them dueled furiously up and down the court. Catchings went up, Holdsclaw went up. Catchings scored.

"You can't hold me," Catchings taunted, smiling.

The taunts increased. Randall drove and laid the ball in. "We've been here two hours and we're already beating ya'll," she said.

"Really?" Holdsclaw said.

Holdsclaw pulled up for a reply, and the ball settled gently into the net.

Suddenly, Teresa Geter, who hadn't said a word all day, rose up from the floor and swatted away a jumper by Stephens. Both sides roared at the same time. The gym filled with the sound of catcalls, a high-pitched *wooooooo*.

They played for over an hour, back and forth, before they finally tired and went to bed.

Who won?

Nobody. And everybody.

The next afternoon, Kellie Jolly stuck her head in my office. Normally, Kellie isn't very expressive. She's a slow-talking sort, who doesn't give much away. But I could see she was in a state of suppressed excitement. There was something overbright in her eyes.

"Well, we played pickup last night," Kellie said.

I sat up straighter in my chair, but tried not to look too interested.

"Really?" I asked, nonchalantly. "How'd it go?"

"The freshmen are the real deal," she said.

"So who won?" I asked.

"It was a draw," she said.

I smiled.

➤ ➤ ➤

I DON'T LIKE THAT WORD, "girl." We don't have any girls on our team. We don't have any sweethearts, or babes, or junior misses, either. And I'm not Mary Poppins. My problem with the word "girl" is that, all too often, the word "little" comes before it. A "girl" is as likely to throw the basketball up in the rafters as she is in the basket. She is equally likely to call you up and tell you she is running off to marry her high school boyfriend, because he is the only one, absolutely ever.

What do I mean by "girl"? First, let's talk about what I *don't* mean. I *don't* mean female. I *don't* mean somebody who wears a skirt and does laundry. I'm not talking about somebody who runs like a girl, or throws like a girl, or cries like a girl, or any of those other traditionally negative usages, either. Crying is fine with me. I do a fair amount of it myself.

When I say I don't like that word "girl," I'm talking about a much finer distinction.

I'm talking about someone who was taught not to keep score.

I'm talking about someone who believes the world is divided into Boy–Girl. A girl thinks that competitiveness is the opposite of refinement. A girl isn't bothered by the limitations society imposes on her. A girl refuses to sweat openly, and doesn't get mad when she loses.

Don't get me wrong. I love *little* girls. You can dress them up, and put hair bows on them.

But I don't have much use for them at this level—the championship level.

Every year, a new group of young women arrives at Tennessee, seeking to win a collegiate basketball title. The first thing I tell them is that we do not win championships with girls. We win with competitors.

Sometimes it feels like I've spent my whole career as a head basketball coach trying to shuck labels. Labels are as confining as a corset. What happens when you get labeled is, people tell you how you are supposed to act. For instance, if someone calls you a girl, what they often mean is *nice* girl. Then they tell you what games nice girls are supposed to play, and how nicely you are supposed to play them.

So the label I want to see attached to our team is this one: National Champions.

The Tennessee players I welcomed to campus in the summer of 1997 were as young and uncertain as any we've ever had. But, as I would discover, there wasn't one among them who could be classified by that single, limiting word, "girl." Or by any other word, either.

The 1997–98 Lady Vols were a team of real complexity. They cried. On occasion, one or two of them swore. Some of them chanted lyrics to songs that came with warning labels on the covers. And yet, they were also the "Lady" Vols. Personally, I saw nothing wrong or contradictory in that, despite the number of pleas we received to remove the word. At least the word "lady" implied adulthood.

The game of women's basketball was changing, and Tennessee was on the leading edge of it. In 1996–97 two new pro leagues were launched, the WNBA and the ABL, giving women the unprecedented opportunity to actually make a living at basketball in the United States. Arenas were filling up with people wanting to see new types of female players, young women who could play up around the rim, and who had pro expectations. But with opportunity and newfound wealth came complications, too. Such as agents tempting players to leave school early for the pros (a topic that I will come back to). Our star player, Chamique Holdsclaw, represented a new level of ambition, and a new brand of athleticism. And she personified complexity.

I had seen overachieving teams, underachieving teams, and teams that came back from the dead. What sort of team would this Tennessee squad be? I had no idea. All I knew was that I didn't want another year like the last one. I wasn't sure I could survive it. The '96–97 Lady Vols had lost ten games, the most ever by a women's collegiate team that still managed to win an NCAA title. We raised a banner in the end, but in terms of wins and losses our 29–10 mark was the worst record of my twenty-three-year tenure, and one of the least enjoyable. We got killed by the traditional powers, teams like Stanford, Connecticut, Old Dominion, and Lousiana Tech, teams we usually matched up with. We lost to teams that had never beaten us before, like Arkansas and Florida. The effort had left us exhausted and numb. I had yelled my way through the whole season.

Even though we were about to start a new campaign, those ten losses still galled me. I cringed at the ugliness of the numerals, 29–10.

I refused to have them engraved on our championship rings.

I didn't want to look at them every day. That may seem silly to you. After all, a record is just a number. But if you were involved in it, in the grueling day to dayness of it, it would matter greatly to you, too.

Maybe you know what our record would be in 1997–98, how the Lady Vols went a perfect 39–0 and won a third consecutive national championship. How we set a new record for the most victories ever by a collegiate basketball team, male or female. And how we created a whole new pace for the women's game.

But what the record can't convey is the cost. It doesn't tell you what happened before and after the games, in the locker rooms and the dormitory rooms. It doesn't tell you about the stress fractures, the dislocations, and the bad knees. It doesn't tell you about the stitches, and the stalkers. Or the fright, the pressure, the family problems, and the death of a young boy.

In the summer before we began our 1997–98 season, I wrote a book, *Reach for the Summit.* At the end of the book, I swore I wouldn't write another.

Well, I lied.

When I said I wouldn't write another book, I didn't know about this team. I had no idea what a remarkable story the Lady Vols would prove to be, and how much they would accomplish. I didn't know what they would do to me.

Usually, it's the coach who changes the team. But in this case, it was the team that changed the coach. That's the story I intend to tell.

It's the story of how I finally lost control.

I never knew it could be so much fun.

Q & A with Niya Butts (Sophomore guard)

What were your early impressions of the freshmen?

When I saw Randall, I thought, she's just too fast. It's going to be terrible for anybody who has to guard her. I hated it for them already.

With Tamika, I'm thinking to myself, "She has everything." And she was so nice, which made it worse. She wasn't going to say anything to you, she was just going to kill you, and not have a word to say about it. You'd almost rather she talk.

Ace, I don't think she even saw who she was passing the ball to sometimes. She'd throw those no-look passes. And I'd say, "I know you didn't see that girl." She'd just laugh.

Then there was Tree. She would block everything that came her way, and she didn't even know why she was jumping.

But it was hard not to like them. You couldn't be mad about sitting on the bench, because you liked to watch them play. If you were a fan of the game, if you loved the game, you couldn't see the way this team played and not be excited by it.

CHAPTER TWO

Teresa Geter Comes over the Mountain

YOU TRY IT. You try to say "Chamique, Tamika, and Semeka," all in a row, and what's more, try to say it during a time-out with a horn section shrilling "Rocky Top" frantically in your ear, 25,000 people screaming desperately, and twelve players gathered in a tight circle looking fervently to you for the answer that will win them the game. You can't do it. You can't. It's impossible.

We had a major "Meek" problem.

I could just imagine it: we'd be in a close game, down to the final seconds, and I wouldn't be able to call a play. I would have the game winner at my fingertips, I would diagram it on my clipboard—and I would stammer incoherently over their names.

For two years, there had only been one Meek. Everybody in the country knew who she was: Chamique Holdsclaw. But now, when you said, "Hey, Meek!" three people turned their heads.

What's more, they called each *other* Meek. They'd walk into the locker room, and this is what you heard.

"What's up, Meek?"

"What's up, Meek?"

"What's up, Meek?"

Not to mention the fact that after the "eeks" came the "a's," as in Teresa, LaShonda, Kyra, and Niya.

The day after the pickup game, the four freshmen wandered into the basketball office. I teased them about my problem. "Tamika, Semeka, Chamique, Teresa . . ." I rehearsed aloud.

I looked at Ace, with relief. She, at least, was easy.

"Ace-ika," she said.

I buried my head in my hands.

In piecing together the 1997–98 Tennessee Lady Vols, we would start with something as simple and fundamental as our names. We had to decide who we were. Every team has its own personality and character. We needed to get to know ours.

The problem with a college freshman is that she has no identity on campus. There was nothing on Teresa Geter's dorm room walls, just blank cinderblock. It didn't exactly look like home. She had no close companions, no boyfriend, no allegiance to campus or coach or team. She might wake up, recoil at her surroundings, throw her belongings in a duffle bag and thumb a ride home. All she had was a locker with her name on it. She didn't even have a nickname yet, that initial sign of belonging and acceptance.

As for me, most everyone called me Pat, players and coaches alike. There was a reason for that: while I wanted no mistake as to who was in charge, I wanted to be approachable, too. If I was renowned as a tough coach, I also wanted to be a caring one. What's in a name? An entire relationship, that's what: loyalty, friendship, knowledge, mutual respect, and the history of shared events. The name "Pat" was a statement. It said, "I might get on you in practice, but here's my home phone number if you ever need me."

So, all joking aside, I thought carefully about what to call the new players. A simple thing like a nickname could mean comfort and acceptance, the first signal to a lonesome freshman that this was her new home.

In those first few days it was obvious they were struggling. They went everywhere together, bonded out of necessity, a foursome of tall young women trailing knapsacks. They sat together in every class. They sat together at every meeting, and at every meal. We called them The Clones.

Over the next couple of days the parents departed one by one, making their long road trips back home. Some partings were more difficult than others. Wanda Catchings stayed three days, visiting with her daughter and shopping for her, telling her to be careful of this and that, not to spend too much time on the phone, and to be sure to study. On the morning she left they were both were a little tearful. But Tamika was ready to get on with it, too. She was already fitting in, a self-possessed presence whom everybody called "Catch."

"Mom, it's time for me to grow up," she said.

Wanda said, "Well I know, but you're still my baby, you'll always be my baby."

"Okay, fine, I'll be your baby, Ma, but I'm not going to be your baby like *that*," Tamika said. "I have to learn things for myself. You have to stop telling me what to do."

She was right. It was time for her coach to start telling her what to do.

Randall stayed too busy to think. She moved at sixty miles an hour, with no middle gear. She was constantly on the run, looking for someone to play one-on-one with, or shooting by herself in the semidarkness of Stokely Athletics Center. We just called her Randall. We didn't have time to call her anything else. She would streak by and I would bark out her name. "Randall!" I would say. "Slow your butt down!"

But the one who really worried me was Teresa Geter. She was expressionless and all but silent. So far, she was still Teresa to us. Her childhood nickname was Tree, because of her build, and that's what our players would eventually call her. She was 6-feet-3, but only weighed around 150 pounds, giving the impression of a thin, wavy sapling. But there was something reserved in her large, quiet presence that made me use her full name. She had large, serious eyes, with eyebrows that seemed to be permanently raised.

Teresa was having the worst time saying good-bye to her family. Robert had stayed over in a hotel for a day, to make sure she was properly settled in. Teresa's first night in the freshman suite had been disorienting. She didn't like sleeping in a strange bed, in a strange room, sharing it with a virtual stranger in her roommate Semeka.

On Sunday morning, Robert came to the dorm to kiss her good-bye. They stood in front of Humes Hall, awkwardly. Teresa was determined not to cry in front of her father, but she had been on the verge of it all morning. As she looked at her dad she knew she wouldn't get through a good-bye scene without dissolving. Suddenly, she hugged Robert once, quick, laughing, and then before he could hug her back or say a word, she turned and ran. She ran hard, sprinting back into the building, and ducked into the stairway. Tears streamed down her face. But at least she hadn't let him see.

Down on the sidewalk, Robert wasn't fooled. He knew his daughter was crying and it broke his heart. But he had been preparing for this. We had talked about it over the summer. I called him up to warn him that Tree might have a difficult adjustment to make, and that I would be getting on her. "She's going to want to come home," I warned him. "But I'm asking you now, please don't let her come back over the mountain."

Robert climbed in the car, and turned the key to begin the drive back through the Smokies into South Carolina. No way was Teresa coming back over the mountain.

➤ ➤ ➤

ROBERT GETER didn't like most babies, but he had felt a weakness for his daughter from the moment he first held her as an infant. It was extraordinary. He was a big man, 6-feet-6, and babies made him nervous. They were too small. But Teresa was different. She was long and sturdy, twenty-three inches at birth, to be precise, and she weighed nine pounds, eleven ounces. No one could believe the size of her, especially since her mother, Joanne, was only 5-feet-3. When Robert cradled Teresa, she seemed to settle in his arms just right, like she belonged there.

When Teresa was four years old, Robert and Joanne asked her what kind of doll she wanted for Christmas. She said, "I don't want a doll. I want a basketball." So Robert, delighted, bought her a ball, and she put her doll in a closet, and never took it out again. "From then on, we never saw the doll, it was just that ball," Joanne says.

Robert was passionate about basketball, even though it had deeply disappointed him. Robert had been a promising collegiate forward at East Carolina and played for a while with a well-known semipro team in New York, the Harlem Professionals. He was flirting with the big time when he caught a bad break, one of those lousy cards you sometimes get dealt through no fault of your own. The Cleveland Cavaliers were talking about signing him when the NBA and the renegade ABA merged. The ABA rosters were absorbed by existing NBA teams. Suddenly, teams were swamped with players. There was no room for a little-known semipro who lacked big league experience.

Even though his pro career was over, Robert never quit playing. He moved back to Columbia, where he was born and reared, took over the rec center at Valley Park and began substitute teaching, and set about raising his family. But he played organized ball until he was forty years old.

Robert loved to cart Teresa along with him to whatever games he was playing in. He would take her to the courts and sit her right on the bench, next to him. She dangled her legs while he played, or she ran around on the sideline, dribbling.

But when Teresa was seven, Robert and Joanne split up, effectively ending Teresa's childhood. Robert stayed in the Valley Park neighborhood, running the rec center, and visiting his children. Robert and Joanne didn't want the kids to suffer for their mistakes, they agreed.

Joanne took whatever work she could find, but with two small children it was difficult to keep a steady full-time job. She washed dishes, cleaned houses, and cooked in cafeterias. She made minimum wage, $4.25 an hour. Even with Robert's child support, it was a lean existence.

Joanne enrolled in a nearby technical college, hoping to get a degree in accounting, and things were good for a while. But she only took half as many classes as she needed to, what with caring for the children. There wasn't enough of her to go around, between work, school, and the kids. She quit school.

Teresa would tell you herself that they lived from paycheck to paycheck, and sometimes the checks didn't stretch very far. She would also tell you that in some ways, young as she was, she felt like another parent. When Joanne worked a night shift, Teresa would feed Robert Jr. and put him to bed, clean the kitchen, and then put herself to bed. Fortunately Robert was always a phone call away. But there were nights, too, when there wasn't anything to eat in the house and Joanne would go to relatives to borrow something to feed her children. Joanne would sit Teresa down and explain the situation. But Teresa always said she understood. She never complained, never talked back.

Finally, when Teresa was in eighth grade, Joanne and Robert Sr. made a decision. Joanne felt she couldn't adequately care for Teresa and Robert Jr. anymore. They were supposed to spend that summer with Robert, but both parents decided it would be best for them to live with him full time.

At school, Teresa made up stories to tell the other kids about why she was living with her father instead of her mother. "I was bad, so she sent me away," Teresa said.

Living with Robert Sr., Teresa had stability, and she had basketball. Slowly, steadily, Robert shaped her into a college prospect, until I came knocking on their door. Robert was deeply proud and relieved to deliver his daughter to college; they could all rest assured now that Teresa's future was secure. Joanne was on solid ground, too. She worked in dietary services at the University of South Carolina.

But much as Teresa adored her father, she never quite got over her separation from Joanne. Every time Teresa tried to talk about it, which was rarely, her eyes filled up. Joanne had an equally difficult time discussing it. "It hurt then and it hurts now," Joanne will tell you. "It will always hurt."

➤ ➤ ➤

ON THE EVENING OF August 24 we held our first team meeting. But beforehand, our staff gathered in my office.

The makeup of our team had completely altered over the summer. We did not have a single healthy senior. Our two leaders from the previous year, Abby Conklin and Pashen Thompson, had graduated. Our only returning senior, Laurie Milligan, was recovering from knee surgery but would shortly be diagnosed with degenerative arthritis and told she shouldn't play basketball again. I had dismissed our only other senior, Tiffani Johnson, for violating team rules. There was some sentiment in Knoxville that I had personally jeopardized our chances at a title by not overlooking the transgression.

Without Tiffani we lacked a physically imposing presence in the middle, someone who could play in the painted area under the basket known as the post. Post players are primarily those who play inside with their backs to the basket, sometimes referred to as pivot players. Tennessee almost always had a presence in "the paint," players with strong physical builds, who could muscle in and hold their positions.

We had plenty of perimeter players, those players who face the basket, who can create offense off of the dribble and shoot the three point shot from beyond the 19-foot, 9-inch circular line. But we didn't have bodies. We needed bodies.

We had always had a post game. Always. A nice, reassuring, wide-bodied presence in the middle to haul down rebounds and play the physical game. I didn't like finesse teams, and I didn't trust them. But as I scanned our roster, that's what we were shaping up to be.

Our prospects for the 1997–98 season depended on the following assortment of young women: Chamique Holdsclaw, our two-time All-American, a 6-feet-2 forward with an exquisitely silky pull-up jumper, who was hearing whispers that she could cash in by leaving school early to move to the pros. Kellie Jolly, the 5-feet-10 point guard who was our most reliable player, but was coming off of surgery to repair torn ankle ligaments, and had had two prior knee injuries. A pair of Tennessee-bred juniors, Misty Greene and Brynae Laxton, who were valuable role players but had seen limited playing time.

This meant three sophomores would have to become contributors if we were to have any kind of chance: Niya Butts, a guard from Americus, Georgia, who had chronic shin problems. LaShonda Stephens, another Georgian, nicknamed Wilt for her height and build, who was penciled in as our new starting center, but who had terminally swollen knees. And Kyra Elzy, a 6-feet-1 guard, who was healthy, but was still developing her offensive game, and had drawn my ire for much of the previous season for being too passive.

And four pure freshmen.

Between their reputations, and the already established presence of Holdsclaw, the experts felt we would be a contender. I was inclined to agree with them—but with some serious reservations. What the experts didn't realize was that some important weaknesses were hidden on our roster. And in me. I had never coached a team this young. And I had never coached a team without a proven post game.

But as our assistant coaches sprawled informally on two couches in my office, I silently counted my blessings. We might be young with four pure freshmen, but we had the advantage of a stable and long serving staff—the best in the collegiate game, I felt.

Mickie DeMoss, 43, was my right hand and best friend of thirteen years. A tiny brunette with warm eyes, reared in the Louisiana delta, she was a person of formidable charm and was responsible for recruiting three of the four freshmen to Tennessee. Mickie had a way of exuding humor and sincerity at the same time, and people just naturally took to her. But she was also a sharp strategist who was bound to be a head coach of her own program again some day (she was a head coach at Florida, in the early '70s). A former point guard who had starred at Louisiana Tech, she had complete floor vision, the ability to see the movements of all ten players as a whole—a quality I sometimes lacked. I knew I couldn't hang on to her forever, and I got an ulcer every summer when the job offers started coming in. So far, she had turned them all down. She liked winning championships and she wasn't sure she wanted to start over at another school.

Holly Warlick, 39, was like a member of my own family. She not only coached under me, she had played for me, too, and she knew my mind as well as I did. As a floppy-haired undergraduate she had starred at point guard for the Lady Vols from 1976–80. She joined our staff in the summer of 1985, at the same time I hired Mickie, and had become an accomplished recruiter and an extremely valuable sideline presence. She had an acute tactical sense and she, too, was probably going to be a head coach in her own right some day. Like me, Holly was Tennessee born and reared; she was a slow-talking Knoxville native with a permanent grin and lived on a five-acre tract with a truck and three Dalmatians.

Al Brown, in his mid-fifties, was the newest member of the staff; he was only starting his third season, but he had been in the game for over thirty years. He was a tall, gray-haired man with a slow-dawning smile and a washboard stomach from running four miles a day. Al had enjoyed a long career in the men's game, the high point of which was reaching the Final Four as an assistant with Purdue. He was in charge of scouting opponents, and his office was wall-to-wall videotape machines. He could analyze a player's tendencies just from a quiver. He could tell you that the point guard was too right-handed, and that the center couldn't go to her left; watch how she moved her eyebrows, or scuffed her sneakers. He was as committed to scouting as Mickie was to recruiting.

As we sat in a semicircle, drinking Diet Cokes, we had a million questions to answer. The Lady Vols were ranked preseason No. 1, and just about everybody was talking about a "Three-Peat," a third straight NCAA title. Expectations were spiraling higher and higher. But if we were excited, we were on edge, too. Nobody seemed to understand how difficult it was to win one title, much less to repeat.

How should we deal with the problem of expectations? I asked them. What approach, I asked the staff, should I take in our first team meeting?

"I think you need to address it head on," Al said.

But as soon as we answered one question, another took its place. How would the freshmen respond to the intensity of the program? How quickly could they learn the system? How would our talent mix? Would we have enough basketballs to go around? How could we avoid dissension and resentment when the freshmen challenged for playing time? Kellie might resent Ace. Kyra and Semeka might have a serious problem over playing time. Tamika and Chamique might butt heads.

We assigned an upperclassman to each of the first year players, as a buddy system. Semeka was Kyra's responsibility. Ace was Kellie's. Teresa belonged to LaShonda, and Tamika to Niya. They would call them in the morning to make sure they were up. They would call them at lunch, to make sure they had eaten, and at night to see if they were crying. That way, they would take responsibility for each other.

The more we talked, the more it became clear that the key would be Holdsclaw. Holdsclaw was the real Meek, and the real deal. For two years, she had been our child prodigy, and she was still maturing. She could be aloof and cautious with her teammates, and she wasn't yet completely trusting of me. But she was always courteous.

She was the only player on the team who called me Coach Summitt.

Chamique needed to grow into herself. She was our high scorer, but now she would have to become a leader in other, more subtle ways. It was obvious that the freshmen idolized her, that some of them had even come here to play alongside of her, and that where she went, they would follow. But how would Chamique react to having four disciples? She might well be threatened by the presence of Catchings, who had a similar style and build. But a mature player would realize that Catchings and the rest of the freshmen could only help her.

"Chamique needs to take ownership of this team," Mickie said. "We need to figure out some ways to make her feel that this is *her* team."

It was time to go downstairs to the locker room. By now, the players were gathered for their first team meeting. Even more than the dormitory, the locker room would be where the players lived out their college existence. For that reason, we had spent a lot of time and money making it like a family room. It had wood paneled lockers, rich blue carpet, and in the lounge area there was a large blue leather couch positioned in front of a 60-inch TV. All around the walls were built-in trophy cases and framed photos of All-Americans, Olympians, and visits to the White House.

The four freshmen took seats on the couch, huddled together, as usual.

I dragged a chair to the center of the room, and looked directly at the freshmen.

"Sit up straight, listen, and participate," I said.

➤ ➤ ➤

AND THAT'S HOW we officially began our season.

Over the course of the meeting, I introduced them to the Definite Dozen, the twelve principles by which we run the program. I outlined them in *Reach for the Summit,* but I'll do it again. Briefly, they are a set of rules meant to foster teamwork.

1. Respect yourself and others
2. Take full responsibility
3. Develop and demonstrate loyalty
4. Learn to be a great communicator
5. Discipline yourself so no one else has to
6. Make hard work your passion
7. Don't just work hard, work smart
8. Put the team before yourself
9. Make winning an attitude
10. Be a competitor
11. Change is a must
12. Handle success like you handle failure

I asked some of the upperclassmen to stand and explain them, and what the overall philosophy of the program was.

I hoped that Chamique would find a way to step forward. She did.

"It's all about buying into the system," Chamique said, addressing the freshmen. "Basically, you have to trust in what Coach Summitt says, even when you might question it inside, and you have to do your part to make it work."

Next, I tackled the problem of the "Three-Peat." It was all we would hear about in the coming months, I said. We would hear about it on campus. We would hear about it in the papers, on the radio. We would hear about it from students, teachers, friends, and neighbors.

"I don't want you to even think about it," I said. "Forget the word 'Three-Peat.' You'd better concentrate instead on the small things. Like getting down in a stance."

I considered what to say next.

"Look, we don't ever have to win another championship," I continued. "Tennessee has enough championships for the record books. We have our place in history and in the women's game. But you do have a chance to win your *own* championship. This is *your* team and *your* opportunity. There is no guarantee you can repeat. You don't win on tradition alone. Look around the walls, and you'll see that a lot of great players have come here. And now they're gone. So this is your team, and your season."

I paused.

"You'll work," I said. "There's a reason it's called work—it's hard. But it's nothing to be afraid of. It's not anything you aren't capable of. No one's ever died from it."

I probably shouldn't have said what came next. But as I looked at the freshmen, staring at me all wide-eyed, I couldn't help teasing them.

"Some have passed out. . . ."

➤ ➤ ➤

THE FRESHMEN WERE WORRIED.

They sat in their suite after the team meeting, worrying.

They were worried about passing out.

Individual workouts would start the next day. After what I had said at the end of the meeting, the freshmen were convinced they would fall over in a swoon.

Tree was especially worried. She silently struggled with her confidence. Ace, Tamika, and Semeka were at least somewhat prepared for what was to come, thanks to a summer of playing for the USA junior national team. Along with Kyra Elzy, another member of the junior national team, they had toured Brazil and won a gold medal in world competition. But Tree had missed making the squad and consequently spent a more leisurely summer. Now she was concerned about keeping up.

In those first few days on campus, Tree stayed just slightly apart from the other freshmen. Ace noticed it first. The four of them would be strolling to class or to a meeting, and Tree would lag by a couple of steps, drifting in their wake. Maybe she simply moved more slowly, because she was taller. Or maybe she felt like she wasn't invited to join the conversation. Either way, Ace decided, it wasn't right. Gradually, subtly, Ace began slowing her step. One pace, two . . . until she fell into step with Tree.

From then on, that's how it was, Semeka and Tamika and Ace and Tree, a united foursome.

The freshmen sat in their suite, each privately unsure of herself, wondering if she was up to playing at Tennessee. What they didn't know was that it was almost a tradition for upperclassmen to paint a terrifying picture of what was to come for the new players. Sophomores, particularly, delighted in scaring the new arrivals, since they had just gone through it themselves. Every class claimed they got worse treatment from me than any class before or after. "Pat was tougher on us than anyone else," they liked to say, when in fact I was the same to everybody. It was the stories that got worse and more exaggerated every year.

Over the summer, Kyra had told Ace, Tamika, and Semeka lots of stories about playing for the Lady Vols. She told them about endless wind sprints and 6 A.M. runs around the track. She told them about the sound of my voice, how it was like a long arm that could reach all the way across the gym and practically seize you by your shirt collar and jerk you up short.

She told them how I would punish the whole team for individual transgressions. For instance, if one player dogged it through a wind sprint, I made the whole team run another one. That way, they were responsible for each other. (Peer pressure was a wonderful motivator.)

Anyone who had gone through our 29–10 season in 1996–97 had run miles and miles of wind sprints. I ran them early in the morning, and I ran them late at night. Kyra still shuddered at the memory of all that running.

Kyra was going to have the freshmen ready.

➤ ➤ ➤

THE FRESHMEN DECIDED to start running that very night.

They laced up their sneakers, and set out on a three-mile circuit of campus. They ran and ran, touring the entire university. They found every building they had a class in.

But Tree wasn't used to to running long distances. She had never really trained like this before. Halfway through the run, she started breathing hard. Then she started hurting. She stopped. She bent double, sucking in air.

"Go on without me," Tree said.

Ace Clement stopped, too.

"Come on, you can do it," Ace said.

Tree shook her head. She waved them on. Tamika and Semeka took a couple of tentative steps, and looked back over their shoulders.

But Ace shook her head. "No," she said. "No, Tree. Come on."

Ace wasn't going to leave Tree behind. It was harder for a big girl like Tree to run at their pace, Ace thought. She needed help.

"Come on, Tree," Ace begged. "I know you can do this. Push yourself. Just try, I know it hurts, but you can get through it. It'll get easier. Come on."

Tree stood upright and regained her breath. Ace was a nice person, she thought. She didn't have to wait for her like this.

Tree started running again.

Every night, that's how it was. They would run around campus for forty-five minutes, Tree a little slower than the rest, with Ace talking her through it.

A few nights later, Ace and Tamika decided running wasn't enough. They walked to the center of campus and stared upwards at a steep rise called "The Hill." Atop it was Ayres Hall, one of the oldest buildings on campus, and built on the highest ground. During the Civil War, a siege was fought around The Hill.

It was eleven o'clock on a humid summer night, and Ace and Tamika were covered in sweat. It was the perfect time and place, they agreed, for wind sprints.

They pumped up the The Hill, gasping, every muscle in their legs trembling. Then they walked down.

And sprinted up the hill again. And walked back down. And sprinted up the hill again. And walked back down. I had sprinted up that hill myself, so I knew what it felt like. Your legs grew heavy and inflamed like molten iron, and your heartbeat accelerated to a *wham-wham-wham* rhythm, until a deep chemical burn suffused your lungs, and your breath sounded like *unhhhhhhh* as you tried to suck a little sustenance out of the night air. It was like trying to breathe through a wet flannel blanket, and all you could think as you went up the hill again was *Don'tletmethrowupdon'tletmethrowupdon'tletmethrowup*. . . .

They did ten sets.

➤ ➤ ➤

TREE TRIED TO BRACE HERSELF for the opening of workouts. Still, it was a shock.

Tree came to the gym for the first time on August 28. These individual workouts were to build fundamental skills, to get to know the coaches, to learn terminology, and to practice some basic techniques. They were a matter of small things: a defensive stance, high hands, low hips, quick feet. I tended to sound like a drill sergeant as I led Tree through each repetition.

The problem with promising Mickie I would try not to yell was that sometimes, a raised voice was the only way to get through to a talented young prospect. Great players often came with a certain stubbornness— that was part of their competitive ego and standard operating equipment. And they frequently came with bad habits that needed breaking. They tended to think, because they were high school stars, that they did everything right and had nothing to learn. But I would be cheating them if I let them think that, if I protected their egos at the expense of teaching them. And I would be misleading them.

You had to break young players down in order to build them up again, properly. It was an uncomfortable process and even a painful one that could result in short-term loss of confidence. But it was all in the name of making them better. If I was about to hurt Tree Geter's feelings, it would hurt her more to let her play with fundamental flaws in her game.

The freshmen had to learn some things the hard way, but I wanted them to do it with me, in the privacy of practice, rather than in front of 25,000 people.

I jumped on Tree after just five minutes.

"Geter, if you don't start getting up off the floor, we're going to have a problem all year," I snapped.

A worried frown creased Tree's forehead. No one had ever told her she was lackadaisical in her rebounding. But she bore it well outwardly at first, just staring at me. She wore eye goggles, so her eyes looked even larger than usual.

A drill later, however, Tree still wasn't getting up off the floor to my satisfaction. She would work hard for one play, and then lean over, pulling at her shorts like she was tired.

I grabbed the ball and bounced it, aggravated. "I can chew, and I can chew, and I can chew," I said. "And you're going to have to respond and respond and respond!"

Now Tree looked on the verge of tears. But it was about to get worse. Five minutes later, Tree was still standing around.

I slapped the floor, hard. The crack sounded throughout the gym.

"You're going to learn how to get in a stance," I said, "or I'll sit you in a chair—without the chair."

I spun on my heel and walked back to half court. Tree just stood there, staring at her feet. After a moment, Holly sidled over.

"It's all right," Holly murmured. "We're going to fix it. We'll get it right now, so it's not a problem later." Tree, comforted, nodded and readjusted her goggles.

It went on like that for weeks. Me yelling, and Tree trying to not to cry, blinking back tears behind her goggles. Tree was desperate to get it right. But it seemed that I hollered at her, no matter what. Afterwards, Tree would sit in front of her locker, staring into it, not speaking.

She must have heard my voice in her sleep. The grim, constant grating followed her everywhere. It was an implacable, clenched-teeth drone that summarized her faults daily, sometimes rising in mock surprise and then dropping again in withering criticism. *You tired? You want to sit? I've got a seat for you—right next to me on the bench!*

What Tree couldn't know was that it was quite calculated on my part. I had been lying in wait for her all summer.

I knew Tree was as laid back as a blade of grass. Now, if there's one thing I can't abide from a player, it's laid back. And it was the one thing we couldn't afford from Tree, especially.

We had to bring Tree along fast.

We didn't have time to coax Tree along because we were scheduled to meet Louisiana Tech, ranked No.2 in most polls, in just our second game of the season. And Tech had Alisa Burras, the best and most experienced low-post player in the country. If Tree wasn't ready, she would get eaten alive.

But Tree didn't do anything fast. I knew that from watching her play in an American Athletic Union summer tournament in Chattanooga. Holly and I had driven over to visit Tree and to get to know her a little better before she reported to school. But we were appalled by the lounging, sometime player we saw. Tree loafed up and down the court, barely sprinting. I couldn't believe a Tennessee signee would represent our program that way. Holly and I were so mad we had to force ourselves not to leave at halftime.

After the game I walked across the gym and found Robert Geter, Sr.

"Robert, I'm going to have to get on her," I said. "She's going to learn to run the court at Tennessee."

Robert smiled and nodded and said, "That's why I'm sending her to you."

In her first few weeks at Tennessee, Tree decided I just didn't like her. But she wasn't experiencing anything that a hundred others hadn't experienced with me. In fact, all of Tree's freshman roommates were in for similar meltdowns. That's what I did with freshmen: I chipped and peeled away at them, a piece at a time. I did it on purpose. Then I put them back together again—in order to fit them into the Tennessee system.

One night, Tree called her mother, Joanne. She couldn't please me, she told Joanne. "No one could please that lady," she said. What should she do?

Joanne said, "You have to learn to love her."

"Why?" Tree said.

"Because she's going to make you better," Joanne said.

After that, Tree didn't call her mom for a while. She wasn't in the mood to hear that she should love her tormentor. I didn't blame her.

It was hard for others to watch. Kyra Elzy felt for Tree, perhaps more than anyone. Kyra had been my target throughout *her* freshman year, for similar reasons. I jumped hardest on players I felt were underachievers. So Kyra knew.

"Every time she yells at you, that means she really likes you," Kyra told Tree. "She thinks you have potential."

Tree said, "Well, I can't tell."

"She does," Kyra said. "She likes you. She really likes you. She thinks she can get something out of you that you're not giving. So take it as a compliment."

It was as hard for me to ride Tree as it was for other people to watch. You didn't need to be clairvoyant to see that Tree was a sensitive young woman. I would ride her, and afterwards I would chew my lower lip all the way home, worrying over whether she would hold up. Each time I barked at her, I thought, *don't you fold on me, young lady.* I agonized over whether I was being too demanding.

One afternoon, Tree wept openly in practice. The tears just slid down her cheeks. If Tree couldn't take much more, neither could I.

So I kept her after practice. We sat down under one basket.

We just didn't have time to bring her along slowly, I explained. I went over our problems with the post game, and told her how concerned I was about Louisiana Tech.

Then I asked Tree, straight out, if I should give her a break.

"Help me be your coach," I said. "Am I being too hard on you? Do you want me to back off? Because if you do, I'll back off right now. I won't say another harsh word to you."

Tree thought about it for a moment. Then she shook her head.

"No," she said. "Stay on me."

So I did.

➤ ➤ ➤

TREE WOULD CRY AGAIN. Her tears didn't stop overnight.

On the morning of September 29, Tree woke up crying. It was her eighteenth birthday, and she had never spent a birthday away from home before. She was homesick. She missed her father, she missed her mother, and she missed her little brother. She talked all the time about Robert Jr. to her roommates, about what she would buy him when she went home for Christmas. They had even told each other "I love you" on the phone one day, something new between the brother and sister.

Tree was lonesome, and the adjustment to campus life was not proving to be an easy one for her. She missed the intimacy of her neighborhood back in Columbia, where she knew everyone she passed on the street. She had the typical freshman sensation of being overwhelmed. The lectures were hard to follow, a lot of the terms and subjects were new to her, and she struggled to take notes at the collegiate pace. She tried to keep up as best she could, but it seemed like she was always behind. She studied for two weeks for her first biology test. She was afraid of failing.

Semeka Randall, in the next bed, heard Tree weeping.

Semeka slid out of bed and padded back to Tamika and Ace's room— she was about to cry herself. She said, "Tree's crying and it's her birthday. We have to do something."

The three of them spent all afternoon planning a surprise. They bought a vanilla cake with white icing; they blew up eighteen balloons and decorated the back bedroom with them; they strung crepe paper, and ordered pizzas.

Word got back to me that Tree was having a hard day. In the afternoon, I called the freshmen suite. I sang "Happy Birthday" to Tree, in my voice that was hoarse from yelling at her. That cheered her up some.

That evening, Ace, Semeka, and Tamika acted like it was just another night in their dorm room. They talked about going out, and decided against it. Semeka said, "Let's just eat pizzas." Tree thought, "There goes my birthday."

When the pizza arrived, Tamika told Tree to stay in the front room. After a minute, they called Tree into the back.

She walked into a room darkened except for a flaming birthday cake.

It was the final icebreaker. Tree beamed. The three freshmen circled Tree, and began to sing. Semeka started first. But she didn't sing "Happy Birthday." She sang their favorite song from the film *Waiting to Exhale*.

As Semeka sang a verse, the others joined in. "Count on Me," they sang.

Tree, touched, started crying again.

➤ ➤ ➤

ON A WEEKEND in late September, after assessing our rookies and returning players, our staff took a retreat to brainstorm about the coming season. Mickie, Holly, Al, and I went off to a resort for three days and poured over our offensive and defensive options. We were determined to come home with the answer to a central question: What style would we play?

Our first impressions, based on the individual workouts:

Ace Clement was a natural point guard, confident and vocal. To add to it, she was 5-feet-11 and left-handed. Randall showed intensity to match her athleticism. She didn't always know what to do, so when in doubt she just went hard to the basket. Catchings was even better than I anticipated, a total player who could work from all five positions. Geter, even though she was not as highly touted, clearly had as much game as any of them. She had soft hands, quickness, shooting touch, and an absolute genius for blocking shots. She could be one of our most versatile players ever at the post, I thought, if she could survive her first few weeks with me.

The problem was how best to use them.

A basic philosophy had been in place at Tennessee for years. We played a controlled half court offensive game, and a famously disciplined man-to-man defense. Was there anything we might want to add or take away or change, we asked ourselves?

And what would we do without a proven post game? After some discussion, we decided the answer was to run. If we couldn't beat other teams with strength, we would try to beat them with speed and an up-tempo style. This group was athletic enough to push the ball up and down the court at a fast enough pace that they might wear out their opponents. But a running game was something new for me. I had spent my whole career as a coach of methodical half court teams.

Then Mickie said, "Do you want to talk about a press?"

I thought about it for a minute. If I was uncomfortable with a running offense, I was doubly uncomfortable with the idea of a pressing team. To press meant applying defensive pressure for the entire length of the court.

It meant playing a "transition" game: after we scored, we would stay in the opponent's end of the court and start our defensive effort right under their basket. It was tricky, because it meant changing direction almost momentarily. If we were going to press, we had to drill it daily, and simulate game situations in our practice. The question was, could you score and then press, and if the press was broken, could you then get back down the court and defend effectively enough to prevent the other team from scoring?

A full court press was a risky proposition. It was a gambler's strategy. It meant leaving one end of the court unprotected. We had tried to press in other years, without much success. The problem was, if our team didn't get up and down the floor quick enough, we would get burned. I preferred a more conservative approach: historically, the Lady Vols had fallen back to half court and played a fundamental man-to-man defensive scheme.

But Mickie, Holly, and Al wanted to try a press. And they weren't alone. Back in the middle of that miserable 1996–97 regular season, when we were in the midst of losing ten games, I had gotten a bold phone call from Semeka Randall suggesting the same thing. The call came the night of a tough loss to Stanford on our home court.

I was low. I stayed up late watching the film over and over again, brooding about our terrible defense. Ordinarily, a classically aggressive, harrying defense was Tennessee's signature. Our philosophy was to pester the opposing team until they simply jacked up a bad shot or threw the ball away or turned the ball over. But against Stanford, our defense was soft. There was nothing aggressive about us. We looked like a sagging wall, about to give way at any moment.

Just as I was rewinding the tape for the thousandth time, the phone rang. It was Semeka calling, from Farringdon Avenue back in Cleveland. She was in the middle of her senior year in high school, but she had watched our game on TV, and she had seen our defense, too.

"I know you're in a bad mood, and you don't want to talk," she said. "I just have one question for you."

"What?" I said.

"When I get there, can I pick up the ball full court?"

Semeka wasn't even here yet, and already she wanted to play a pressing defense. Not only that, she wanted to play ninety-four feet of it. She wanted to play it from one end of the court to the other.

Now, listening to Mickie, Holly, and Al, I considered an occasional press. Nah, I thought. It was tempting, but too risky, too much of a commitment. I still preferred our good old standby, a tough, half court, man-to-man defense. That's what we should work on, I said.

We drove home, and I forgot all about the press. But then, on October 17, we met for our first full organized practice.

I had seen the Lady Vols working in twos and threes during individual workouts. But nothing could have prepared me for what I saw when Holdsclaw, Jolly, Elzy, Catchings, Randall, Clement, Geter, and Stephens and the rest of their orchestra hit the floor together for the first time. I could only imagine what the pickup game must have been like. It was hard, as I watched them play, not to let my jaw drop. Their collective talent was beyond anything I had encountered at Tennessee.

Everything they did, they wanted to do perfectly. And most of it *was* perfect.

In my mind, I always had a picture of how the game should be played: controlled, methodical, in half court increments. I saw it almost in slow motion. But as I watched these young women move around the court, just doing the simple things like ball handling and passing, the picture began to change. It began to speed up.

And then it kicked into fast forward.

They could move from baseline to baseline, and sideline to sideline, at a pace I had never experienced before. For the first time, the court didn't look huge to me. They made *it* look small.

Next, we tried a little defense.

They were like vultures, attacking the ball. From that phone call, I knew Semeka was aggressive. Turns out, the whole freshman class was that way. They absolutely hawked it.

Despite certain shortcomings—Geter still needed to learn a fifth gear,

Randall needed to take better shots—they were breathtaking. I had no idea.

I walked over to my staff. I said, "We're going to press."

With most freshmen, you start slow. You reassure them that they belong, and you make painstakingly sure that they don't run home. You get 'em on the hook. Then you go after them.

But this team, I understood, was coming after *me*.

A couple of days later, Niya Butts stopped Tree in the locker room. "Hey, Tree," she said. "Do you mind if I give you a new nickname?"

Tree looked at her, curious.

"You're quiet," Niya said, "but underneath it all, you aren't. You're smooth. Big Smooth."

Tree thought about it. She decided she was pleased. Big Smooth. It sounded good.

"I guess that's okay," Tree said.

We knew who we were.

It hadn't taken long.

Q & A with Chamique Holdsclaw
(Junior forward, All-American)

Why do you call her Coach Summitt when everybody else calls her Pat?
Just out of respect.

Really?
Yeah. She's not one of my peers, you know. I'm not going to call her Pat.
Doesn't sound right.

Do you trust her?
Oh, definitely. Everything she told me when she came to my house, it's
true. From day one. She told me, "If you buy into me and my system, I'll
make you the best player you can be. If you work hard, you'll see it." And
here I am. I mean, we got into it a couple of times. I felt like she was
pushing me too hard, and I thought, "My God, this lady doesn't like me."
She got on me left and right. She wouldn't let me breathe. Anything went
wrong, it was, "Chamique! Chamique!" Do this. Do that. She had me running for days. But it just shows that she cares. Now when she's not making
me run, I say to her, "What am I not doing right?"

Did you feel it was your job to get this team through the season?
For my first two years here I was kind of the baby. But now I was older, and
I was the player who had the most significant role. And they were kind of
like my team—I earned the right to call it my team.

CHAPTER THREE

Chamique

EVERY EVENING in a graffiti-scored New York City housing project overlooking a disconsolate stretch of the East River called Hell Gate, a girl with limbs as thin as winter branches would stand under the streetlights, bouncing a basketball in a steady *whap-whap-whap* rhythm on the cracked asphalt. Periodically, the whapping would stop, followed by the clang of a shot slipping through an iron rim, and the thrum of a backboard trembling. Chamique Holdsclaw would shoot the ball up and out, perfecting the pull-up jumper that would take her on a similar arc, up and out of the projects. Thousands of boys in housing projects across the United States similarly whiled away their time. But Chamique was different. First of all, she was a *she*. Second, she could shoot the ball like no other *she* ever had. She could shoot it from the three, or off the dribble, or on the reverse. She could shoot it up and over all the thick-shouldered guys she played street ball with. Now, as a grown woman, she shot it so well, from so many half-suspended positions in the air, that leagues, agents, and sneaker companies quivered to sign her to guy-sized contracts, and all of the homeboys who used to make fun of her big feet and said, "She's a girl, she stinks" were bragging that they grew up with her, and all of them, agents and homeboys alike, had to admit that she just might be the most important ballplayer, man or woman, to ever come out of that wretched park with broken swings.

Astoria Houses is a housing project in Queens, New York, the kind of place where the odd empty bottle and vial litter the front steps of the recreation center where Chamique once played. It is made up of a set of bleak towers arranged around the barren waterfront. But it is also the home of hardworking people like Chamique's grandmother, June, who raised her on a hospital clerk's salary. The basketball courts within the courtyard of Astoria Houses, like any number of other high-rise, low-income urban complexes, have produced a spate of ambitious young players. Some of them obtained college degrees from places like St. John's or Georgia Tech. Every now and then a rarity like Kenny Andersen, the Queens-bred guard for the Portland Trailblazers, even made it to the NBA. But Astoria had known nothing like Holdsclaw, who surpassed them all when it came to fashioning herself into a street legend.

She was the player the women's game had been waiting for, 6-feet-2 of near angelic leaping ability and a headliner of Michael Jordanesque charisma. Her talent, coupled with the startling growth of women's professional basketball, gave Chamique a level of recognizability no female player had before. She was, in my estimation, the future, the kind of impact player and star of breakout proportions capable of significantly expanding the popular appeal of the sport. I had high hopes that she could become the first million dollar baby of her gender.

I don't give out compliments easily. But I had no problem stating straight out that Chamique was the best player in the collegiate game.

Why? Because she stayed in the air. Chamique could linger up around the glass, while everyone else was jumping, and falling again. Her supple fingers could retrieve the ball and flick it in the basket while everyone around her fell away, dropping back to earth. Perhaps you had to be a player to understand the full range of her game, to know just how liquid her jumper was, and how limber her drive to the basket. There were times when she changed position in midair. She would move, meet an opponent, and seem to shape-shift. Suddenly, there she would be, on the *other* side of the basket, with an open shot. The entire Tennessee bench would bury their heads in their hands in disbelief.

And she had never lost. At anything. In every year of competitive basketball Chamique had ever played, she had won a championship. As an eighth grader, she won a city championship. In four years as a star at Christ the King High School in Queens, she won four straight state titles. Then, in her first two seasons as a collegiate player, she had led Tennessee to back-to-back NCAA Championships. Could she lead us to an unprecedented third straight title? It looked good.

But we had a problem. Talk was rampant that Chamique might finish out her junior year and then jump to the pros. Her stardom placed her, and us, at the center of two potential bidding wars.

One was forming between the young rival pro leagues, the WNBA and the ABL, each anxious to secure her marquee talents. Another was shaping up between the powerful sneaker companies, who recognized Chamique as a potential marketing gold mine.

She offered a big city rep and a battery of nicknames, Meke, a. k. a. Mique, a. k. a. Meek, a. k. a. The Claw, that seemed ready-made to sell shoes. There was already intense jockeying over her. We were seeing a full court press.

Here were some of the alternately disturbing and exhilarating rumors swirling around our prodigy and leading scorer: that she would leave school early to play for the New York Liberty of the WNBA. That she would leave school early to become the first $1 million player for the ABL. That she would have her own "name" shoe, and double the endorsements of any other player thus far. That Michael Jordan, a Nike stockholder with his own sneaker and apparel division, wanted to personally sign her to a deal.

Although the WNBA and ABL had policies against accepting undergraduates, no one believed the rules could hold up. On the men's side of the game, underclassmen had been dropping out of school to enter the NBA draft for years. The women's leagues were fledgling, and no one had challenged them legally—yet—but someone was bound to. There was too much money at stake. Spencer Haywood opened the floodgates in the men's game in 1969, when he left the University of Detroit for the NBA after his sophomore season. In 1970, Haywood signed a six-year contract with the Seattle Supersonics worth $1.5 million. Consider the state of affairs he unwittingly wrought: plunging education levels but steadily spiraling salaries in the NBA, personified by Kevin Garnett, the high school player who in 1997 would bypass college altogether, signing with the Minnesota Timberwolves straight out of high school for an estimated $125 million.

Would Chamique be the person to lead such a devolution in the women's game? She had a chance to be the first woman with real bargaining leverage. A testament to her potential clout was that at least one of the two pro leagues was willing to bend or break its rule against signing underclassmen—seemingly set in stone—in order to procure her. ABL commisioner and co-founder Gary Cavalli said that if Holdsclaw declared herself ready, he would consider signing her. "We'd be foolish not to at least have that discussion," he said. The *Wall Street Journal* even did a piece on her marketability, calling her talent "sublime."

So I was concerned. I was concerned about Chamique's state of mind. I was concerned that she do the right thing for her future. And I was concerned for our team.

I didn't want the pro question to become a distraction; we had too many other things to worry about. If we didn't get it settled, it could consume us all season.

Something else was worrisome, too. Truthfully, I had never fully understood Chamique. In her first two seasons, I treated her gingerly. She had a deep reserve—witness her refusal to call me Pat. And she had a duality that baffled me. On the one hand, she was urgently driven. On the other, she was a delicate, almost frail-seeming young woman, so soft-spoken her voice was a near whisper, and she covered her mouth to hide her braces. She had a charming habit of collapsing into short high-pitched giggles, a whoop-whoop-whooping sound that was all the more improbable given her height. There was something elderly in her mannerisms, the result of being raised by her grandmother. She had an eerie habit of fanning herself and exclaiming "Goodness!" or "Oh, Lordy."

"I don't know how I do some of the things I do," she once whispered to me. "I do surprise myself. But I can't *act* like I'm surprised."

She had puzzling dreams, reveries of flight and paralysis. She would dream of jumping after a loose ball and trying to save it before it went out of bounds. She leaped through the air in her sleep, spinning and off balance, the ball just out of her reach. She would fall until the floor loomed up at her, and then start awake. Sometimes she dreamed she could not move at all. Her mind would be alert but her arms and legs inert and benumbed. She had the dreams often, when she dozed in class, or in study hall, or on airplanes. She would jerk awake to find that people were staring at her. Were they good dreams, or anxiety dreams?

She didn't know for sure—which was how we both felt about the waking developments in her career.

➤ ➤ ➤

JUNE HOLDSCLAW NEVER KNEW what might arrive in the mail from her granddaughter. Chamique was always sending the most surprising things. Bibles, videotapes, photographs. Once, June opened an envelope and a gold national championship ring fell out. It was the ring Chamique won at Tennessee as a freshman in 1996. Another time, June opened a package and a national championship wristwatch fell into her lap. Sometimes, Chamique mailed to her grandmother the most elaborate, electric-hued, cutting edge pair of sneakers she could find. "I can't have you coming to my games looking old," Chamique teased her.

Chamique claimed she gave her grandmother something more significant than knickknacks, rings, or books. "I give her youth," she liked to say. Chamique would call home and say, "Hi, Grandma." And June would shoot back, "S'up?" All hip. The sound of her grandmother talking hip-hop would send Holdsclaw into a set of whoops.

The deep relationship between grandmother and granddaughter began when Chamique was eleven. Her story is no different than that of a lot of kids from the Queens projects. She told me the saga one day on an airplane flight.

Chamique's mother, Bonita, got pregnant when she was nineteen. Bonita and Chamique's father, William Johnson, a former football player for South Carolina State, had another child, Davon, who is three years younger than Chamique. But Bonita and William split up when Chamique was eleven, and Johnson returned to South Carolina, where he did his best over the years to support his daughter from afar, working as a mechanic.

Bonita, meanwhile, remained in Jamaica, Queens. She struggled to make a living and raise two small children in the city alone, but it was difficult, and shortly after the split, June stepped in. She took charge of both Chamique and Davon for nearly two years while Bonita got back on her feet. "She had me when she was pretty young, and she had a hard time with the responsibilities," Chamique said. "She couldn't deal with the problems I presented."

Life with her grandmother wasn't always smooth, either, but June Holdsclaw was intent on giving Chamique a sense of stability. June was a gentle, easygoing woman from Camden, Alabama, who both doted on her granddaughter, and yet held her to a firm set of rules. Chamique was expected to be in the house after dark, no hanging around outside. Idleness was not permissible. She signed Chamique up for every conceivable after-school program. June's philosophy was to keep Chamique as busy as possible, for two reasons: to distract her from her domestic situation, and to keep her safe from harm, given the menacing surroundings. "As long as you live in my house you go to school and to church, you don't sit around, and you aren't out on the street," June said.

It seemed to Chamique that June was always volunteering her services. She enrolled Chamique in glee club and in jazz dance and in ballet classes at the Bernice Johnson Dancing School in Queens. Chamique looked awkwardly long-legged in her pink tutu, and she had no flexibility. The teacher could have hit her with a stick and she still wouldn't have been able to stretch, she claims.

On Sundays, June insisted that her granddaughter accompany her to services at the local Lutheran church. Chamique would sit in the pew, frustrated and snapping her gum, while her grandmother told her to sit up straight. Chamique yearned for a traditional southern-style evangelistic church, something with movement. These days, Chamique attends a Baptist church in Knoxville, but she is too embarrassed to stand and sway, certain that she will betray her lack of timing. "I have better rhythm than Chamique Holdsclaw," Mickie DeMoss likes to joke.

The generational difference between June and Chamique was never more clear than when they went shopping for sneakers. June resolutely bypassed the thick-treaded, brightly colored Nikes, Adidas, and Reeboks. Instead, to Chamique's utter outrage, June headed straight for the generic section. "You're trying to buy me skips," Chamique would say, furious.

They would argue for twenty minutes in the back of the store.

"I want those," Chamique said, pointing.

"You aren't going to get them," June said.

They warred over the shoes, but eventually, Chamique won out. "It was downhill after that," June likes to say. In reality, June wanted to give Chamique everything. She would never make more than $25,000 a year as a medical records assistant at Jamaica Hospital in Queens. But she tried not to deny Chamique much, if she could help it. Neither did the rest of the family. Chamique was raised as if by committee: in addition to being parented by her mother and father and June, Chamique was watched over by her maternal aunt, Anita, and her uncle, George Spells. They ferried her to basketball games and made sure she had the latest basketball wear.

Clearly, the game captivated June's granddaughter. Chamique played scattered, unruly games of pickup with the other small children in the courtyard playground, or at her Queens Lutheran grade school, where the boys called her "The Skinny One." One afternoon when June was walking home from work, she saw a cluster of boys holding tryouts for a Police Athletic League team under the supervision of Tyrone Green, a young bank executive who had grown up in Astoria Houses, where he had helped found a community center and an eight-team PAL league.

June asked if her granddaughter could play.

The boys took a vote, and the verdict came in: no girls allowed.

But a year later, a twelve-year-old Chamique appeared before Green and his troupe of ballplayers. Green saw a skinny kid with big feet, tall and frail looking.

"I want to play," she said.

Right, Green thought.

Chamique picked up a ball and began to dribble. Okay, Green thought, so she can dribble. He put her on the team, over the protests of the boys.

"Why are you letting her play, Mr. Green?" the boys asked. "She's a girl, she stinks."

Chamique became the team's leading scorer.

> > >

EVENTUALLY, Bonita asked that the children return home to her in Jamaica, Queens. Davon went, but Chamique, by then thirteen, declined. She was a handful, with an awkward arrangement of knees and elbows and "a smart mouth," as she herself puts it. She announced that she wanted to remain with her grandmother. "I'm not going," she said. Chamique's reasoning was that she was at peace after the upheaval of her parents' split, and didn't want to change households again. She was established, going to school and playing basketball, and she didn't want to disrupt it.

So Chamique stayed at Astoria Houses. She began starring in the pickup games that formed all over the complex. Every morning at eight o'clock in the summers, the same group of boys appeared at June's door, asking for Chamique. One of those boys was Ron Artest, who went on to become a 6-feet-6, 233-pound basketball star at St. John's. When Chamique was thirteen and Artest was twelve, they played together on their neighborhood Boys and Girls Club team.

Chamique started. Artest sat on the bench behind her.

"It was crazy how good she was," Artest remembers. "She could slap the backboard. When you're twelve or thirteen, that's like dunking. She'd take people to the hole, she'd play down low. Everybody respected her."

There were four sets of courts in the courtyard of the housing complex; front, back, side, and middle. Chamique ruled the middle courts. She and her cadre played every afternoon, in all seasons. They would shovel snow from the courts to play. They would play into the night. Chamique would wolf down supper, and then run back outside.

Every night, you could see the frail-looking girl, shooting jumper after jumper. She would shoot until way past dark, until June would throw open the window of their apartment, and yell, "Chamique, it's time to come in."

Chamique would scowl and run up the stairs. "Grandma, don't yell out the window," she said. "It's so country."

June didn't mind if Chamique stayed out late to play ball. Basketball seemed safe compared to some other activities around the complex. Chamique wasn't one to lounge on the park benches, where trouble could be found. She saw only the basketball courts, and the safe environment inside of her grandmother's apartment.

There was a regard within Astoria Houses for those promising ballplayers who might make it out of the project. Chamique was treated no differently—as long as she held her own on the court. As the boys she played against got bigger and better, Chamique had to find more creative ways to score. It was called keeping your face. She developed a compulsion to play against the better players, to seek out bigger, stronger opponents, whether in a pickup game or in her choice of schools. The logical one for her to attend was St. John's Prep, a reputable Astoria institution with a solid program. But then Tyrone Green told her about Christ the King. It had the best girls' program in the city, he said.

Christ the King had an impressive record of sending players on to college. Under head coach Vinny Cannizzaro, twenty-seven girls from

Christ the King had received college scholarships as of 1997. Green called up Cannizzaro, a tough former police officer he knew fairly well. "You've got to see this girl," Green said. The coach got on a bus. He wandered over to some neighborhood courts near Astoria Houses and watched the skinny eighth grader. What he saw amazed him. *She's going to change everything,* he remembers thinking. *She's going to change the way the game is played.*

Attending Christ the King meant riding the bus an extra twenty minutes each way, but it also meant a chance to win championships in the highest division of play in the city. Yet it wasn't enough for Holdsclaw to dominate girls' basketball. She started riding the bus all over town. She would seek out games against grown men, the hardest guys on the most competitive courts. She prowled other housing projects in Astoria, places named Queensbridge and Ravenswood, looking for games. She met players such as Derrick Phelps, who went on to North Carolina, and Dwayne Edwards, who would play for Texas–El Paso. They took it at her, and they took it at her hard. She held her own.

When Holdsclaw was sixteen, Green took her to a three point shooting contest in Jamaica against some of the top teenage boys in the city. She won it.

As an eleventh grader, she was escorted by Green to a city tournament pitting an all-star girls' team from New York against a team from Philadelphia. When officials discovered the New York team was one player shy, Green volunteered Holdsclaw. She protested that she hadn't brought any sneakers. Green found a pair of size 12s for her, two sizes too small. She squeezed into them. Then she hung thirty points on the board.

With feats like that, Chamique developed not just a city reputation, but a national one. When she was a junior at Christ the King, the recruiting onslaught began. She was romanced especially hard by Virginia and Connecticut. But Holdsclaw's compulsion for challenges is what led her, somewhat improbably, to Tennessee.

➤ ➤ ➤

I HAD NEVER RECRUITED a New York player before. It seemed to me Chamique was a long shot; why would a streetwise, big-city talent choose Tennessee? But Mickie was bold enough to go after her. When I suggested Chamique was out of our reach, she was adamant. "We're recruiting her anyway," Mickie said. "We're at least going to make the effort." I said it hardly seemed worth it, if we didn't have a realistic chance. "We're recruiting her," Mickie repeated. I shrugged, and said okay.

In September of '94, Chamique agreed to let us come to New York to pay her a home visit. Mickie had worked her magic, befriending Chamique and earning the regard of June. We got on the plane, hoping for a miracle.

"Whatever you do," Mickie cautioned me in advance, "don't say anything about how big her feet are."

Once we arrived in New York, Chamique's high school coach, Vinny Cannizzaro, the former police officer, offered to escort us to Astoria Houses—he didn't want the two southern magnolias going by themselves. We found a parking spot near the complex and met up with Vinny, who walked us through the neighborhood, past the Korean markets and front stoops full of guys lounging in the heat. They whooped and whistled at us. "If anybody says anything to you, just ignore them," Vinny said.

We arrived at Holdsclaw's building. We stepped through a dank entrance hall and into a dark, rickety elevator. As we rode up one floor, an empty beer can rolled at our feet. Profanity was scrawled all over the walls.

Mickie said, "She has to look at this every single day."

I thought, "I'd love to take her home with me."

But when we stepped into the Holdsclaw apartment, we found a tidy, comfortable living room. The windows were thrown open to let some air in, and we could hear the stoop men, still yelling, amid the incessant street noise. But June and Chamique were surprisingly naïve and soft-spoken.

I introduced myself. Chamique took me in.

I had on a tailored suit, a pair of high heels that made me just over six feet tall, and vivid red lipstick.

"You look fake!" Chamique exclaimed.

I smiled despite myself, and announced that I was real. June invited us to sit down. She pointed to a sofa that took up most of the tiny living room.

"Be careful you don't trip over those big feet of Chamique's," June said.

Mickie and I exchanged glances, and grinned. Everyone relaxed. I sat down and composed myself. I said to Chamique, "We want you to talk to us about coming to Tennessee."

But to Chamique it sounded like "We wahnt yew . . . "

Chamique burst into her *whoop-whoop-whoop* giggles. She covered her mouth with her hand.

Fortunately, June warmed to the southern accent. June didn't know a lot about basketball or the Tennessee program, but she liked the idea of sending Chamique south. When she was a girl, some of her friends had gone off to Knoxville College, and come home with degrees. It was June's ambition that Chamique become a teacher, too. Plus, there was something in our southern voices and manners that reassured her. She felt even safer with us when we began to talk about the principles of the Tennessee program.

Chamique asked the question every prospect wants an answer to. "Will I get to start as a freshman?" she asked. "How much will I get to play?"

Other coaches had assured Chamique of a starting role and unlimited playing time. Both Holdsclaw women expected a similar answer from me.

I frowned.

"I've never promised a player a starting job," I said. "And I never will."

I held my breath, thinking we had just lost her. But Chamique just nodded and, if anything, seemed encouraged. Later, she told me that she liked it that I didn't try to please her. Everyone else had promised her the world. She decided that even if I looked fake, there was something trustworthy about me. I didn't pull my punches with her. Instead, I went out of my way to challenge her. Mickie and I said things like, "Are you *ready* to play in front of 25,000 people?"

By the end of the visit June had made up her mind. "I like the discipline," she told Chamique after we left. "They're strict. I don't allow a lot of coming and going, and they don't either."

> > >

WE DIDN'T FULLY UNDERSTAND what sort of player we had acquired until Chamique's first freshman practice. That day, she took the ball down the court alone against three male practice players. I watched closely, interested to see what she could do.

She feigned to her left, dribbled behind her back, then cut right. She split the first two guys. That left one defender. Driving the basket, she met up with him, switched hands, smoked by him, and went up for a reverse layup. She spun, and kissed the ball neatly off the glass, leaving us all agape.

It was a moment that would repeat itself over and over. She was our go-to player from that moment forward. Chamique had an appetite for the important shot. As a freshman, she actually interrupted me late in a close game with Vanderbilt to demand the ball. I was having an intense sideline conversation with our assistant coaches during a time-out when I felt a tugging on my jacket. I turned around to find Chamique yanking on my sleeve.

"Give me the ball," Holdsclaw said. "Give me the *ball*."

In front of 15,000 people, she wanted the ball.

I said, "Okay, okay."

I sat down, and smiled, and thought, "Four more years of this."

But Chamique struggled when she first arrived at Tennessee. Not on the court—she made All-American there, leading the Lady Vols to the 1995–96 national championship. No, she struggled in other ways. She wasn't accustomed to the homogeneity of Knoxville. There were exactly two kinds of people there, she noticed. White people, and black people. *Where are all the Koreans?* she wondered. *Where are the Asians, and the Latinos?*

And she struggled with me. She couldn't decide whether she liked me or not. She wasn't accustomed to raised voices, after growing up with the gentle June Holdsclaw. The first couple of times a member of our coaching staff hollered at her, she fell to pieces. Midway through Chamique's freshman season, we suffered a particularly tough loss to Mississippi. Mickie, Holly, Al, and I stood outside of the locker room, discussing our terrible performance. As we talked, we heard Chamique giggling in the back of the locker room. Mickie went nuts. She marched back there and snarled, "Maybe you can explain just what's so funny?" Chamique burst into tears. As it turned out, Chamique was as upset as any of us. Giggling was her way of dealing with it.

Early in Chamique's sophomore season, I upbraided her for what I felt were subpar practice habits. In tears, she threatened to leave school and go home. "I hate it here, I'm leaving," she wailed. She was going to call her grandmother, she announced. That was fine with me, I said. I stalked out of the locker room, leaving Mickie to comfort her.

That night on the phone, June sided with me. "Oh no," June told Chamique. "No, no, no, no. When you walked out my door, you made a decision. I expect you to stay there for four years. You're graduating from Tennessee."

Gradually, however, Chamique and I developed much better communication. I marveled at her skill, and told her so. She had a fascinatingly idiosyncratic game. She played as if she had hinges in her arms and legs. Accompanying that peculiar physical ability was an intuitive scoring instinct; she was a body magnet for the basket, but you never knew from what direction she might come at it. Trap her in an improbable position, and she would find some contorted way to get the ball to the hole. She became notorious for her loose, twisting reversal moves and second-effort tip-ins. Afterwards, she seemed to barely know what she had done. "Dang, how did I score twenty-four points?" she would say.

Chamique could singlehandedly take control of a game. During a

1997 regular season meeting with Georgia, we trailed by eleven points with 2:42 to go. Chamique proceeded to score fifteen points in the time left. She buried shots from all over, including a trio of three-pointers, to tie the game and send it into overtime.

Then she scored eight of our twelve points in overtime.

➤ ➤ ➤

HOW COULD I EVER GET to the bottom of such a perplexing young woman, I wondered? She was soft-spoken and aggressive, childlike and grandmotherly, giggly and moody. Mature on the floor, and yet very young away from it.

But Chamique was being forced to shed the last of her naiveté under the mounting pressures brought on by the question of turning pro. Over the summer, the issue had grown burdensome, even disillusioning. She was thrilled to receive fifteen birthday cards—until she realized they were from total stangers, all of them agents seeking an entree. She was receiving missives and entreaties from people promising to negotiate multi-million dollar deals on her behalf. Perfect strangers were calling her grandmother's apartment.

Everybody wanted something from her. Agents wanted to sign her, sneaker reps wanted to meet her, and the Lady Vols wanted her to lead them to a third championship. Everywhere she went, she was asked about the pro question. It was taking its toll on her. What *she* wanted was some peace and privacy.

I could tell Chamique was tense. And it got back to me that some of that tension was spilling over to the team. The freshmen craved Chamique's attention, but Chamique was a junior with her own apartment off campus. And she was sick of people pulling at her. She was friendly with the freshmen, but she didn't have the time or emotional energy to be a mother hen to them. What's more, I heard that Chamique and Kyra had a personal issue to settle, one of those things between undergraduates. It seemed to me we needed to clear the air.

Each week, our players held a "team-building" meeting among

themselves, with no coaches present. The only staff member in the room was a sports psychologist, Nina Elliott. When I heard about the problems, I called Nina and suggested she ask in the upcoming meeting whether there were any issues that needed to be dealt with. Nina did just that.

Two hours and a half hours later, some major resentments had been aired. Once Nina gave them the opening, the meeting quickly deteriorated into a roomful of tears. Chamique and Kyra weren't speaking. Meanwhile, the freshmen felt Holdsclaw was stand-offish. Chamique and Kyra argued across the room with each other, in one of those "she said, you said," arguments. Then the freshmen started in, complaining that Chamique hurt their feelings by ignoring them.

Tamika Catchings was especially hurt. "You were the person that I was so excited to come here and play with," she said, tearfully. "I wanted to play with you and be cool with you. But now that I know how you are, I don't know if I want to be friends with you."

Chamique talked about having pressure on her. Tamika said, "You know what, girl? Everybody has pressure on them. Maybe not as much as you, but I know what pressure is. Don't take it out on the team. Go off by yourself and take it out the trees, or something."

Nina stepped in to referee. She suggested that someone neutral needed to explain what the problem was. Everyone agreed that Kellie Jolly would be the best person to do that. Kellie was sort of like Switzerland on our team, quiet and neutral. But she also radiated integrity. Kellie would tell the truth as she saw it. Kellie hazarded the opinion that Chamique had a lot of problems and responsibilities to deal with, and was trying to mature. No one should hold her back.

Chamique chimed in, trying to explain herself. She couldn't be all things to all people, she said. So many people wanted a piece of her. Plus, she was simply older than the freshmen. "Look, I'm grown," she said.

After two and a half hours, everyone cried again. But this time it was friendly crying. They hugged, they cried some more. Then they started laughing, and all went to dinner.

It was the only instance of serious dissension all season.

What the other players couldn't understand was just how disheartened and distrusting Chamique had become, thanks to some ugly lessons in human nature. In a nasty incident over the summer, one agent even used Chamique's roommate to get to her. We had to be guarded: NCAA rules were specific about what constituted amateur status, and any gifts or cash overtures from an agent could cost Chamique her remaining eligibility. Our antennae were up.

As a sophomore, Chamique lived with a track athlete from Houston. Every so often, an older woman would call for Chamique's roommate. If Chamique happened to answer the phone, she would chat casually with the lady. One day, according to Chamique, the woman on the other end of the phone said, "You're Chamique Holdsclaw? I didn't know that's who I was talking to." She introduced herself as an attorney.

Not too much later, the woman called again. This time, she said, "You know, if you ever need help, my boss can provide you with whatever you want." Holdsclaw laughed off the overture, considering it a joke.

But then, the next summer, the so-called attorney showed up at the trials for the USA national team in Colorado Springs. One afternoon, after play had been concluded for the day, she approached Chamique and said hello. They talked casually, and the woman suggested they visit. Holdsclaw agreed. They left the gym and went to Chamique's room at the Olympic training center dormitory.

Watching the exchange from across the gym was Mickie, who was helping to run the trials, as were several other coaches from around the country. Mickie uneasily eyed the stranger talking to Chamique. She thought she knew everybody in the business. But she didn't know this woman. Mickie decided to ask around about her, just in case. As she and a group of fellow coaches climbed into a car to go to dinner, Mickie said, "Does anybody know who that woman was?" Someone remarked that they thought she was an agent or an attorney from Houston.

"Stop the car," Mickie said.

Mickie jumped out of the car and sprinted into the dormitory and down the hall to Chamique's room. She burst through the door and found the stranger sitting in a chair, chatting up her star player.

"Have you ever seen a dead body?" Mickie demanded.

The woman stared at Mickie, speechlessly.

"If Pat Summitt knew about this, she would *kill* you," Mickie said.

The woman protested that she was simply a friend and an attorney. But Mickie ordered her out of the room anyway. Afterwards, she and Chamique talked. Clearly, she was going to have to be more careful, Mickie said. The Tennessee coaches wanted to protect her, but she would have to learn to protect herself, as well. "Look, I don't want one dime of your money, and neither does Pat," Mickie said. "We just want what's best for you. If that's going pro early, then that time will come and we'll discuss it, and you can make the best decision. But the time is not now. You don't need to be dealing with agents, or any other people trying to get into your life."

Chamique learned a hard lesson from the incident. "Why would a thirty-year-old want to be my friend?" she said. Meanwhile, the numbers of agents and sports management companies trying to contact her only mushroomed. Another attorney sidled up next to her while she was watching a summer tournament in Manhattan. He slipped her a card and whispered that she would be worth $6 to $8 million in endorsements if she turned pro.

One day in late September, shortly before the season began, I asked Chamique to meet with me. We had a long talk. We needed to get organized, I said. We needed to put the pro question to rest. Otherwise, it would eat us all alive.

Chamique assured me she intended to return for her senior year. "Everyone thinks I'm leaving, but right now I want to stay and get my degree," she said. "I don't want to be the one to set a negative trend, instead of a positive one. I don't want to be the player who brings it down a notch."

However, whenever Chamique was asked about turning pro by a member of the media, she had a disturbing tendency to leave the door ·

open. I knew that when the dollar signs started showing, she might feel differently. She had a lot of decisions to make.

The challenges at the collegiate level were, for her, fewer and fewer. With all of that talent, Chamique was easily bored. Without some fresh obstacle or goal, I was afraid she could feel confined at Tennessee. The key to getting a commitment out of Chamique would be to somehow keep her interested. In a word, to challenge her.

And she had a dilemma, I knew. She had enormous financial considerations. When the time came, I promised her, the Tennessee staff would do whatever we could to help her find a reputable agent.

There was one person whose opinion would carry more weight than mine, I knew. Her grandmother. Chamique burned to liberate June from her small apartment in Astoria Houses. June would talk dreamily about some day retiring back down south. But June was adamant that Chamique get her college degree. Pleading poverty over education didn't appeal to her—or to her granddaughter, either, deep down.

June wanted her to get a degree. But Chamique knew June was struggling, too. It was expensive to support a prospective Olympian and a future pro. Chamique needed pocket money in her travels with the national team. She needed clothes for public appearances and awards banquets. Also, she needed insurance. We advised June to purchase $250,000 in disability insurance for her granddaughter. June bought a Lloyds of London policy for $1,800. It was a huge expense for her.

There was so much for Chamique to think about. But for the time being, Chamique would continue to call the old Astoria neighborhood home. Occasionally, she would hear that someone she grew up with had met with an ugly fate. A boy she used to play ball with was shot and killed while trying to rob someone. A girl she went to grammar school with was pregnant.

Mostly, she saw the same old people doing the same old things. With one notable difference. There was no skinny girl with an exquisite pull-up jumper, haunting the middle courts. She was gone.

Now, in her place, several of them ran the courts.

One afternoon Tyrone Green, Chamique's old rec center director, watched the girls shoot around. One of them, a thirteen-year-old named C.J., wandered over to him. He struck up a conversation with her.

She informed him that she was the next Chamique.

"I hope you are, honey," Tyrone said. "Oh, I hope so."

Q & A with Kyra Elzy (Sophomore guard)

Did you know your dad much growing up?

No.

Where is he now, do you know?

That's funny, Pat and I were just talking about this. He lives in western Kentucky. He left when I was a baby.

Do you have a relationship with him?

No. It doesn't matter. He's a stranger to me.

Does the drive on this team come from so many players raised in single-parent homes?

I think it does. To my family I've made it. I made it out, you know? And hopefully, I'll make some money and take care of my family, so my mom won't have to work. So basically, as far as my father is concerned, I don't want anything he has. I'm two years from graduating from college without his help. I've made it here on my own. I'm on the downside of things. I'm skating down.

CHAPTER FOUR

Family Matters

SMALL INTIMACIES FORM A TEAM. You measure them for their uniforms, and ask them if they prefer blue or orange practice shorts. You distribute their Adidas sneakers, and tease them about their less-than-delicate shoe sizes. You go over their physicals, and examine the scars from old injuries. These are the tiny but vital stitches of personal knowledge that draw you together. If you're the coach, you just hope they don't unravel on you by halftime.

It was in the name of team bonding that I held Family Night. The idea was that everyone would bring pictures of their family and we would talk about where we were from. To the players it sounded corny, another one of Pat's down-home remedies. But I insisted. We needed to try something fresh. We had too many new players, and possible hot spots of dissension. One thing I knew: a single alienated influence, a player who decided to remain a stranger, could slip the knot and undo this team.

I scheduled the meeting for one night in mid-October.

We gathered in the locker room and sat in a circle. We would go around and talk about our backgrounds and the people who were closest to us, I said.

I could see some of the veteran players lifting their eyebrows. Close? Pat, trying to be close? It was a foreign concept.

Closeness was not something I had always cultivated in the past, I'll admit. I wasn't the most understanding coach. For years, the only thing I thought about was whether the opponent was in a zone or man.

Understand the *players,* off the court? What for? The only time a coach should be close to her players was when they needed a talking to, eyeball to eyeball, I thought.

When I first started at Tennessee in 1975, I was an inexperienced twenty-two-year-old head coach—with four players who were twenty-one. I kept my distance. I thought a coach was supposed to show a team how to win, help them graduate, and make sure they stayed out of any trouble that couldn't be handled with a phone call to their mothers and daddies. I set up strict player-coach boundaries. I felt I wouldn't be able to do my job if I cared about them too much. I built a wall of reserve, and I thought that reserve was the same as authority.

I got it wrong. It was fourteen years before Tennessee won its first national championship. I was so busy being tough, I didn't understand the value of getting to know the players on a deeper level, their real strengths and vulnerabilities. You didn't let 'em see you smile until Christmas, I thought. That became my personality. *Do it,* I said. And I expected them to just do it.

Then, in 1987, we won our first title. And four more in the next ten years. What changed? For one thing, me. Over the years, I matured and learned from my experiences. I was forced out from behind my desk to deal with drugs, alcohol, injury, broken hearts, and emotional break-downs of every other description. I was confronted by unwanted pregnan-cies, drinking problems, a player in a near-fatal car wreck, and countless instances of love gone wrong. I had even handled the occasional violent boyfriend, and obscene caller. I had dealt with several parents who tried to tell me how to coach, and a few who thought I just plain didn't like their daughters. There was one mother who, I was certain, would kill me given the chance. Whenever she showed up at a game, I half expected to see a rifle and scope.

I was learning that a coach is far more than a strategist or a disciplinarian. You are a peculiar form of crisis counselor and interim substitute parent.

But I was still figuring out the coach-player relationship. The complexities and intimacies of it continually made me uneasy. I was extremely close to some players, like Bridgette Gordon, our all-time leading scorer from 1986–89. But with others I had never found a middle ground. Even the most confident players took a while to decide they weren't afraid of me.

I was tired of trying to interpret players, of hoping to divine the inner feelings of a Chamique Holdsclaw from halting talks in my office. And I was unnerved by the loss of Tiffani Johnson. I had tried for three years to reach her, and failed.

I didn't know what music they listened to. I heard strains of melodies drifting from the locker room that I seldom recognized. When the players talked among themselves, I didn't get half of their references.

Maybe I was softening with age, but I wanted to understand them better. But was I capable of it? With this team, it seemed especially important to know more than just their personalities on the court. I needed to know their characters off it. The more trusting my relationships with players, the better teacher and coach I could be to them. With four freshmen, four young blanks looking for so many answers, trust would be paramount. The task was to blend them together with a complicated star player, Chamique, and somehow build a team.

But the funny thing was, to a certain extent the players didn't *want* to know *me* better. I was a fixed entity. I was Pat, their famously rigid and upright coach, practically cast in bronze. They knew me by my reputation, and by the numbers: five national championships in twenty-three seasons, and fourteen Final Four appearances. They were as resigned to my persona as they were to the Statue of Liberty. They were even reassured by it. Kellie Jolly once said they *liked* seeing the veins in my neck stand out when I got mad—it psyched them up.

Lately, I felt like toying with their perceptions of me. It was fun to throw away my rectitude and watch their reactions. For instance, one afternoon, it got back to me that the team planned to get a stripper for Niya Butts' birthday. They were crushed when the stripper didn't show up.

After practice, I called them into a circle. I was wearing sweats. I said, "Niya, I heard you didn't get a stripper for your birthday. So I'll strip for you." Then I started to pull off my shirt.

You could hear their scandalized shrieks out on the sidewalk. They scattered like a flock of birds, flying to various corners of the court and hiding their faces. But I was only kidding. I pulled my shirt down.

Now, I'm not saying I wanted to become their best friend. And I didn't intend to act like an eighteen-year-old in hopes of becoming their confidante. But I sensed that this team might need something more from me than past teams had. They were so young.

Not long after Semeka Randall arrived on campus, she wandered into the office and stuck her head in my door. I was out; what a surprise. It must have seemed to Semeka like I was always out. I was either traveling, or at a speaking engagement, or in a meeting. Semeka was hurt. We had developed a great phone relationship during her senior year in high school, talking several times a week; she called me at home at all hours. But now that she was here, it seemed like I didn't have time for her. Okay, she thought, so that's how it's going to be. Fine. She didn't need me.

But the fact is, she did. Semeka went from my office to Mickie's. Mickie was busy, too. Semeka stood in Mickie's door, watching her sort through the correspondence on her desk. Finally, Mickie looked up, and saw Semeka staring at her, her big brown eyes shiny and calf-like.

"Whatcha need?" Mickie asked, absently.

Semeka said, plaintively, "I need some love."

Mickie got up from her desk and threw her arms around Semeka.

So maybe that's why I called the Family Night meeting. Maybe I was still learning that it was more important to listen to players than to lecture them. And maybe I was finally secure enough in myself to be closer to them.

Maybe I was both charmed and taken aback to learn that Tamika Catchings wrote poetry.

I opened the meeting.

We would explain who we were and where we came from.

> > >

THE FIRST TIME KYRA ELZY remembers laying eyes on her father was as a sixth grader. In a courtroom.

Kyra's mother, Sheryl, and her father, Bobby Jones, split when Kyra was still a baby. Bobby moved to Paducah, where he eventually started a second family. Meanwhile Sheryl was left alone back in LaGrange, Kentucky, a twenty-one-year-old mother who had to find a way to raise her small daughter by herself.

Sheryl worked every waking hour. She became a prison corrections officer in LaGrange, but on the side she worked two and sometimes even three extra jobs to support herself and Kyra. She punched a cash register at a local grocery store. She dished out soft serve ice cream at a Dairy Queen.

She also took odd jobs around the apartment complex where they lived. There were several steep flights of stairs on the back of the apartment complex. Sheryl would vacuum the stairs every week to earn some extra cash. Three flights up, and three flights down. Even so, to hear Kyra describe it, despite all that hard work they didn't have enough money to get across the state. One pair of sneakers had to last a year.

The day Kyra saw her father for the first time was when Sheryl and Bobby met in court to decide child support issues. Kyra had to appear with her mother. Kyra gazed at the strange man sitting across the room. She has seen pictures of him, shown to her by her mother, but now here was the real article, in the flesh. "Gosh, that's my dad?" she asked. Sheryl nodded. Kyra left the court without speaking to him.

Sheryl worried constantly about Kyra. She was putting in so many extra hours, and working late shifts from 3 P.M. to midnight, that she barely saw her daughter at times. They were lucky to have Sheryl's brother, Robert Elzy. Kyra considered him more of a real father than her own. When Sheryl was working too hard to look after Kyra, Robert Elzy would take her home with him. Other times, Kyra was a classic latchkey kid. She would let herself in the apartment and fix her own dinner, do her homework, and put herself to bed.

All of the Elzys looked after Kyra. She was the hope of the family, they said. She could be the first female Elzy to win an athletic scholarship, and that meant a chance to do something besides working paycheck to paycheck in LaGrange. Kyra was a cross country runner as well as a basketball star. When she wasn't at practice, or running, she would help Sheryl vacuum all those stairs in the apartment complex. But Sheryl didn't want Kyra's help unless she had finished her homework. "You *have* to pass, you can't fail," Sheryl said.

Kyra got through her adolescence with no major problems, and became a nationally renowned player as a high school junior. All of the major schools began recruiting her, and Tennessee was at the forefront. The day I visited her at home, Kyra filled me in on some of her family history. She told me how hard Sheryl worked, and she said her dad really hadn't been in her life. I didn't make any judgments about the situation then, and I still don't. I just told Kyra I was sorry, and that I wished it had been easier for her.

When Kyra signed with Tennessee, it made all the local and state papers. One night, her phone rang. It was Kyra's father, Bobby. He wanted to say hello, he said. He had heard that she was a high school All-American.

Kyra listened, and felt nothing. Bobby tried to make conversation with her, but she didn't really respond. She didn't know this man, and she had nothing to say to him, she decided. After a couple of brief exchanges, she hung up.

Then one afternoon, Kyra's father called me. I picked up the phone in my office. "This is Kyra Elzy's dad," he said. "I hear Tennessee is recruiting her. I know she's quite fond of the place, so I'd like to know a little more about it. Would you send me some material?" I said I would be happy to. But Kyra had told me enough about their relationship, or lack of one, that I didn't feel comfortable offering more than that.

From then on, I would hear from Bobby occasionally. He wrote me a letter after she signed. In another instance, he called asking for a media guide, and wanted to get on our mailing list.

One evening when Kyra and I were on the phone, I admitted that I had heard from her father.

"Your dad called me," I said.

"He didn't!" she said, disbelieving.

Kyra kept her temper with me. But it clearly galled her. When we talked about it later, she acknowledged it had made her angry. "Oh, I was outraged," she said. "How was he going to call and write? It was like some distant member of the family."

Kyra felt that she gotten through all of those difficult years, raising herself while her mother worked three jobs, without Bobby. She might have needed him then, but she didn't any more.

"I don't know him," she said.

➤ ➤ ➤

As we went around the circle, I began to wonder if there was an echo in the room. After Kyra's story came Ace's.

Ace was a year old when her parents split. Her father, Richard, a musician, stayed in touch with her until she was thirteen. Then one day, she said, she stopped hearing from him. She said he had moved to Florida, and she hadn't really seen him much since.

➤ ➤ ➤

Mickie DeMoss had seen her father just a handful of times in her life. He left when she was either two or three, she can't remember. She was raised by her mother, Wilma, a tiny but forceful character who worked as a waitress and ran a general store and barroom in Waverly, Louisiana, called the Delta Grocery and Lounge. Wilma worked night and day, rarely getting home before 11:30 at night. Mickie fed herself, got herself up for school, and generally raised herself. It was understood that Wilma would never permit Mickie to work as hard as she had to.

She was going to send Mickie to college if it took her last breath, so her daughter would never have to scrape or depend on anyone else to support her.

Mickie could do a fair imitation of her mother. She loved to collect what she called Wilma-isms. Like this one: "If you never open your mouth, nobody will know you're a fool."

My personal favorite was "You can't ruin ruin."

Mickie saw her dad when he came to her high school graduation and again five years later when, one day, she happened to be driving through Arkansas. She looked up and realized she was in Eureka Springs, where he lived. She asked around, and found out he still resided there. She drove by his place, and there he was. She walked straight into his front yard. He recognized her right away, before she got within ten feet of him. "Is that Mickie?" he said. He knew her because they looked just alike. They talked for a while, casually, but they had little to say to each other. The resemblance, no matter how strong, couldn't make them family, Mickie decided. And she hadn't seen him since.

There was one detail, which I knew about, that Mickie didn't tell the team. Mickie was a grown woman before she had her first Christmas tree. I knew that, because I bought it for her. Shortly after she came to work at Tennessee, we were sitting around the office one day during the holiday season. I asked her, "Do you have your tree up?"

Mickie said, "I've never had a tree."

I got up from my chair and grabbed the car keys. "Let's go," I said, trying to hide the fact that my eyes had filled up with tears. I insisted we buy her a tree, and all the trimmings, too.

On we went around the circle. Chamique's voice broke talking about her grandmother. Then Semeka spoke, and Niya, and Laurie. All of them told stories of divorces, of mothers working two jobs to get by, and in some instances, of fathers they barely knew. One variation was Teresa Geter's: she talked about her father, but couldn't bring herself to talk about Joanne because she knew she would cry if she did.

As the meeting wore on, something began to dawn on me. An important statistic was hidden on our roster, and it wasn't exactly the kind of stat you find in a box score. It was more significant and human than that. In fact, it was heartbreaking.

I gazed around the room in disbelief, wondering if I could be right. I checked my math.

I looked from player to player, counting.

Nine of our twelve players were raised in single-parent homes at some point in their formative years. Including all four freshmen.

What's more, so was half of our coaching staff. Among the coaches, just Al and I were raised in two-parent homes. Holly's father died when she was a sophomore in high school. Her mother, Fran, worked as a hotel manager, so she was gone from seven in the morning until seven at night. Holly had to be the other adult in the household. She cut the lawn, did the cooking, and fixed things when they were broken.

As each player talked, the mutual sympathy filled the room. Emotions bounced off the walls.

What had I gotten us into? I wondered.

Frankly, I had never dealt with such a complication before. We had had one or two players before who came from difficult family circumstances. But I had never seen wholesale orphaning like this.

I had trouble grasping it. I didn't want to make judgments. But I didn't understand it, either.

How could you not *want* a Mickie, or an Ace, or a Kyra, I wondered? But I knew this, too: I couldn't afford to feel sorry for them. One thing you learn as a head coach is that you can't save people from themselves. Coaches in general think they can—some of them even have God complexes, or images of Father Flanagan dancing in their heads. But the truth is this: an eighteen-year-old is already a defined human being.

They didn't need me to save them.

Every one of those players had already been saved.

➤ ➤ ➤

BRIEFLY, I described my own childhood. I was the fourth of five children, and the first girl, in a cash poor farm family from Henrietta,

Tennessee. We were so hard pressed that I slept in a baby bed until I was six. My parents, Richard and Hazel Head, built their own dairy and tobacco farm out of nothing in Montgomery County, Tennessee. The crow's feet at the corners of my eyes came from long days sitting on a tractor in the tobacco fields. I started setting tobacco when I was six or seven.

Richard Head didn't know what to do with a daughter, so he raised me like a combination of a fourth son and an extra field hand. If I made a mistake I got whipped. If I cried, I got whipped harder. As I got older, my three brothers enlisted me as the fourth player in their nightly basketball games. I learned how to play ball in the top of a hayloft. My father nailed an old iron rim and strung some floodlights up around the tin roof, and we would play brutal games among the haystacks, shoving each other across the pine floor. There, too, if I cried, I got whipped. The solution was obvious. I didn't cry.

The barn is still there, except that it leans sideways, blown off its foundation by a tornado a few years ago.

My parents worked every waking moment to scratch out a better living. They opened a general store in Henrietta, and after school, I would work behind the counter. Once a week, I sold large bags of sugar to the local bootlegger. I remember my mother lugging milk cans across the cement floor, a surface so hard that it wore her ankles down to nothing and she had to have surgery. Then my parents opened a hardware store, tobacco warehouse, feed mill, laundry, gas pump, and beauty salon—mostly because Henrietta didn't have those things. They also built houses. When my father wasn't starting a new business he worked two other leased farms and served as the county water commissioner. All that work took a toll on his body; he had a quintuple bypass, two ministrokes, and two knee replacements, but he still tends to his tobacco fields every day.

When I went off to college at the University of Tennessee-Martin, I was so shy and country that I was afraid to open my mouth. Back home my family called me Trisha. (It came out *Treee-sha*). But at Tennessee-Martin, everyone assumed I was Pat. I was too timid to correct them, so that's who I became. The only place I felt comfortable was on the basket-ball court. Back then, there was no reward or reason for playing ball other than love of the game. There were no athletic scholarships for women, no money for decent uniforms, or hotels. On the road, we slept on mats in the gym of whatever campus we visited. But the thing about it was, I needed the game more than it needed me. I needed it to prove my worth in a family of brothers, who had never once cleared their own plates from a table or poured their own ice tea. And I needed it to earn something—anything—from my father in the way of attention.

My father wasn't good at expressing love or pride, much as I knew he felt those things. He was too tired from setting tobacco or getting the hay in to have anything left over in the way of talk. He was tall—6-feet-5—so everyone called him Tall Man. But that wasn't what made him imposing. It was his stare, a blue-eyed death ray. When my father looked at you, you thought it might set your clothes on fire. I'm told I inherited his look, which everybody calls The Stare. A for-mer player, Michelle Marciniak, says I can "look down" into your eyes. I can stoop to chin level, grab you in eye-lock, and rise back up again, taking your head with me. My father could make people step backwards involuntarily just by gazing at them.

Although I grew up with my father in the house, I went without a hug from him for forty-three years. And I went without much in the way of praise from him. Like him, I had trouble expressing my feelings and developing relationships. But my mother, Miss Hazel, was as openly caring as he was reserved, the kind of mother who was always frying a chicken and shelling butter beans and churning homemade ice cream at the same time that she was asking you what was wrong. I love and respect them in different ways.

Finally, one night in 1996 when Tennessee beat Georgia to win a third national championship, I won a response from my father. That night, I climbed up in the stands, and he put his arms around me and hugged me. The following year, when we won the championship again, despite that ugly 29–10 record, I got a second hug from him. And this time, he said in my ear, "Somebody around here knows how to coach.

Maybe Mickie, or Holly, or Al." Which was Richard Head's way of paying me a compliment, telling me he was proud.

The rest of the particulars I related in *Reach for the Summit.* How the other thing I inherited from Richard Head—that's what I call him, Richard Head—was his drive, that overwhelming feeling that no matter how far ahead you got, you were still behind. How in 1974 I was named head coach at Tennessee, as just a graduate student. How I taught three courses in phys-ed at the same time I was taking four courses to get a masters degree, while coaching the basketball team, and rehabilitating a knee injury in hopes of making the Olympic team. I would run three miles at 6 A.M. after studying past midnight, teach three classes, supervise a two-hour practice, attend four classes, drive myself through another two- or three-hour workout, and then hit the weight room. But I got the degree, and in 1976, at twenty-four, I was the oldest member of the U.S. team that brought home a surprise silver medal from the Montreal Olympics, the first time women's basketball was played in the games.

In 1980, after a three-and-a-half-year courtship, I married a country banker named R. B. Summitt, who was as patient and quiet as I was noisy and impatient. And who was as proud of our teams as I was. In 1990 Tyler Summitt was born. I nearly delivered him on an airplane over Virginia, on a harrowing recruiting trip that may have been worse for Mickie DeMoss, into whose arms he almost fell. The pilots wanted to make an emergency landing, but I refused to let them set the plane down anywhere but Tennessee, so my son could be born in Knoxville, with his father watching. Have you ever seen anyone try *not* to have a baby? Fortunately, Tyler waited, just like his father. Almost immediately, he displayed a disconcerting tendency to fall sound asleep during big games.

So that was my story.

When the team meeting finally ended, two hours after it began, we all understood one thing, if nothing else, about each other: basketball was no game to us. It wasn't just a way to earn a varsity letter or eventually a better living, although that was important motivation for us. For Kyra Elzy it was a form of requital. *I'll show him what he walked out on.* For

Ace Clement, a redemption. *If I'm good enough, I'll be loved.* For Chamique Holdsclaw, an exploration of her own value. *I'll find my true worth.* For Tamika Catchings, an offering of self-expression. *I feel all of this.*

It made them walking contradictions, sweet and mean and fragile, all at the same time.

> > >

JUST BECAUSE I wanted to know them better didn't mean I backed off. Over the next month, I made each of the freshmen cry. But at least now they knew *why* I drove them, and *who* was driving them. Tree cried when I hollered at her for being slow. Semeka cried when I told her she played too fast. Ace cried when I yelled at her for trying to throw thread-the-needle passes. Tamika cried when I told her she didn't know how to play defense. In the locker room, they would sit huddled together, saying, "Man, we're going crazy. If it wasn't for basketball, we wouldn't even be here."

Things were right on schedule.

Then, on the night of November 14, something happened that would affect me for the rest of the season, and for the rest of my life. I went to bed thinking about basketball, like I did on any other night. In just a few days, we would open our regular season against Mississippi. I closed my eyes, and slept. And while I slept there was a crack, and a flash.

It began as a pleasant social evening. R.B. and I went to see *Les Miserables* with Mickie, our nanny and friend Latina Dunn, and our best friends in Knoxville, Lex and Mary Margaret Carter. Mary Margaret, a surgical nurse, had gone to school with me at Tennessee-Martin. We belonged to the same sorority, Chi Omega. She was a sweet-natured brunette who still had something of the sorority girl about her. Lex, owner of his own construction firm, had blond tousled hair and spectacles, and a soft, easy voice.

Lex and Mary Margaret vacationed with us, and we went to

Tennessee football games together every weekend. They were boosters and friends of the Lady Vol program, and often traveled with the team. All of our coaches and players knew them on a first name basis.

At the intermission of the show, I chatted casually with Lex. He was in a mood to talk about his three sons, Alex, Cullen, and Caleb. But he especially talked about Caleb, sixteen, the youngest and the last one living at home. They had gotten closer, he said. He was glad he was doing better at balancing family and work, and that he had more time for his third son, he said.

We got home at about midnight, and turned in. An hour later, at 1 A.M., the phone rang. I grabbed at the receiver, afraid there was an emergency with one of our players. Instead, it was Mary Margaret. She was incoherent. She was at the University of Tennessee Medical Center. From what I could understand, still half asleep, she was telling me that one of her sons was dead.

I bolted out of bed and threw on a shirt and a pair of slacks. I pushed past 90 mph going to the hospital. I found Lex and Mary Margaret slumped in a couple of chairs, in shock. It was Caleb, they told me. He had been shot.

It happened at a Friday night party of teenagers. Someone found a handgun, and began playing with it. Caleb had just arrived. He was standing in a doorway, watching the boys fool with the gun. The gun went off, and a bullet struck Caleb in the head. He died instantly.

I spent most of the night at the hospital, trying to console Lex and Mary Margaret, making necessary calls, and helping with arrangements. Finally, at about 4 A.M., we dragged ourselves back home. I fell into bed and slept for a couple of hours.

Before practice that day, Mickie explained to the team what had happened. No one was sure if I would show up for work. But with our opener against Mississippi coming up, I felt I should try to make it in. I arrived late. But I might as well have stayed home.

I knelt on one knee at the end of the court, staring into space. I watched the team run up and down the length of the court, but I didn't really see them. I couldn't stop thinking about the folly of putting boys and guns together in the same room, and how vulnerable children are.

Caleb Carter was a thin boy with a straight line of blond bangs. I had known him for the better part of his short life. Every summer, he worked as a go-fer and equipment manager at our basketball camp. The gym directors and assistant coaches argued over who got to work with him, because he was so pleasant and hardworking, a silky-haired kid with an open disposition. My son, Tyler, thought Caleb hung the sun and switched it on. Earlier in the summer our families had vacationed together in Jackson Hole, Wyoming. We went rafting and hiking. Tyler followed Caleb everywhere. Only a few weeks before Caleb's death, our families had hiked to the top of Mount LeConte, one of the higher peaks in the Smokies. We stood at the top and stared over the expanse. It was one of those views that made you feel like your heart was wide open.

Two days after Caleb's death, a memorial service was held at Lex and Mary Margaret's Presbyterian church. Hundreds attended. The death by gunshot of a sixteen-year-old boy was not uncommon in some cities, but in Knoxville it was near unheard of.

As the minister began to eulogize Caleb, I struggled to hold myself together. Mortality wasn't a tragedy, the minister suggested. Caleb was in the arms of the angels, ever perfect and unbroken. He would not know pain or disappointment. I could see Lex and Mary Margaret rise somewhat at those words.

Tragedy was being forced to *live through* something like this, I thought, as the minister continued to speak. Caleb was at peace; he would not have to survive the various losses, loves, hates, moments of truth, and disappointments that make a life. He wouldn't have to know the heartsickness of losing a family member. Or the inevitable disenchantment and erosion of confidence that was adulthood. Or the solitary, bone-wearying struggle of single parents to make a living and raise a beloved child by themselves. There would be no marital mistakes for Caleb either, no collapse of love ending in angry, baffled divorce.

Sometimes, I thought, it's all we can do to pull ourselves through the wreckage of our own lives.

I cried as bitterly as I ever have.

And then I realized I was scaring my own son.

Tyler sat between R.B. and me. He had never seen me, his mother, his near six-foot tower of confidence and reassurance, fall apart. I was the safest thing he knew. Four nights out of five he jogged across the house in the middle of the night and crept into our bed. I would spoon him, my arms around his little body, and feel him breathe in and out. In those moments, I could feel his heart banging in his chest, and I would swear that it beat harder than the ordinary child's. If he was having a bad dream he would twitch, and throw his arm across my neck.

I'd say, "What is it, baby?"

"Aliens," he would murmur.

In the church pew, Tyler stared up at me, tearfully. He was having a hard time grasping the idea that Caleb was dead. But to see me cry was more alarming than anything.

"It's all right, darlin'," I said. "I'm just sad."

But the loss of Caleb shattered every ounce of certainty I possessed. All of a sudden I had an acute sense of the ground shifting under me, and of how much you could win and lose in a day. I had the uncomfortable feeling that I was living at one hundred miles an hour, and that I was kinder and more attentive to a million strangers than to the people closest to me, whether R.B. or Tyler. Or our players.

There's no time, I thought.

The day after the service, I tried to go back to our team routine. But it was difficult not to think constantly about Lex and Mary Margaret. And it was difficult not to reappraise my relationships with the players.

I had four years to know them.

Having a son had already altered my relationships to a certain extent. When I was pregnant with Tyler, every forkful of food I ate was for him. He made me more open and able to express myself. He needed so much, and I found I was capable of giving it. Now that he was a boy, he needed different things, but he still needed reassurance and safety and love the way he needed food and water. Our players were the same way. Just because you're grown doesn't mean you stop needing, I realized. You just need different things. And in some ways, you might need more.

The coach-player tie is not unlike that of a parent and child, I decided. It doesn't have to be—but I elected to coach that way. This team was a family. We were a combination of close and embattled. We skirmished over private territory, over what was my business, and what wasn't. We were mutually capable of inflicting wounds straight to the bone. It might seem like I had all the power. But I didn't. If I could bench them, they could deny me their trust. We were locked in a never-ending tug of war; I wanted their all, and they craved my attention and approval. It was tempting to withhold it, because it could be a valuable tool—like me with my father, they were willing to do almost anything to obtain it.

And just like parents and children, we were precious to each other. Only we'd never admit it.

But I was ready to admit it.

How well, you may wonder, could a forty-five-year-old coach with a pronounced taste for orange blazers really understand a dozen undergraduates? Probably about as well as a mother understands her daughters. You gain a deep understanding of your child's heart. You'd just rather not know all the specifics.

On November 18, Caleb Carter was buried on his family farm in Fayetteville.

That same day, our season began.

PART TWO

>>> No-Limit
Soldiers

Q & A with Ace Clement (Freshman guard)

You're not in touch with your father?

No. He wasn't always there for me while I was growing up. He remarried and started another family and basically wasn't a part of our lives from then on. It broke my heart. I think during those years you really need fatherly advice. Now he's trying to come back into our lives. He's been writing me letters. But it's my choice. Sometimes I don't even read the letters.

How do you think it shaped this team that so many players came from single-parent homes?

I think it drives you. We wanted to go out and prove that we could survive. We got through all the adversity. And look at us now, look at what each of us has accomplished.

What about your relationship with Pat? Did it shape that?

Yeah. She could be rough, but I like that. People don't see the other side, how loving and caring she is. You know, when you come from single-parent families like we do, and then you come across someone like Pat, who cares and worries about you, boy, you take advantage of it. You hang on to it.

CHAPTER FIVE

Glamour Girl

Ace Clement was on the bench. She had never sat on the bench for the start of a game. Ace didn't do the bench. It was not her area. It felt wrong, all wrong. It felt . . . conspicuous. Everybody was looking at her, she thought. They were wondering why she was sitting here, while the other freshmen were shuttling on and off the court, playing against Mississippi. The freshmen were on the court and she was here, on the bench, and she felt like every ticket-buying spectator in the arena, every paid-admission fan, was staring at her. And they were all thinking the same thing, probably.

"They think I suck," she thought.

The Mississippi game was more than just our season opener. It was the much-anticipated debut of the four freshmen, the first time they would play together in Tennessee uniforms. Only now the crowd would see just three freshmen instead of the Fab Four, because Ace Clement was on the bench.

Then, mercifully, an announcement came over the loudspeaker: Ace Clement would not be playing, due to injury. So at least there was that. At least the crowd would know that she was hurt.

➤ ➤ ➤

ACE WASN'T JUST A GLAMOUR GIRL, although that's what we called her. The word glamorous didn't begin to do justice to Ace Clement. That was just a silly locker room routine. It started as a running joke between Ace, Chamique, and LaShonda Stephens. There were some players who were more concerned with clothes and looks than others. And then there were Ace, Chamique, and LaShonda, who raised primping and prissing in the mirror to an art. The three of them started a club, and dubbed themselves the Glamour Girls. It was a hilarious, self-mocking act, and they played it to the hilt. They air kissed. They flipped their hair, and talked in sing-song send-ups of high society voices.

Ace *was* glamorous, of course. She was a real live Miss Hawaiian Tropic, a genuine beauty with lustrous brown hair and brown eyes, who, through no fault of her own, couldn't sit in the cafeteria without being surrounded by the entire starting backfield of the football team. But her looks were profoundly deceiving. In the end, they told you absolutely nothing about her. To understand who Ace really was, you had to see her on the basketball court. You had to see her in practice when she dove headfirst for a loose ball.

We always practiced against guys. I wanted us to become accustomed to jostling with players well over six feet and weighing 175 to 200 pounds. That way, when we had to play teams that were physically imposing, we would be used to it. One afternoon, we were just killing the guys. We led them by thirty points, with four seconds to go on the clock. Suddenly, there was a loose ball. Ace dove for it, a full body skid. She retrieved it, got to one knee, turned around on a speed dribble, raced down court— and got a shot off before the clock expired. With a thirty point lead, she was still desperate to score.

So that's who Ace was. If being a floor mop would help Ace win, then she was willing to be a floor mop.

There was nothing glamorous about the headlong, self-sacrificing, obsessively dedicated way Ace played the game. There was nothing glamorous about the vicious way Ace had been treated by other young women because of her looks. There was nothing particularly glamorous about being the youngest of six kids raised by a single mother with a bad back.

There was nothing glamorous about being hurt, either. Or how she got injured in the first place. Or what it did to the rest of her season.

Ace's injury started out as just a sore foot. We were in the middle of a routine practice in early November when I called for a set of wind sprints, to punish the team for some transgression or other. Ace's foot had been achy for several days, but she figured it was a result of heaving herself up and down The Hill. When I ordered the wind sprint, she obligingly went to the baseline and took off running. As she did, her foot slipped around in her sneaker. In the next stride, she felt a dull pain.

Ace decided to ignore it, and kept sprinting. But every time she put her foot down hard, the pain increased.

I won't tell anyone, she thought, *maybe it will go away.*

Bad decision.

Ace kept running on her sore foot for a couple more drills. But with every sprint, every pivot, every give and go, the pain got worse. Finally, she went to our trainer, Jenny Moshak.

"My foot hurts," she said.

"Okay, we'll check it out," Jenny said.

Ace didn't want to tell me she was hurt. She tried to hide on the sidelines during practice. But I caught on, and wandered over. "What's wrong?" I said. Ace said her foot hurt.

"We'll take care of you," I said, reassuringly. "It's going to be all right."

I didn't want to let on how concerned I was, because Ace looked worried enough as it was. I tried not to panic. But inside I felt faintly sick. Not Ace. We couldn't lose Ace. Not now, with the season just about to begin.

A couple of days later, an MRI confirmed the bad news: Ace had a stress fracture.

With a stress fracture, you rehabilitate conservatively. The only cure for it is time and complete rest. Ace couldn't believe it. She was not going to sit out the start of the season over a stupid sore foot.

We had a dilemma. Not only did we have our season opener against Mississippi coming up, but only three days later, on November 21, we were scheduled to host Lousiana Tech—the team that many were calling the favorite to win a national championship.

It was potentially one of the most important games of our entire regular season.

And I wasn't sure we could win it without Ace Clement.

In just a few short weeks of practice, Ace had pushed Kellie Jolly for the job of point guard. At first, I was tense over the thought that I would have to choose between the two of them. Then I realized I didn't have to make a choice. It didn't matter who started, because we needed both of them. The way this team ran up and down the court, we required more than one point guard. After ten minutes of constant sprinting, Kellie and Ace would be bent over, pulling at their shorts.

The point guard is the quarterback, or traffic cop, of the team. She calls the plays and directs the offense. Kellie and Ace brought different touches to the position. Kellie was a tough, durable, and quietly brilliant player. She had a sure grasp of how to run the offense and how to get the ball in the hands of the right people at the right time. Ace, on the other hand, played at a breakneck pace, relying on intuitiveness. She could seemingly wedge the ball in an inch-wide opening, or sling it up the court in the blink of an eye. Ace thrived on pushing the tempo, and she liked to score. It was a case of choose your weapon. Did you prefer the beautifully crafted rifle, or the rapid-fire machine gun?

Both would play. We had to find a way to get some minutes out of Ace, foot or no foot, not only to give Kellie a breather, but because Ace would need big game experience when we entered postseason play in March.

Jenny, Ace, and I had a conference. Jenny said Ace certainly wouldn't be ready in time for Mississippi. She might be ready for Tech, but even then, she wouldn't be fully healed.

Could she play in the Tech game? I asked, straight out. She could, Jenny said, but it would mean a calculated risk. Ace wouldn't damage her foot further by playing. But she could set herself back.

Ace agreed to sit out Mississippi, if it meant she could play against Tech.

Ace slept with a bone stimulator attached to her foot. She drank milk all day, because the calcium was supposed to help the bone heal. She would sit on the sidelines with two or three cartons in front of her, swilling from them.

Before the Mississippi game, Ace tried to go out on the floor with the rest of the team. But as she jogged through the shoot-around, she felt that persistent zap of pain in her foot. She had hoped that it would magically go away. Finally, she limped back to the locker room. There was no way she could go. Her foot was inflamed.

"I can't even do a layup," she said to Jenny, her breath hitching.

Ace and I sat glumly on the bench for the tip-off against Ole Miss. Ace was down because of her foot. And I was down because of Caleb.

Directly across the arena from me I could see the seats that Lex and Mary Margaret always sat in. They were empty, of course, because they were burying Caleb. I felt flat, and uninterested. It was hard to care about a basketball game.

I told our assistant coaches, "Y'all, I need some help tonight."

The five Tennessee players who took the floor for the opening tip-off were Chamique Holdsclaw, Kellie Jolly, Kyra Elzy, LaShonda Stephens, and Tamika Catchings. Ace watched them, enviously.

After four minutes of play, we led by only 4–2. Then I put Semeka Randall into her first official collegiate game.

We now had three Meeks on the floor.

And something happened.

In the next six minutes, we scored fifteen unanswered points.

Semeka fired the run for Tennessee. She had two steals, and penetrated for four spectacular driving layups. On the bench, we all began to slowly straighten, and I even smiled a little. This was what I had hoped for on that first day in practice. It was that possibility I had seen a shadow of. We led at halftime, 42–21.

In the second half, we poured it on. I kept trying to clear the bench and not run the score up. But every time I made a substitution, a new wave of Tennessee players would attack the basket. At one point, we led by as many as forty. Final score: 92–54.

Semeka Randall finished with twenty-four points, Chamique Holdsclaw with twenty-three, and Tamika Catchings with thirteen.

From that night on, they were dubbed by the press "The Three Meeks."

Ace burned to join them, from her hated seat on the bench. When would it be her turn? She had so much to prove, to herself and to others. She wanted to show that she could play with this team.

She wanted to show how far she had come.

➤ ➤ ➤

Ace didn't bring a picture of her father to Family Night.

Ace's mom, Sue, was a twenty-two-year-old corporal in the Marine Corps when she met and married Richard Clement, a fellow Marine and an aspiring singer. Sue left the Marines, and they started their large family. The six kids had come, every year or two, one right after the other. Sue was one of those involved, energetic mothers who was always at a Little League game. The neighbors affectionately called the family The Brady Bunch.

Unfortunately, the Clements didn't remain as happy as their TV counterparts. Shortly after Ace, the youngest, was born, Sue and Richard separated.

Sue was alone with six kids between the ages of one and fourteen, and she did not have a college degree. But she did have confidence in herself. Not only was she an ex-Marine, she had also done a stint as a police officer. Sue soldiered on, juggling the rearing of six kids with various jobs.

She started a sewing and embroidering business out of her home, called Initially Yours, stitching names and logos on uniforms. For a while she worked as a quality control supervisor for a company that made vinyl siding. Then she was a product manager for a company that made custom-molded plastic parts. She sold cars. She hunted down lost packages for UPS. She rose to the level of sales and marketing manager for a company that sold carpet and floor covering.

In what spare time was left over, Sue worked towards a college degree, played softball on a semipro slow-pitch team, and earned a few extra dollars umpiring softball games.

But then Sue developed a herniated disc. When she came out of surgery, she wasn't the same. She couldn't remember things, and she would get vertigo and fall down. It turned out she suffered from short-term memory loss, a result of complications on the operating table. The condition was bad enough to keep her from working full time. From then on, the family struggled financially. But Sue had her savings and her military pension to help them get by.

In the meantime, her youngest child was turning out to be a prodigy. When Ace was in the third grade, Sue got a call from a concerned teacher, asking for a conference. "I don't know how to handle this," the teacher said.

Ace had a disturbing habit, the teacher said. Whenever she made a mistake on a piece of paper, she wouldn't just erase it—she would rub out the whole paper.

Then she would go back to the beginning, and painstakingly start over.

"You don't have to erase the whole thing," the teacher said to Ace.

"No, it's got to be right," Ace insisted.

Ace did something else that was peculiar. She used both hands to write. She would start each line with her left hand, but when she reached the middle of the page, she shifted the pencil to her right hand.

She would write half the page with her left, and finish with her right.

"What should I do?" the teacher asked.

"Let her be," Sue said. "It's not hurting anything, and it doesn't matter whether she's left- or right-handed. When she's ready, she'll decide."

Ace had idiosyncrasies on the playground, too. When her junior soccer coach asked her whether she kicked with her right foot, or her left, Ace answered, "Both." By the time she was in the sixth grade, Ace had the ability to finesse a ball almost magically. She could feint and make all of the players on the field go in one direction, and then kick the ball in the other direction and race across the open field by herself.

She wasn't like the other kids who were good at things. It was as if she had an extra sense. It was more than just good field vision.

She saw without looking.

"I don't know what it is, but I can see all around me," she said.

And she could make a ball move through the air seemingly just by thinking about it. With most athletes, there is a pause, while thought translates to action. Not with Ace. Thought and action occurred simultaneously.

But children torture each other for being gifted. On the sidelines, parents would tell their kids, "Did you see what Ace did? Why can't you do that?" So the other kids, naturally, shunned her, or teased her.

Ace would go home crying. "Mom, if they would only talk to me," she sobbed. "They'd like me if they talked to me."

As Ace's reputation grew, it didn't win her friends. Only enemies. In seventh grade, she didn't eat lunch in the cafeteria all year. The other girls threatened to beat her up, just on general principle for being too talented and too pretty.

"If we catch you in here, we'll beat the crap out of you," they said.

Every day at the lunch hour, Ace hid in the library.

At home, Ace took it hard.

"They're so mean to me," she would cry to Sue, "and they don't even know me."

Sue said, "Look, you don't have to play at this level. You can just play pickup."

"No," Ace said, grimly. "I'm going to play."

But a bad year got worse. At the same time, Ace felt she was losing contact with her father. According to Ace, when she was thirteen, her father moved to Florida and dropped almost completely out of her life.

Ace struggled miserably through the rest of her childhood. The summer before she was to enter eighth grade at the local junior high school, sentiment against her took another nasty turn. One afternoon, her older sister, Michelle, was sitting around at a local swimming pool, when she overheard a group of girls talking about the new kid, Ace, who was about to enter high school.

"Wait 'til she gets here," one of the girls said. "I'll slash her with a blade."

Michelle ran to a phone and called Sue, who immediately pulled Ace from the school.

It seemed like every night Ace would cry in her bed. And night after night, Sue sat on the edge of the bed and rubbed her daughter's back. "Everyone has a cross to bear, and this is your cross," Sue said.

Ace finally found a school where she was happier, Cardinal O'Hara in Philadelphia. As a senior, she won every award and accolade available, and led Cardinal O'Hara to the Catholic League championship. She amassed 2,256 points to break Wilt Chamberlain's city record of 2,205, which had stood for forty years, and her picture appeared in *USA Today*. Her Cardinal O'Hara jersey was retired, making her only the second female athlete to receive the honor. (The first was my old friend Theresa Grentz, head coach of the Illinois women's basketball team.)

Ace had wanted to attend Tennessee since she was a seventh grader, when she came to Knoxville to play in the AAU national championships. The final game was played in Thompson-Boling Arena, and that's where I first saw her. I went to every game she played in the tournament. Ace's team won the title, and Ace won me. I even skipped a family boat outing to see Ace play in the championship. That afternoon, I told her I wanted to be her coach some day. "You'd look good in orange," I said. Ace said she wanted to play for me, and she meant it. In February of her junior year, she committed to come to Tennessee—a full twelve months before the rest of her class made their decisions.

One morning during Ace's senior year, a letter from her father arrived. He wanted to get back in touch.

Ace wrote back a mature, carefully measured letter. She had too much going on in her life and too much to deal with in preparing for college to take on any added emotional upheavals, she wrote.

If a time came when she felt she needed him, Ace wrote, she would call.

But Ace was determined not to need him.

➤ ➤ ➤

THE PRESEASON POLLS were split over who was No.1, us or Louisiana Tech.

On the evening of November 21, I cooked a huge dinner for R.B., Tyler, and my parents—meatloaf, chicken, mashed potatoes, corn, green beans, cabbage, asparagus casserole. I was nervous, and that's what I did when I was nervous: I cooked, or I scrubbed, or I did laundry, load after load after load. After I served dinner, I hopped into my car and drove to Thompson-Boling Arena, running late, applying my makeup in the rearview mirror at stoplights, and clenching my teeth when the red lights didn't turn green fast enough, muttering, "Change, change, come on, change!" Then the traffic backed up a block from the arena, so I drove down the shoulder of the street, and nosed the car up to a cop.

He peered in the car window, and said, "I guess I can let *you* in."

I said, "I don't know. They might do better without me tonight."

I took the corner into the parking lot on two wheels, pulled into my customary semi-legal spot in the eaves of the arena, waved at the security guards, and strode through the back halls until I arrived at a heavy orange door. I punched the highly unoriginal combination to the lock on the door, three-two-one, which adds up to six, the number of titles we were going for. Then I was in the comfortable familiar pandemonium of our locker room, with that same familiar knot developing in my lower lip, which I was biting in an effort to hide the tension.

You bet I was tense. So tense that earlier that day, Mickie and I were short with each other on the phone. She was as uptight as I was. She called with a question about some arrangements I'd made for the team on an upcoming road trip to Martin, Tennessee, but really, I think she just needed to vent. I listened for a minute, and then I said, "Don't *start with me today, Mickie. Don't even go there. Not today. I can't take it today." We hung up, and didn't talk the rest of the afternoon, which suited both of us.

Louisiana Tech was probably the toughest team we would face all year, and we knew it. And here we were, having to play them in just the second game of the season, with four inexperienced freshmen, one of them injured. According to *Sports Illustrated*, Tech was the favorite to win the national championship. Not only were they perennial contenders, but they had a team full of veterans, all five starters returning from a team that had reached the NCAA regional finals the year before.

The only good news was that we got to play them at home. The traffic outside was from a crowd of 16,490 that showed up at the arena to help us out. Before tip-off, we raised the banner from our previous championship, and passed out our new gold rings to the members of the 1997 team.

The rings with no record on them.

The Lady Techsters ran on to the floor. They wore loose, flowing, light blue jerseys and shorts that made them seem even more athletic than they were. At center they had Alisa Burras, an agile block of muscle who was capable of pulling down as many rebounds as she put up points. She was routinely in double digits. Tamicha Jackson was a darting little guard with no compunction about shooting the ball; she could and would launch it from anywhere on the court, and make it. Monica Maxwell was their other big threat, a versatile forward who created shots out of nothing. They were a streak team; they might be stone cold one minute, and yet five minutes later you could find yourself trailing by twenty.

In the pregame locker room, I calmed myself by writing a few notes down on the board in magic marker. "Nobody talk to me 'til I've finished this," I said. I wrote in neat block letters, listing just a few fundamental things, like GET ON THE BOARDS and TRANSITION DEFENSE.

Then I gathered the team around, and asked for quiet. The Lady Vols sat facing me, each player on a wooden stool painted in team colors with her number on it. There were all kinds of visitors in the locker room. We

usually invited ten or twelve "guest coaches" made up of boosters, donors, and special guests, who observed us in pregame and at halftime
from their positions against the back wall. I was brief.

"If I were you, I would look at this as an opportunity," I said.

I said we would start by "doubling down" on Burras. My big fear was
that Burras would be too much for our young, thin post players, Tree and
LaShonda. Doubling down meant that we would send another player
down to help out in defending her.

Tree was offended. For days now we had talked about nothing but
Burras, and she was getting tired of it. As if no one trusted her to do a
good job. Tree just sat on her stool, quiet as ever, but she decided she was
insulted by the idea that she needed help.

It was time for tip-off. Ace passed by me on her way to her seat on the
bench, as the rest of the Lady Vols took the floor. I wandered over and
put my hand on Ace's shoulder, as she tested her still-tender foot.

"Be ready," I said. "Just be ready. Because when we need you, I'm
going to turn to you. It might just be for two or three or four minutes. But
be ready."

We started uncertainly. La. Tech came out fast and took an 11–4 lead
with 16:19 to go in the first half. I called time-out, and told everybody to
calm down. We composed ourselves and the crowd got into the game,
and we climbed back in it, tying it up. For the next five minutes, we
seesawed back and forth.

With about ten minutes to go in the half, I turned to Ace on the
bench. "Go get Kellie," I said.

Ace looked surprised for a second. Then she jumped up, and raced to
the scorer's table, requesting a substitution.

In her first collegiate play, Ace had to inbounds the ball. As she stood
underneath our basket, La. Tech's defense swarmed in front of her. Ace
couldn't find an opening. On the sideline, we tensed; if Ace couldn't get
rid of the ball in five seconds, La. Tech would get possession. At the last
second, Ace intentionally threw the ball at a La. Tech player who had
her back turned. Ace literally smacked the ball off her unsuspecting
backside. It bounced once on the floor. Ace calmly stepped in bounds,

picked the ball up, and got a shot off. It was a smart, headsy solution. Mickie, Holly, Al, and I exchanged glances.

We trailed by just a point at halftime, 36–35.

But back in the locker room, I fumed. We were playing well enough to win, if we would get over being tentative. The only reason La. Tech was leading was because they were outrebounding us, and because we hadn't played aggressive enough defense.

"This is *your* game!" I barked. "If you want it. All you have to do is get on the boards."

I wheeled on LaShonda and Tree.

"You need to grow up, right now," I said. "And you can take that as a challenge."

I turned back to the rest of the team. "Let your defense be your offense," I said.

That phrase would be our rallying cry for the rest of the season. It meant we were going to the press. If we could force La. Tech into turnovers and bad shots, we would create some opportunities for ourselves. Grab a steal or a rebound, and we might run off a few points before they knew what hit them.

But back out on the floor, we couldn't seem to gain an advantage. The problem was exactly what I feared in preseason: we were getting eaten alive in the post. La. Tech's big athletic bodies were too much for us, especially Burras. She drove straight to the basket—through what I disparagingly call our matador defense—to give La. Tech a six point lead with 17:52 to go.

I decided to give some of our starters a breather. I turned to Teresa Geter, Semeka Randall, and Ace Clement on the bench, and one by one, waved them into the game. Holdsclaw came out and sat next to me.

Burras drove at us yet again.

All of a sudden, Tree rose up off the floor. I saw her goggles, glinting under the lights.

She swatted away Burras' shot.

Our bench leaped to their feet, throwing their fists in the air.

Burras drove again. Tree rose up. And swatted *another* shot away.

It seemed like Tree Geter had gone crazy. Her face was twisted into a scowl, and she was swaggering and shaking her fist. Next to me, Chamique, normally so reserved, was jumping up and down and hollering like a banshee.

Tennessee's ball. Ace whipped it up court like she had fired it out of a slingshot. Tree drove straight into the paint, right at Monica Maxwell, and snaked in a little layup. Mickie, Holly, Al, and I traded amazed looks. "*Tree?*" Mickie said.

"Geter's been eatin' her some raw meat," Holly said.

A few seconds later, we grabbed a rebound, and here came Tree again, taking the ball straight into the teeth of La. Tech's defense. Tree ducked inside—and layed the ball in.

Tree had singlehandedly cut La. Tech's lead to two, 43–41 with 16:11 to go in the game. I paced the sidelines.

All around me, our bench players leaped up and down, screaming and waving their towels. Next to me, Holdsclaw kept up a constant whooping. *Now we're talking*, I thought.

Burras kept at us, though. Twice in a row she swept straight to the basket to increase Tech's lead to five again, 48–43. But here came Tree right back, storming the La. Tech baseline to bring it back to three.

We pressed. A slow roar built in the arena as the press gathered momentum. After every score, we applied instant pressure on the inbounder. We trapped the entry pass, we trapped the sidelines, we trapped the half court. We harassed the ball for ninety-four feet. And the more the crowd roared, the more intense our defensive pressure became.

We tied the game at 50–50 with 10:56 to go, when Randall sank the front end of a one-and-one from the free throw line.

I stared at the floor, counting heads. Holdsclaw was still next to me, I realized. Where was Kellie? I looked around. There she was. Further down the bench.

Then it struck me. We had *four freshmen* on the floor.

Four freshmen, and a sophomore, Kyra Elzy, were leading our comeback over the best team in the country.

No sooner had the thought occurred to me than Tamika Catchings paused from three point range. She squared up. Then she floated upwards and launched a long bomb.

It fluttered through the net, and the arena erupted. We were up, 53–50.

We never looked back. Holdsclaw's return to the game was the final blow to La. Tech. We went up by eight, then ten, then twelve.

At the two-minute mark, I realized how hot it was in the arena. I shook out my suit jacket, and sat back, exhaling. It seemed like it was the first breath I had taken all night.

"This one's over, folks," I said to Mickie, Holly, and Al.

They grinned and we all leaned back in our chairs. Final score, Tennessee 75, Louisiana Tech 61.

For the night, Tree had twelve points, five rebounds, and *five blocked shots*. It wasn't just that she established a presence for us in the middle, it was the way she did it, those sweeping rejections that made the Lady Techsters alter their aim, and hesitate.

We scored twelve unanswered points on our crucial run, thanks to the press.

And Tree, sleepy, slow-moving Big Smooth, had ten of them.

Holdsclaw had her usual effortless seeming twenty-four points, and eleven critical rebounds. But the four freshmen were the difference, and their spiritual leader was Ace, who, half-limping with her ponytail flopping, had controlled our offensive tempo, shouted orders, and waved signals, in total charge.

In the locker room, I called the team together and pointed out what they had done. "I don't know if you realized this," I said. "But we went on our run with four freshmen and a sophomore on the floor." The upperclassmen mobbed the freshmen with congratulations. Kellie Jolly marched straight over to Tree. "I want you to know something," she said. "We couldn't have won this game without you on the floor." I saw Robert Geter enter the locker room. He moved into a corner quietly, but beaming.

As soon as I finished speaking, the managers brought in stacks of pizza boxes, and the players descended on them. Robert Geter grabbed his daughter in a hug. Holly sprawled in a chair, sipping on a Diet Coke, and razzing Tree. "Smoooooooth," Holly teased her. "Big Smooth."

Mickie wandered over to me, and said, "Man, these kids aren't afraid of anything." Then she moved around the room, giving players elaborate secret handshakes that consisted of a lot of palm rubbing and finger snapping.

Ace limped towards the training room, an ice bag wrapped around her foot. I grabbed her, and gave her a squeeze. "I'm proud of you," I said.

Ace's ears were still ringing from the crowd noise. Her head felt muffled, and she had an adrenaline-wasted feeling, like she did after a long night on a dance floor with loud music.

It feels like coming out of a club, she thought, euphorically. *A real loud dance club.*

> > >

BUT THE GAME COST US, in the end. Ace's foot wasn't fully recovered. We had taken a calculated risk in playing her, and we paid for it. When she woke up, it was sore again. And this time, it stayed that way.

One week turned into two. And two weeks turned into three. And three weeks turned into a month. Pretty soon, I wondered where the player I knew had gone.

The week of November 23, we flew to Martin, Tennessee, to play my alma mater. Lex and Mary Margaret Carter decided to make the trip with us. There was a ceremony to name the gym floor after me, and they were looking for an excuse to get out the house. A grief counselor had warned them that the loss of a child could affect the most solid marriage. "Oh, no, not us," they said. But only a day later they found themselves arguing about how soon to clean out Caleb's room. So they decided to travel. They drove six hours down to Martin, where we all stayed in a tiny motel. They seemed calm on the exterior, but it was a brittle calm. They were like glass that had been dropped, but not broken, and had a thousand tiny cracks. Touch the glass the wrong way and it would fall to pieces.

We beat Martin, 73–32. It was strange and sort of pleasant to walk on my own name, painted on the floor. But the game itself wasn't so pleasant. In the first half, Semeka Randall came down hard on a rebound, lost her balance, and fell squarely on her left shoulder. She got up and rejoined the play, but on the next possession she got tied up in a fight for a rebound. Suddenly, she grabbed her arm, in such pain she couldn't stand up straight.

She hobbled over the sideline, where our trainer, Jenny Moshak, examined her. "It's dislocated," Jenny told me.

Semeka burst into tears. As Jenny rigged a shoulder sling, Semeka sat at the end of the bench, sobbing. Ace limped over, and put her arms around her. They sat together at the end of the bench, a couple of walking wounded.

Late that night when we got back to Knoxville, Semeka went to the medical center for an exam. The worst case scenario was surgery, with a six- to eight-week rehab, Jenny said. Fortunately, word came back the next morning that it was just a minor separation. She would be okay in a week or so.

That afternoon, Semeka and Ace wandered into the gym. Ace was on crutches, and Semeka in her shoulder sling. We stood there, sort of depressed at the sight, when Mickie spoke up.

"Look, it's the Johnnies," Mickie said. Then she started singing, "When Johnnie comes marching home again, hurrah, hurrah."

We all burst out laughing. Even Ace.

I was concerned: we could afford one injured player, but not two. Not against Stanford.

➤ ➤ ➤

OUR NEXT ROAD GAME was a Thanksgiving trip to meet Stanford in the San Jose Arena. Stanford was a powerhouse, with an All-American in

Kristin Folkl, and an impressive consistency—they had reached the Final Four for three consecutive years. What's more, they were coached by the woman who had led the U.S. to an Olympic gold medal in Atlanta, Tara VanDerveer.

It was a big game, and I was dying to play Ace. But we couldn't risk setting her recovery back any further. We might scrape by without her, I thought. But we couldn't play without Semeka, too, and hope to come home without a loss.

Stanford had killed us the previous year, 82–65. What's more, they had done so on our home court. Kellie told the freshmen, in no uncertain terms, "We owe them. We have a score to settle."

We flew out to California. While I always eat pregame meals with our team, I don't hang out with our players much on the road. But on this trip, something interesting happened. I discovered I wanted to spend time with them. They were so funny, such cutups, that you couldn't be around them long without laughing.

The freshmen took liberties, and I allowed it. Why? Maybe because I missed Caleb, and maybe because they were such sweet, open kids. Semeka thought nothing of wandering into my hotel room, and stretching out on the floor. Tamika would stroll in with a lollipop in her mouth, and flop down on the couch. They liked to tease me. Especially the Glamour Girls, Ace, Chamique, and LaShonda. They convinced me to wear black jeans. Then a few of them decided it would be funny to try to talk me into wearing shorter skirts. "You should wear a miniskirt," Kyra said, eyeing me with a calculating look. Ace nodded, sagely.

"You've got the legs for it," she said.

I politely declined.

They ragged each other incessantly. They teased LaShonda for her long legs, calling her Wilt the Stilt because it looked like she had no feet. They teased Niya Butts for her shin splints. Niya wore long Ace bandages and protective plates on her shins when she played. They called her "Forrest Gump."

In San Jose, we took the team out for a gourmet Thanksgiving meal. It was one of those fancy places heavy on presentation, where you couldn't tell the food from the table decorations. You half expected to have your coffee served in a sandalwood box. But it was a new experience for some of the players—they giggled and poked their forks at the unfamiliar ingredients. I kept forgetting how young they were. Semeka didn't think the mashed potatoes were real. Tamika kept marveling, "We get to stay in our own hotel rooms."

All of my guardedness and reserve was falling away with these players, and I wasn't sure I minded. But it left me feeling full of anxiety, too. Handling young women was a delicate matter. You had to know when to push, and when to pull, when to be tough, and when to ease off.

Take LaShonda Stephens. She was a sensitive young woman from Woodstock, Georgia, with a voice as small as her body was big. I could tell that LaShonda, a sophomore center, was struggling to run with the freshmen. She was a tall lumbering player, with tiny hands and chronically painful knees that required an hour of treatment after every game. The thing I liked most about LaShonda was that she tried, on every single play, and she never complained. But in a way, she was *too* quiet. I knew I hadn't reached her yet, and I knew she was low on confidence; she wasn't sure she belonged in the starting lineup.

The day before the Stanford game, I pulled her aside.

"I'm the head coach," I said. "I've been doing this for twenty-four years, longer than you've been alive. Are you telling me I'm *wrong* to start you? Have I made that big a mistake? Am I that poor of a coach?"

"No," she said.

"Well, then, go out there and play," I said.

We rode a bus to Fisherman's Wharf in San Francisco, and wandered the waterfront, souvenir shopping. A bunch of us hopped on a cable car and rode it up and over the hills. Then we got back on the bus and went over the Golden Gate Bridge. We pulled over to take pictures, and as we disembarked from the bus, LaShonda tripped on her little feet and slid all the way down the steps of the bus.

"That's a hard fall coming from that tall," Tamika said.

They fell about laughing.

But underneath it all, I was concerned. There were two games I thought we could lose in the early part of our season. One was Louisiana Tech. The other was Stanford.

➤ ➤ ➤

Stanford led us early.

It was one of those nights when everything fell for the other team. Everything. No matter where the Cardinals shot the ball from, it slipped through the rim. They made a scorching 57 percent of their shots in the first half.

We didn't guard anybody. Stanford had their way with us in the paint, exploiting that lean and inexperienced post game of ours that was driving me crazy. We were just plain soft, I decided. Why didn't Tree and LaShonda just move out of the way for them? The only positive was that we were scoring almost as frequently as Stanford.

We trailed, 45–44, at the half.

Normally, I meet with our staff in the hallway first, and discuss things. Talking with Mickie, Holly, and Al gives me a chance to think about what just happened on the floor, and decide what I want to say to the team. It keeps me from flying off the handle.

But on this night, my temper won. I told our staff, "I'll be right back."

I stormed into the locker room with my blue-eyed death ray, and I did something I rarely do. I cussed.

"Is anybody going to play any defense?" I raged. "Is *any*body going to guard *any*body? You're selfish. You're just plain selfish."

I figured that was about enough. But then something else occurred to me.

"And who the *hell* on this team is *ever* going to take a charge?" I demanded.

I stalked back outside. After meeting with Mickie, Holly, and Al for a few minutes, I returned in a calmer mood. I composed myself, and quietly gave them our suggestions for second-half defensive changes.

"It's a forty-minute game," I reminded them. "The mentally tougher team will win. We've never been able to beat this team in a shooting contest. So you better defend them."

We were a different team in the second half, thanks to Kyra Elzy's defense on the ball. She harassed their guards, using those long wavy limbs of hers. It seemed like she had six arms instead of two. We held Stanford to just five of twenty-nine shooting. They never got an easy look again.

We won, 88–70. But it was the *way* we won that made me feel so much better. Kellie, playing without a breather from Ace, put in thirty-six full minutes at point guard and never made a serious mistake. It was a great unsung performance. Meanwhile, Chamique threw in twenty-five points, Tamika hit a career high twenty, and Semeka, even with her sore shoulder, had seventeen points and a career high eleven rebounds.

The Meeks had struck again. Each was an individual, but together they were a leaping, twisting, scoring ballet. I didn't know the body had that many parts.

The only drawback was Semeka's attitude. She missed, by my count, thirteen shots from five feet or less, probably as a result of her sore shoulder, and got frustrated. When I sat her down late in the second half, she was sullen. When Semeka decided to go into a funk, you could feel it all up and down our bench. She wouldn't look at me as she took her seat. I drifted down the bench, and sat next to her, and tried to talk to her. She was silent.

"Semeka, we're going to have a relationship," I said. "We can have a good one. Or we can have a bad one. It's just a question of what kind. But we're going to have one."

In the locker room after the game, Semeka vaulted into my arms and hugged me. "I'm sorry," she said.

After the game, I ran into my old friend and mentor, Billie Moore, who had coached the 1976 U.S. Olympic team to a silver medal. Billie was retired from coaching and living in southern California. She had come to watch the Stanford game with a critical eye. But she was overwhelmed by our talent.

Billie said, "Holy smokes, Pat."

I said, "I know."

"Who's going to ever beat this team?" she asked.

I said, "I don't know."

"There's only one team capable of beating Tennessee," Billie said.

"Who?" I said.

"Tennessee," she said.

➤ ➤ ➤

IT WAS TIME TO GET Ace back on the court.

When we returned home from California, it had been two full weeks since she had played, and she was bored silly. While we practiced, Ace would ride a stationary bike, or bounce on a small trampoline. She couldn't even shoot, because the fracture was in a place in her foot that served as the takeoff point for a jumper.

She would sit on the sidelines, drinking her milk, guzzling from pint-sized cartons.

But finally, she was cleared to play. I breathed a sigh of relief. In the first week of December, we went to New York for a four-team invitational called the Marriott Big Apple Classic. We would be playing at Manhattan College in Riverdale, in a gym with pull-out bleachers. The competition was solid but not unduly threatening: our opponents were George Mason, a school from Virginia, followed by our host, Manhattan College.

It was a perfect opportunity to work Ace back into the lineup. And it would be a chance for Chamique to come back to New York to play.

I wanted to give the team a good time in New York. Ace, especially, needed it. We took them out on the town. We got tickets to the Broadway musical, *Grease*, and all of the Lady Vols went. The show was opened by an emcee, who joked with the crowd to get them warmed up. Our group was so loud and silly, he couldn't help noticing us. "Where you from?" he asked. Our players yelled back, "Tennessee." He invited them on stage.

Ace leaped out of her seat. Then Semeka jumped up, and Niya, too. My mouth hung open. They were completely unself-conscious in front of the packed Manhattan theater. They joked with the emcee, and then they struck up a dance, hip-hopping around.

So much for shy, inhibited teenagers.

At intermission, I decided to walk over to the All Star Cafe sports bar to watch a Tennessee football game. Semeka and Kyra asked if they could join me. We strolled through midtown Manhattan, got a table and watched the game. We drank hot chocolate, and I found myself kidding around with them like an undergraduate.

But the next day, I turned into a head coach again.

There wasn't much drama to the George Mason game—we won, 98–68. But it was a nice showcase for Chamique, which was the real reason we were there. I made it a policy to play in the hometowns of each of our players, or at least as close as we could get. This one was for her.

But increasingly, Chamique's homecomings were more like events, sometimes fraught with tension. Everybody knew when Chamique came back. She was the talk of Astoria. That day, fifteen different family members showed up to see her, including nephews and nieces, and dozens of old childhood friends, teammates, and coaches. She was less happy to see a bevy of agents and shoe company executives, all of them wielding business cards and jockeying to meet her grandmother. One shoe company rep even asked Mickie for a personal introduction to June. Mickie said, "Look, anything Chamique does will be handled in a professional manner."

Uppermost in Chamique's mind was not the glad-handing of shoe executives. She was more concerned with performing in front of her family. I could see Chamique was frazzled, and she had complained of stomach cramps the day before. But she put up twenty-four points, and hauled thirteen rebounds. It was a bravura performance, all things considered.

But Ace's performance was less encouraging. According to our medical staff, her foot was healed. The problem now was her head.

Ace was still in some pain, I knew. Her foot was tender. But there was a point at which the only way to strengthen it was to play on it—and we had arrived at that point. The medical staff said it was a matter of pushing through the pain.

I sent Ace into the George Mason game early. "Go get Kellie," I said. She hopped up and trotted to the scorer's table. But as soon as she stepped on the floor, I could see she was favoring her foot.

Ace had trouble getting into the flow of the game. She would kick at the gym floor, testing her sneaker. And her timing was off; she hurried her passes. Late in the game, she came to the bench and sat down. She unlaced her sneaker and pulled it off, and began massaging her foot.

I whipped my head around.

"What's wrong?" I said.

She said, "It's hurting me."

I said, "Put your shoe on."

Ace looked at me, questioning.

I said, grimly, "Put it back on."

Ace hesitated.

"Look, we wouldn't let you play if you weren't okay," I said. "You need to suck it up and play through this."

"I'm trying," she said.

"Then you'd better get tougher mentally," I snapped. "The best thing you can do for that foot is go back out there and play."

By the end of the game, Ace had scored seven points. But I wasn't happy with what I saw. She was babying her foot.

I had compassion for Ace. After all, I was responsible for letting her play against Louisiana Tech, which may have set her back. I was still chewing a hole in my lip over that one. But compassion wasn't what she needed; Ace was being checked regularly, and her foot was sound. She was feeling sorry for herself, and it was my job to snap her out of it.

I wandered to the end of the bench.

"I ought to sit your butt for the next two months, and make you watch everyone else play," I said.

But that's what ended up happening. In the next few weeks, it became clear that Ace wasn't the same player she had been in preseason. She was back on the bench—and this time, it wasn't because of injury. It was because she wasn't playing well.

It seemed like the injury had killed all of her momentum. Mentally, physically, emotionally, she grew sluggish. She put on weight. She was distracted in practice. She went through the motions, she ran hard, but her mind wasn't always focused. At times, I'd insert her into a game, and she would turn the ball over in the first few minutes. I would substitute for her, and she'd be back on the bench.

The trick to dealing with a lonesome, homesick freshman was to keep her so busy she would fall mindlessly into her bed at night. We tried to keep Ace busy. She rushed from meeting to meeting. She met with academic counselors. Fitness trainers. Medical staff. We gave all of the freshmen endless checklists of things to do—some of it devised simply to keep them from brooding. We made them memorize their social security numbers, and their class schedules.

But with the injury, and then riding the bench, Ace had too much idle time on her hands. Too much time to think.

Whenever she talked to her friends back in Philly, they all asked the same question. "When are you going to start?" She didn't have an answer. "I could care less," she shot back. Nobody understood how tough it was, and that starting wasn't important on this team. She just wanted to be a part of it.

She had worked so hard, she had slaved to be a contributor. From that very first pickup game, she had been determined to prove she could hang with the upperclassmen. And now it was all going on without her.

Maybe she should go back to Philadelphia.

I could see what she was thinking. I tried to talk to her gently. We had long conversations, in which I told her to buckle down and concentrate on her schoolwork and practice, take it one day at a time. She would pull out of it. But not playing well nagged at Ace. Maybe she didn't belong at Tennessee, she thought. There was nothing for her in Knoxville if she couldn't play.

Ace called her mother. "I don't like it here," she said. "I just don't like it. There's nothing to do."

Sue said, "Give it time."

"Maybe I should transfer," Ace said. "I don't know what I'm doing here."

Sue tried not to panic. It killed Sue to see Ace struggle. Her worst fear was that Ace would make a bad decision, out of pure frustration. Every motherly bone in her body wanted to comfort Ace. But Sue felt like I did; Ace had to push through this on her own somehow. She was a tough love mother, and she didn't want to give Ace an out. No, Sue decided, Ace wasn't going anywhere if she could help it.

"Things will make sense, if you just give it time," Sue said. "Go talk to Pat."

But nothing made sense to Ace.

One day in early December, Ace received a letter addressed to her in a semi-familiar hand. The return address was Florida.

It was from her father.

Ace tore it open, and began reading. He had seen her play on television, Richard wrote. She had blossomed. She had grown so much. He wanted to be in touch with his daughter again. Even though she couldn't see him, he could see her, and he wanted to be reunited.

Ace threw the letter away.

Then she got an e-mail from him. One afternoon she was online, when she got a message signal. Anxiety ran through her body. *Why is he doing this?* she thought. *He'll just leave me again. That's what he does. If I let him back in my life, he'll hurt me more.*

The letters started arriving once a week. Sometimes twice a week.

Some of them she read. But some days she couldn't bring herself to open them. She would hastily toss them in the trash.

Ace thought about the way the season was going, how promisingly it had started, with her performance against Louisiana Tech. But somehow, it had gotten away from her. If she didn't watch it, Ace thought, pretty soon she wasn't going to be playing at all. Ace had learned about inner strength from her mother, Sue. So it wasn't surprising when the realization struck her. There was only one thing she could count on, Ace figured. Herself. She would stay at Tennessee, and she would play.

It was up to her.

Q & A with Harvey Catchings (Father)

**What do you remember about those games between
your two daughters in the driveway?**

Do you want the blood and the gore? Let me put it this way. Neither one
wanted to lose. When you have a situation where no one wants to lose,
and they'll do anything and whatever it takes to win, needless to say it got
a little bloody.

**How did you feel watching Tamika play against her
sister in the Illinois game?**

I just hoped they both performed well. You cheered for both. You couldn't
win. But you couldn't lose, either.

**Did Tamika come to you about her problems
adjusting at Tennessee?**

One time after practice she called me in tears, because Pat had come down
on her hard. I just told her, "In order to be the best, you have to be
broken down. When you're broken down, you can analyze where you are,
and make the decision to be better than you thought you were." What she
realized was that everything Pat was telling her was enhancing her game. It
made her more potent. There were still a lot of weaknesses in her game.
When I walked into camp as a rookie in the NBA, it was almost like the
veterans were saying, "We're going to beat this kid to death, make him
quit." And I said "No, I'll rise up." I was just hoping she'd do the same, rise
up. So she got very little sympathy from Daddy.

How do you think divorce affected your daughter?

I think whenever kids are placed in an environment where they don't have
total support from a mother or a father, where something is missing, you
get kids who will either be overachievers, or underachievers. When you are
around others who are also gifted and talented, and intelligent, it makes it
easier for you to be an overachiever. You want to be a part of it. 'Mika
knew that although her mother and I were not together, all she had to do
was pick up the phone and say, "Dad, I need you." I was there. One of the
things I have yet to understand in this life is how a man could not want to
be involved in his child's life. That blows my mind. I can't envision my life

without my children. When a child is without a father, you have anger, and you have someone trying to build self-esteem. "Why did my dad leave me? What could I have done differently? What did I do to make him go?" They don't realize it's not about them. It's about the strength of the man himself.

CHAPTER SIX

Catch

WE WERE GETTING KILLED.

Illinois was killing us. And not by ten or twelve. Try twenty.

Illinois, ranked fifth in the country, came into Thompson-Boling Arena on December 12. After just a few minutes, I paced the sidelines, as if I was measuring the square footage of the court. I squinted, I chewed my lip, I threw my clipboard. My thoughts went in a circle as I followed the game action, watching the Illini take a wrecking ball to our team. I should've . . . they should've . . . we should've. . . .

None of it mattered.

Illinois was killing us.

On the court, our players stood around, staring at fixed points in space. They looked like they were on a museum visit instead of playing in a nationally televised game. For the umpteenth time, Illinois drove straight through us for an uncontested layup. I stomped my foot. On the bench behind me, I could hear Mickie, Holly, and Al's feet doing the same thing. They stomped as if in synchronized frustration. I glanced at the scoreboard. It read 41–19.

We were down by twenty-two points.

It was embarrassing enough to trail by double digits. But to be down by such a stark, appalling difference pushed us beyond embarrassment into helplessness. At first, our bench had looked like an enraged dance troupe, pointing, waving, and angrily hurling towels. But now, down 41–19, we were sunken in gloom. Everyone sat with their elbows on their knees, and their chins in their hands. How does water feel as it's going down the drain? That's how we felt. We were ready for a close, tough game. But we weren't prepared for this . . . carnage.

Tamika Catchings knew what would happen if Illinois beat Tennessee. Her sister, Tauja, would never stop talking. Never. Tamika and Tauja had been playing one-on-one for virtually their entire lives, they had bloodied each other and lorded it over one another since early childhood, and now here they were, opponents for real. Trash-talking rivalry laced with love was the foundation of their entire relationship. So Tamika was determined to beat her sister. Maybe *too* determined.

Across the court, Tauja had her own resolute thoughts on the subject. Before the game, a reporter had asked Tauja what would happen if Tamika stole the ball from her.

"I'd have to nail her," Tauja answered.

It was an irresistible scenario, surrounded by media hype: Tauja, the Catchings' elder daughter, was a quick-slicing sophomore guard for Illinois with an average of twelve points per game and a growing national reputation. Tamika, meanwhile, was on pace to break the Tennessee freshman scoring record. But if it was an intriguing matchup, it was also a potentially difficult one for the central characters.

Outwardly, Tamika had seemed unfazed by the idea of playing her sister. In the days before the game, she hadn't really talked about the situation, so I assumed she was handling it. But then, on the afternoon of the contest, Tamika said to me, almost as an aside, "I just don't want to be matched up against her." I knew then that Tamika was more emotional about meeting Tauja on the court than she was letting on. I said, "Well, okay, but if it comes down to it you may have to."

Harvey Catchings had flown in from Chicago, and Wanda Catchings had come in from Dallas. Harvey and Wanda had been divorced for over five years. They were cordial when they needed to discuss something concerning their three children, Kenyon, twenty-two, Tauja, twenty, and Tamika, eighteen. But I knew that Tamika couldn't help feeling torn when they were in the same room. There were times, after a game, when she didn't know who to go to first, her mom or her dad. It was a no-win situation.

On the afternoon of the game, Tamika, Tauja, and Wanda visited together at the Illinois team hotel. Tauja didn't have much time, because the Illini were on a tight travel schedule. But Tamika radiated pleasure in seeing her sister, if only for a few minutes; it wasn't often they got a chance to all be together any more. Then it was time to go.

"Good luck, we're going to beat you," Tauja said.

"Yeah," Tamika said. "Good luck." She didn't want to start anything.

In the Tennessee locker room before tip-off, Tamika had been so keyed up that the other players laughed at her. Normally she was quiet and still. But on this night, she was jitterbugging all over the place.

A few hours before tip-off, I had run into Harvey in a hallway at the arena. He was a tall, courtly man who still cut an athletic figure. He was just finishing an interview with ESPN as I arrived, and I stopped to say hello. "Glad you came," I said. Harvey replied, "I'm excited to see them both play." But it was obviously a difficult position for him.

"It's too bad someone has to lose," I said.

➤ ➤ ➤

AND NOW IT LOOKED like it was going to be us.

Wanda Catchings tried to view the game as a happy occasion. She didn't want to view it as Tamika against Tauja. It was her job as a parent to support both, she figured. So she did just that. She sat in the stands and cheered for both. When Tauja got away on a fast break, she would leap to her feet and scream for Illinois. Then Tamika would muscle inside for a layup, and Wanda would clap and sing "Rocky Top."

But it was becoming one-sided. We were playing awful. Just awful.

We couldn't shoot a BB into the ocean. Everything we put up seemed to clang off the rim.

Meanwhile, the Illini were making everything. Absolutely everything. They were a big, able team, with five different players averaging in double figures—including Tauja. Moreover, they were extremely well coached by Theresa Grentz, an old friend and colleague of mine. Theresa and I had met back in 1973 as teammates on the World University Games team. She was a tough-talking Yankee, so I called her Pennsylvania; she called me Tennessee. The Illini were like Theresa, frank and contentious. If things got any further out of hand, we'd have a hard road coming back.

Chamique went up for one of her can't-miss jumpers, and the ball rolled all the way around the rim and fell away. I shook my head.

We were in a funk. I'll tell you just how out of it we were. Semeka Randall actually thought we were leading. She really did. She sat right next to Holly Warlick on the bench, and was convinced we were ahead.

Semeka glanced up at the scoreboard, and thought, "Oh, good, we're up by ten." She glanced up again and thought, "That's nice. A twelve-point lead."

Then she looked up again. Something was wrong. She did a double take, and reeled in shock.

"Holly!" she said in alarm. "We're *losing!*"

Holly stared back at Semeka.

"Well, dang, Semeka," Holly drawled. "What did you think we were doing?"

The misery continued. It seemed like every time I looked up, Tauja Catchings was loping down the court for yet another freebie layup. I knelt on the sideline, alternating between discouragement, encouragement, and wrath. I whacked the court so hard I bent my gold rings, and my hand began to hurt.

We scored just two points in the last 8:30 of the half.

Even the Meeks were helpless, completely without game. The three of them, Tamika, Semeka, and Chamique, were a combined 6–20 from the field.

We went in to the locker room at the half trailing by seventeen points, 41–24.

I was calm.

I looked at a stat sheet and assessed the damage with Mickie, Holly, and Al. It wasn't my imagination: we had been horrible. We had made just 23 percent of our shots. Now, that was beyond playing badly. That fell in the category of plain bad luck, major voodoo.

It was important that we remain composed. The team was already spooked enough. They had played hard, that wasn't the problem. The problem was that the shots weren't going in. What they needed was some reassurance, not a tongue lashing. We all knew how matters stood.

I spoke reasonably.

I said, "Okay. Y'all are down by seventeen. This is embarrassing. But you can get it back."

Our players stared at me, their faces slack with surprise. They expected a vintage Pat rage. But strangely enough, I wasn't concerned with winning and losing. I was more concerned with how we would handle the situation. If we lost, well, okay. Truth was, I felt that losing a game or two might be good for this team. Toughen 'em up. Losing strengthened you, it revealed your weaknesses so you could fix them. That's why Tennessee played at least twenty ranked teams every season, because we believed a schedule that tested us would prepare us to win it all in the end. I even said aloud to our assistants, "If we don't lose a game, I don't see how we can win a title. But if we lose a game or two, we've got a pretty good chance of winning the whole thing."

I strolled to the front of the locker room and I asked the team a question.

"What are you *not* doing?" I asked.

They said, as a group, "Rebounding."

"You've been doing it all season, haven't you?" I said. "So let's go back out there, and do it."

I waved the stat sheet. I turned on Tree.

"How many rebounds did you have?" I asked.

She didn't reply.

"Zero," I said.

Silence. I went down the list. Tamika had four.

"Well," I said to the team. "It can't get any worse. You've seen everything they can do to you. Now listen. You can still win this game. But you can't get it all back at once. Take it one possession at a time."

I paused. I could see Tamika was seething with embarrassment and frustration. She had played hard but, for her, terribly. She had just six points, with a couple of free throws.

"I'll tell you this much," I said. "If we're going down, we're going down fighting."

"Catch" was about to play some serious catch-up.

> > >

TAMIKA WAS NOT EVEN A YEAR OLD when she touched a basketball for the first time. Harvey Catchings would walk in the house with a ball under his arm after a long day at practice, and his three kids would greet him at the door, grabbing for it. They would pry it out of his hands and roll around on the floor with it, trying to dribble.

Tamika's earliest memories were of going to various gyms and arenas to watch her father. Perhaps her most idyllic childhood memory was of seeing him in the final game of his career on a court in Gorizia, Italy. After the game was over, all of the men threw flowers to their wives in the stands. Harvey tossed a bouquet up to his family. The bouquet rose in the air, and Tamika, only seven, stood on tiptoe and came down with an armful of flowers. Tauja, too, grabbed some of the bulbs. They were already competing.

Harvey and Wanda moved their family to the Chicago suburb of Deerfield, Illinois, where Harvey built a new career as a businessman and a broadcaster. As the kids got older, they began playing the game seriously. When Tamika was in the fifth grade and Tauja was in the sixth, they asked Harvey to be their coach.

Harvey said, "Do you guys really want to learn how to play this game?"

The two girls said, "Yes, Daddy."

"No," Harvey said. "That's not what I'm talking about. If you really want to learn how to play, I can teach you the proper fundamentals. But it's going to take work. If you aren't willing to work, tell me now, and we'll keep it a playground thing. But if you want to be good players, then I can help you. I'll give you the same drills I gave your brother."

And that's what he did. The little girls struggled with drills meant for grown men. Harvey taught them how to square up on their shot, and the right technique for a fast break. He coached their grade school team, making it a family affair. But the sisters were so good he had to sub one of them out. It just wasn't fair to the other girls—if Tamika and Tauja were in at the same time, no one else got to touch the ball.

As Tamika and Tauja grew more competitive, they played increasingly bitter games of one-on-one in the driveway. Instead of ending with a final score, the contests would end in fights. They would go at it, elbows flying. If Tauja scored on Tamika, then Tamika would bump her. The next time Tamika would drive, she'd intentionally give Tauja a hip. Tauja would get mad, and literally trample Tamika on her way to the hoop.

Tamika would pick up the ball, and throw it at her.

And then they'd brawl.

Harvey would come outside to find his adorable daughters bloody. "Okay, you know what?" he'd say. "Give me the ball. The game's over."

Tauja would go back to her dolls. But Tamika would pout. She'd jump around and pretend to play the game without a ball. She would take imaginary jump shots.

But the family games ended early one morning, when Harvey and Wanda announced they were divorcing. It was the start of Tamika's seventh grade year. Tamika wasn't really aware of what was happening. All she knew was that one night her parents went out dancing, and the next morning, she was having a talk with her daddy.

"Me and your mother have decided to split up," he said.

And then he started crying.

Tamika had never seen her daddy cry.

"We'll still be able to see each other," he said, tears running down his cheeks.

"Okay," she said.

Tamika was too young to understand. What she really wanted to do was go back outside to play basketball with her friends.

But as time went on, Tamika learned the meaning of divorce. The breakup literally divided their family. In the first few months after the split, Tauja missed her father badly and announced she was going to live with him. Tamika was caught in the middle. She didn't want to part from her sister, but she couldn't bear to leave Wanda. She chose to stay with her mother. Tamika and Tauja would see each other at their school, Stevenson High School in Deerfield—and then go home to separate houses.

Tamika watched her mother struggle with the hurt of divorce, and with trying to make a second life. Wanda was frank with her daughters: she wasn't prepared to be single and self-supporting. She went to work as a teaching assistant, but education was hardly a lucrative field. Tamika and Tauja were hard on her. They would tell her, "We won't ever end up in your situation." Wanda didn't take offense. She agreed—she didn't want them to end up that way either.

Tamika was developing into a loner. None of the other girls at school wanted to play ball as hard or as long as she did. If she went without a basketball for forty-eight hours, she went through withdrawal. She didn't want to do what other girls did, which to her mostly seemed to be gossiping behind each other's backs.

On a spring afternoon at the end of her sophomore year in high school, Tamika came home from school, and said, "Mom, let's move." Tamika sensed that her mother needed a change, and the timing seemed right. Tamika and Tauja had led their Deerfield high school team to a state championship. Tauja was a senior preparing to graduate and enroll at Illinois; Kenyon was already in college at Northern Illinois. Tamika knew Wanda needed a fresh start, and wanted to help.

"Mom, I'm ready to leave," she said.

Wanda said, "You sure?"

"Yeah," Tamika said. "I'm sure."

Wanda started looking for a new town. She was from Texas originally, and that year, Tamika played in a tournament in Grapevine, Texas. Wanda decided she liked the surrounding area, and found an apartment in Duncanville, a suburb of Dallas, and landed a job in the school system there. Later, she moved into reservations with American Airlines, so she could use their benefits for free flights to see her children at college.

No sooner had Tamika enrolled in the local Duncanville high school than she led them to a state championship. Then, I came calling. On the day that I first met Tamika, I knew I wanted her at Tennessee. Initially, I set out to recruit her simply on the basis of her talent, but after just a few minutes of conversation, I practically wanted to adopt her.

"You want to see my room?" she asked me.

"Okay," I said.

Her room was almost militarily neat, except for the walls. Plastered all over them were motivational slogans and posters of NBA players and the 1996 USA women's Olympic basketball team.

We sat on her bed looking at scrapbooks, and talking. Not everybody could play at Tennessee, I said. It took a certain character, someone who not only wanted to win, but who wanted to get better.

"You want to see my closet?" she asked, shyly.

"Okay," I said.

She proudly showed me the uniform she got for playing on the USA junior national team. Then she pointed to all of her favorite clothes.

Out in the living room, Mickie, Wanda, and Tamika's high school coach, Sara Hackerott, visited. After a while they wondered what was keeping us. Finally, Tamika and I broke off our conversation to sit down to dinner with them. By the end of the meal, I had decided that recruiting was a dangerous thing. You shouldn't get too attached, I reminded myself.

We might not get Tamika to Tennessee. Tauja was already projected to be a star at Illinois, and Harvey had his heart set on Tamika going to Illinois too, so he could watch them play together.

You took a shine to a kid, and then they signed with another school, I told myself. So I tried not to get in too deep. But I couldn't help it with Tamika.

Picture a kid with a smile as pure and unaffected as early morning sun, and that was Tamika. Picture a kid with such an open and unspoiled nature that you could read every single thought and emotion that crossed her face. Picture a kid who was a ramrod straight 6-feet-1, but still called her father "Daddy."

Picture, too, a young woman who hid behind her openness. Who, despite the sociable veneer, would often sit withdrawn and alone on her high school bus, writing in a notebook. Whose idea of a nice evening was to have a friend over, and to sit in her room, silently passing the notebook between them, writing poems, words, and thoughts to each other, without saying a word aloud. Who was so easy to like, but who was careful in liking others, because she was susceptible to being wounded. Who not only hated fake people, phonies, but who sensed them almost instinctually. Truth ran through Tamika like the blood in her veins. She was not capable of insincerity.

Yesterday I saw you walking down the road
I called out your name, hoping you would turn around
But obviously you didn't hear me
I sensed pain in your body by the way you were walking
I sensed sadness in your soul by the sag of your head

TAMIKA CATCHINGS

That afternoon, when we left Wanda Catchings' apartment, I sat in the car and said to Mickie, "It's going to kill me if we don't get that kid. It's going to kill me."

We got her.

And she got me.

➤ ➤ ➤

I PROBABLY SHOULD HAVE talked to Wanda Catchings more before Tamika arrived at Tennessee. Who, I wondered, was this juvenile who showed up on campus in place of Tamika? Where was the sweet, dimpled young woman I had recruited?

Wanda could have told me about that smile. Tamika was prone to tantrums as a small child, Wanda later informed me. Wanda remembered her youngest becoming so enraged if she didn't win or get her way that she would throw herself on the floor and literally bang her head on the ground. When Wanda threatened to discipline Tamika, she would show that dimpled, radiant grin, and Wanda, disarmed, would let her get away with it.

"That smile has *got* to stop," Wanda would warn her, exasperated and charmed at the same time.

I knew exactly how Wanda felt.

Tamika was not accustomed to being criticized by coaches. It came as a shock the first time I tried to correct her on a few things. Tamika couldn't understand it. What could she possibly be doing wrong?

Our initial bone of contention was her defense. Tamika *thought* she knew how to play defense. But defense is a foreign language to a freshman. Tamika was aggressive and played hard, she went for everything, every steal, every pass. But in doing so, she'd take herself out of position, or not use her feet properly. Her fundamentals weren't there. When I addressed it, she didn't listen and kept repeating the same mistakes. Obviously, she thought she was right.

So I made her cry.

"Get your butt down in a stance, and get your hands up!" I said.

Tamika would look at me, blankly, and go back to doing the same old thing.

"Get your hands *up!*" I said.

Tamika had only been told how great she was. She'd had so much success—after all, she was the Player of the Year in high school. Her defense had always been fine before.

About the fourth or fifth time Tamika repeated the same mistake, I lost patience.

"Am I going to have this problem with you for four years?" I asked.

Tamika grew sulky. She got a glazed look in her eye, and acted like she didn't care if we ever won a game. Now I was furious. But I checked myself, and waited until after practice to talk to her.

I sat her down behind the basket.

I said, "You're acting like a baby, and a prima donna."

Tamika just stared at me.

"Look, you're one of best freshmen I've ever had here," I said. "You've got to know I'm thrilled to have you, and how much I care about you as a person. Now, why did you come here?"

She said, "To be the best."

"Okay, so then let me coach you," I said. "It's my job to teach you, and to get you ready to play."

But the next day, we tangled again. I got on her about her defense, and stayed on her. Tamika bent over, pulling at her shorts, like she was out of breath, but really, it was to hide the fact that her eyes had filled up with tears. She was more emotional than I realized.

After practice, I sat her down under the goalpost again.

I said, "Do I need lace gloves to handle you? Is that how you want to be?"

Tamika said, "I'm not used to being yelled at like that."

"Am I not supposed to coach you?" I said. "Am I not supposed to do my job?"

But Tamika was stubborn—she would tell you that herself. She went back to making the same mistakes, and when I started yelling at her again, she closed off, and gave me that look. Or she watered up.

A lot of players think they are being coachable because they give effort. But the really coachable ones are those who correct their mistakes. Tamika wasn't correcting hers.

A few days later, we had our grand final run-in. The gym was full of people watching us practice. This time, when I corrected her, telling her to get her hands up, Tamika didn't appreciate the fact that there was an audience. She got that glassy look in her eye, and checked out. She started acting like she wasn't trying.

I snapped at her, "You'd better try."

She shot back, "I *am* trying."

Nobody had warned Tamika that the one thing you didn't want to give me was any backtalk. The only answer I was seeking from her was "Yes." Backtalk was a bad precedent. I started the next drill, and then I pulled Tamika over to the sideline.

"Am I going to have this problem with you all year?" I said.

She said, "No."

I said, "I'll send your little butt right back to Texas. You need to stop acting so stubborn and start thinking about this team. You're not only going to get yourself in trouble, you're going to get them in trouble, too. You're being selfish."

This time, I didn't sit her down after practice for any soothing talks. I went back to my office without saying another word to her. The Lady Vols learned quickly that my silence was worse than my yelling. When I didn't say anything, or when I spoke most softly, that's when you knew you were in real trouble.

A few minutes later, Tamika stuck her head in my door. She was showered, and contrite.

"I'm sorry," she said. "I just got frustrated. It will never happen again."

And it never did.

We talked for a while in my office. "I don't mean to shut off, but that's how I get," Tamika said. "I'm not used to coaches yelling at me. That's not the way I learned."

I explained to Tamika that if I saw her doing something that was going to harm the team, like playing unsound defense, it was my business to stop and correct it. "You just have to trust me," I said. "It's important that you focus on the message of what I say and not the volume. You know I'm an intense coach. But I'm only here to help you."

Coaching young players is sort of like driving with my son in a car. He always has his seatbelt on, but if I have to stop short, I still throw my arm across him. It was the same with me and these freshmen. I couldn't help throwing an arm across them, if I thought it was for their own good.

But I was learning something about Tamika. She was perhaps the most sensitive person on the team, and the most introspective. That was at least partly a result, I thought, of the fact that she had suffered from a hearing impairment all of her life.

➤ ➤ ➤

THE WORLD was a whisper to Tamika.

Tamika was two years old when her hearing problem was diagnosed. It was termed senso-neural hearing loss, a condition in which the mechanisms in her inner ears showed permanent damage, and it was probably congenital. Her older brother, Kenyon, had it too.

There were four categories of hearing loss: "mild," "moderate," "severe," and "profound," and Tamika's hearing loss was described as "profound." More specifically, it prevented her from hearing certain pitches and tones. The pitches and tones that she had the most trouble with happened to be those that people employ when they talk.

Tamika had trouble hearing voices.

As a small child, Tamika had worn hearing aids in both ears. But when she reached fifth grade, she suddenly refused to wear them. She was at that age where fitting in had become desperately important, and when some kids teased her at school, she grew self-conscious. The hearing aids seemed bulky and conspicuous to her. She preferred to read lips and risk missing things rather than be made fun of.

Tamika had gotten through four straight years of high school, and now a portion of her first year in college, without being able to hear a lot of what was said to her. But she compensated so well that most people didn't realize it. She was a good student who covered herself by studying hard. The only telltale sign that she had hearing loss was in her speech; sometimes she left out sounds, or her pronunciation sounded lazy.

I knew Tamika had some sort of hearing problem when I recruited her. I called Tamika's high school coach in Duncanville, Sara Hackerott, and asked her about it.

Sara said, "It's never been a hindrance on the court."

So I never addressed it in conversation with Tamika. I just assumed it wasn't a problem.

But when Tamika got to Knoxville, I began noticing small things. I saw that she always made eye contact and positioned herself close to me when I spoke in practice. But if her back was turned, or she faced away from me, she missed some, if not all, of what was said.

The real tip-off was when she missed curfew. On our road trip to Stanford, she showed up in her room at 11:30 instead of 11 P.M. like the rest of the team. When I asked her why she was late, she admitted she hadn't heard the announcement.

Then our associate athletic director for media relations, Debby Jennings, told me that some of the local press had noticed that Tamika had a slight speech problem. They were were asking if she was hearing impaired.

In games, I became concerned about the crowds and the huddles. Tamika was our quietest player on the floor, she rarely communicated in a way other than nodding or shaking her head. I believed the reason she didn't talk more on the floor was because of her hearing. Also, I thought there were instances in which she missed the offensive signals. We were such a verbal team that I felt she needed to hear better.

I consulted with our trainer, Jenny, and Debby. We agreed we should approach Tamika about getting a hearing aid. I knew that there were some new ones that were so tiny they were unnoticeable. I broached the subject one day in the training room after practice, with Jenny present. I figured it could be a sensitive issue with Tamika, so I eased into it, carefully.

I told Tamika that when I was twenty-nine I got braces to correct my crooked front teeth. I added that I had seen some new hearing aids that were very small, and would she consider wearing one? Tamika said she had worn one before, and she wasn't sure she was comfortable with it.

I said, "I wear contacts. I wear orthotics. If you have a problem or a handicap, why not fix it? It's nothing to be ashamed of."

Tamika said that her old hearing aid was too big and she had been teased some. I said, "You're going to be a great player and a role model. You're going to go to a lot of press conferences, and your speech is going to be an issue. So let's take care of it."

It took a while longer to convince Tamika to wear it, and then to work out the health insurance, and to get her to a doctor to have her hearing tested. When the hearing aid arrived, I was relieved to see how tiny it was. I don't know if the team ever noticed that Tamika even had one in. We never said a word about it. We just moved on.

After a few days, I asked Tamika casually, "How's it going?"

She said, "It's okay. It's just weird hearing myself talk."

➤ ➤ ➤

EVEN THOUGH WE WERE DOWN by seventeen to Illinois, our shots had to fall sometime, I told myself. We couldn't go the entire game without our shots falling. It would just be too unnatural.

As the Lady Vols took the floor for the second half, Mickie, Holly, Al, and I tried to stay positive and level-headed. Holly kept saying things to them like "It's all right, baby doll, we're going to get back in this game. Just force some turnovers, and we're back in it." Mickie was chattering, saying, "Stay on the boards! Stay on the boards!"

Al pulled Tamika aside. Each of our assistants had their own relationships with players. Holly was a fountain of offensive options, as well as laughs. Mickie doled out attitude adjustments, and worked most closely with our post players. Al was good at analyzing the opponent and providing a psychological edge.

Al whispered in Tamika's ear, "This game is going to come to you. You were just overexcited in the first half. Relax, and I promise, your shot will fall."

Holdsclaw came out and made the first four points of the half, pumping in her little jumpers. That cut it to thirteen, 41–28.

Illinois took a twenty-second time-out to consider that.

Mickie looked up at the clock, and said, "If we can get it to ten with ten minutes to go, we'll be all right."

And then we pressed.

And I mean, *pressed.* It was a full court suffocating attack, led by Kellie and Kyra. As soon as the ball came inbounds, Kellie and Kyra would set a trap, clawing at the ball. Just watching it made *me* feel claustrophobic. Imagine having a blanket thrown over your head, and being tied up with a rope. That's what our defense looked like.

Now the Illini's attempts were rolling off the rim, like ours had done in the first half.

The game began to seesaw. The Illini went back up by eighteen, we inched it back to eleven. The Illini still led by 50–39 with 12:32 to go.

On the floor, Kyra watched one of the Illini players lean over, pulling at her shorts, the sure sign of someone who is trying to catch her breath and can't quite do it. *Okay,* Kyra thought, *it's our time to go. It's our time to go* now.

Kellie chanted, "Steal and score, steal and score."

Kellie quickly swiped the ball away on Illinois' inbounds pass, and made a layup, to roars.

"Steal and score," she said, to no one and everyone.

We had it down to single digits.

The Illini turned the ball over again: Tamika deflected a long inbounds pass, and Chamique recovered it beyond the foul line. Chamique whipped the ball to Kellie, who set up for a three point attempt.

When Kellie Jolly set up for a three, it looked like she was dipping her toe in the ocean. You could see what was coming.

She edged her right toe out.

Uh-oh, I thought.

Kellie took aim—and lofted a gorgeous arc that settled cleanly in the basket. The Thompson-Boling Arena crowd exploded into utter pandemonium. In just a little over ten seconds we had cut it to six, 50–44, thanks to Kellie Jolly's five straight points. "Steal and score, steal and score," Kellie kept saying.

Next, it was Semeka's turn. She slipped up on an Illinois guard and tipped the ball from behind. Kyra lunged to the floor for it. Semeka took off, and Kyra hit her with a pass. Semeka drove the baseline for a lay-in.

Illinois brought the ball up the court—and Semeka leaped in the air to slap away another pass. As Tree recovered the loose ball, Semeka was already streaking towards the opposite basket. Tree flung the ball, and Semeka caught it on a dead run. Semeka gently laid it in to a deafening eruption from the crowd.

I kept thinking about what Mickie said, that if we could get within ten, with ten minutes to go, we'd be all right.

After a couple of messy exchanges, we ran off four more straight points. Chamique barreled down the baseline, and got clobbered, earning two free throws. She sank both for our first lead of the half, 54–53.

I gazed at the clock. There was 9:25 remaining.

There was no reversing the momentum now. Ace got a steal and a pull-up jumper to make it 56–53 in Tennessee's favor at the nine-minute mark.

Illinois took a time-out. We had outscored them 32–12 in the space of just eleven minutes.

Tamika blocked a pass from Tauja, chased it, and took the ball all the way for the layup. A Holdsclaw leaner widened our lead to 62–53.

I sat back, and allowed myself to be amazed. Now it was showtime. With thirty-two seconds left, Ace whipped a no-look pass to Chamique for an easy layup.

Chamique pointed at Ace. "That's not bad," she said, coolly.

The buzzer sounded. We had won, 78–68.

In the locker room, I grabbed another stat sheet and scanned it quickly. Holdsclaw had nineteen, Randall had thirteen, and Jolly had ten.

And Tamika Catchings had a career high twenty points, with thirteen rebounds.

At that moment, I knew I had never coached a team so combustible. Or so willing to run full out, ninety-four feet, for forty minutes.

Afterwards, Tamika met her sister in the hallway.

Tauja just smiled and said, "We almost got you."

Tamika smiled back. "But you didn't," she said.

Tamika and Tauja met up with Harvey, who was still marveling over what he had just seen.

Harvey embraced Tauja. "You played great," he said. Then he turned to Tamika. "And you played great," he said.

A few minutes later, Niya Butts and Kyra Elzy ran into Wanda Catchings wandering in the hallway outside of our locker room. They bore down on her.

"Come on, tell us the truth," they said. "You know you were rooting for Tennessee."

≻ ≻ ≻

On December 18, we traveled to Alaska for a tournament called the Northern Lights Invitational. It was a selfish bit of scheduling; I had always wanted to see Alaska. Also, it was another chance to give our team an exotic experience. But I almost regretted it on the flight, which was a monster. We went from Knoxville to Atlanta to Salt Lake to Anchorage. It took about thirteen hours, door to door.

The highlight of the trip was a sledding expedition. Two players at a time rode the sled behind a team of six dogs. I won't forget the looks in their eyes as they climbed aboard, or Semeka Randall screaming with laughter at how bad the huskies smelled.

We beat Akron, Texas A&M, and Wisconsin in that order to claim the tournament title. The Meeks were defining themselves. The three of them were named to the all-tournament team and were in double digits all week. Against Texas A&M, the Meeks had 73 of our 105 points. Holdsclaw had 29, Randall 23, and Catchings had 21 points, with a dozen rebounds.

There was one bit of unpleasantness in Alaska. Kyra Elzy and I had a war of wills. It all started when I pulled her from the Texas A&M game in favor of Randall, and she gave me a look as she came to the bench. An outsider probably wouldn't have even noticed it. But I said, "Don't you catch an attitude with me."

Kyra did the worst thing she could do, which was to snap back at me. She said, "I'm not catching an attitude."

I said, "You catch an attitude with me, I won't play you for the rest of the game."

In the next game, Kyra didn't play as much as she was accustomed to. I wasn't punishing her, it just worked out that way.

Now Kyra was angry; she thought she was sitting on the bench, all because of one sullen look. Kyra decided she wasn't going to talk to me, or listen to me. When I spoke to her, she refused to make eye contact. Well, I certainly wasn't going to reward her for that kind of behavior.

Mickie would sit next to Kyra on the bench, and say, "You're going to play. She's just sending you a message."

But when we headed home from Alaska, we still weren't on good terms. I decided I would let Kyra enjoy her Christmas break. But a day or two later the phone rang. It was Kyra, calling to apologize. "I just wanted to say I'm sorry," she said. "I didn't want to go all through Christmas like this."

I said, "I'm glad you called. I really appreciate it. I feel better now."

The reason I was hard on Kyra was because she was a key to our team chemistry. I didn't want any of our players to resent yielding the floor to a teammate. Usually, Kyra would come out of a game and tell Semeka as they passed on the sidelines, "Okay, your turn." With enough confidence in ourselves, we didn't need something as petty as ego. This team was beginning to act like they were above ego, and I liked that about them.

On the way home, we passed through the Atlanta airport again. It was

December 21, and we were all flying home to different destinations for the holidays.

While we were lounging at the gate, Betsy Roberts, our assistant athletic director for development, handed me a quarter that she'd found. Betsy knew how superstitious I was. I was especially superstitious about lucky coins. Particularly pennies.

But a coin was only lucky if you found it lying heads up. If it was tails, I wouldn't look at it twice, much less pick it up. This quarter was heads up, so Betsy retrieved it and handed it to me. "I know you prefer pennies, but I found you a lucky quarter," she said. I thanked her and stuck the quarter in my pocket.

A few minutes later, I went into the rest room to freshen up. I entered a stall, and looked down, and saw something in the bottom of the commode.

It was a penny.

It was a heads up penny.

Dara Worrell, our ticket manager, was also in the rest room. I decided I needed a second opinion.

I said, "Dara!"

Dara poked her head in.

I said, "Look in that commode."

Dara gazed at me strangely.

"No, really, look," I said.

Dara glanced down once, quickly, as if she was afraid something in there might be alive.

I said, "Dara, do you know what that is?"

She said, "Well, it looks like a penny."

"It is!" I said. "But it's not just a penny. I think it's a heads up penny. Do you think it's heads up?"

She looked again, and said, "Yeah, it is."

I said, "I got to have it."

"Pat, no," she said.

I said, "How can I get it?"

I looked around the bathroom. There was a plunger in the corner. I grabbed it.

I caught the penny with the plunger, and tried to drag it up the side of the bowl. But right at the top, it fell out and slid back down in the water. I tried three or four more times with the plunger, splashing around without success.

It was time to board the plane.

I said to Dara, "I don't care. I've got to have it."

I set the plunger down. I rolled up the sleeve on my right arm. I was wearing an orange and white flannel shirt. Then I took my rings off.

Dara turned green.

I reached in and got the penny.

Then I went to the sink and turned on the hot water. I lathered up. I washed the penny, and my whole arm.

I started to hand the penny to Dara. "Hold this," I said.

Dara didn't want to hold it. I had to wrap it in paper before she would touch it.

I said, "This is it. We're gonna win a championship. You remember this."

I went out to the gate, where several of our players, boosters, and Betsy were waiting to board. I told them the whole story.

All of a sudden they didn't want to stand next to me.

Someone piped up, "Do you know how many people go through the Atlanta airport each day?"

I didn't care. I had gotten what I wanted.

And that's how we broke for the holidays, with a perfect 13–0 record, and a lucky penny. It had been a long autumn, and we all needed a rest.

But when I got home, I had trouble sleeping. There was something in the back of my mind, a thought or a sensation, trying to force itself forward. Ever since the Illinois game, I'd had a feeling of something impending. It wasn't a bad feeling. It was good. In fact, it was something wonderful. So wonderful, I was afraid to voice it.

The thought woke me up in the middle of the night.

This was the team I had worked twenty-four years for.

Q & A with Kyra Elzy (Sophomore guard)

Was Pat more affectionate with this team?

I think I hugged Pat more this year than I even looked at her last year.

Why do you think that was?

I think it may have started with the freshmen. I think they kind of paved the way with her. Especially Semeka. The rest of us never would have gone up to Pat and tackled her like that. We always knew Pat was a human being, even though last year she didn't act like it. But this year, we could let down our guard with her.

How so?

I mean, we could say, "Pat, I don't like your hair today." That would've never happened. I would be like, "Pat, I don't like your outfit." Everybody relaxed around her. We'd be singing on the bus, and dancing. We were more open and uninhibited. It felt like we were a bunch of sisters.

Let's talk about your knee injury. Pat took that hard.

You know, it was strange. When I hurt my leg, after all that we had been through, the person I wanted, the person I was screaming for, was Pat.

Which Pat do you prefer?

This one. I'd have to say I prefer this one.

CHAPTER SEVEN

Stitches and Sideshows, or, "Who Will Guard Nykesha Sales?"

IT WAS HARD TO BELIEVE that the state of Connecticut could cause me so much annual trouble. You went to Connecticut for quaint little inns, or antique markets, or old whaling towns, but not for ballplayers, right? Wrong. Unfortunately, the mere word "Connecticut" practically made me take to my bed with worry. In the last few years, basketball had become a chief export of the state—a development that, while good for the game, was galling to those of us who lived in Tennessee.

When Tennessee and Connecticut met, the color clash alone was violent enough. Not to mention the game itself, which had a tendency to rob the loser of any hope for the rest of the season, and leave them inconsolable. On one side, you had the day-glo, orange-clad, shriek-voiced southerners of Tennessee, singing "Rocky Top" often enough to induce epileptic seizure. On the other side, you had the blue-clad, deep, bass Yankee tones of the UConn loyals, chanting "Go Huskies!" while wearing dog collars and gloves shaped like paw prints.

It was a culture war. It pitted regional custom, colliding team colors, and perennial national rankings—the three things that made up that cheerfully poisonous and childish state of affairs known as a great college rivalry.

And we didn't have much time to get ready for it. We were to meet Connecticut in Thompson-Boling Arena on January 3.

The day after Christmas we had our single worst practice of the year. Our players had been home for five days, and they still had the taste of turkey in their mouths. Vacation was over, the excitement of beginning the regular season had worn off, and we had a long winter semester ahead. While they were eager to *play* UConn, *practicing* for UConn was the last thing they wanted to do.

I knew what they were thinking. They had one foot at the mall, and one on the court. They wanted to catch those after-Christmas bargains. But we had to snap out of it.

Throughout the holiday, a thought had nagged at me. "Who will guard Nykesha Sales?" Sales was UConn's All-American, a brilliant senior guard who posed our biggest problem. She was eating the opposition alive, averaging over twenty points, but statistics hardly did justice to her game. She was six feet of constant movement, a head-to-toe scoring threat who could take you off the dribble with either hand, or bury you with a three. We had to find a way to limit her touches.

All through the holidays, I fretted over the Sales problem. It was a half-buried anxiety, one of those vaguely worrisome sensations like leaving the iron on. I watched her on film incessantly. I even watched film on Christmas day.

So I was ill-tempered when our team took the court so lethargically the day after Christmas. No matter how hard I smacked the floor, I couldn't get them going. I was beside myself. Didn't they know what we were up against? Was there nobody who understood about my obsession with Sales?

No. Especially not Tree Geter.

"You lounge lizard," I said.

We worked out for two and a half hours. At the end of practice, I called them into a circle. I said, "Fine. If you can't handle having a few days off, then we just won't *take* days off."

I made them practice *twice* the next day. It was my way of exacting some payback for the 26th.

Like I say, I knew what they were thinking: why is this lady always after us? How come she's never satisfied, no matter what we do? Why can't we just go out and play? So I answered them.

"You've got to commit, right here in practice, because right here is where you get better," I said.

As good as we were, we still hadn't approached our potential. I was beginning to have an inkling of just what this team might accomplish—if they put their minds to it. The more I watched them play, the higher my expectations rose. I no longer felt that losing a game might be good for us. I wanted more—I wanted to see what they were truly capable of, I wanted to exhaust every last possibility in their bodies. It was kind of like having a fast new car. "Let's see what this baby can *really* do."

But Connecticut was just the sort of game that could blow out our tires.

The Huskies were coming into Knoxville ranked No. 3 in the country, and on a fifty-two-game regular season winning streak. They had Paige Sauer, a strong young presence at center, and a secret weapon in a bank shot artist from St. Petersburg, Russia, named Svetlana Abrosimova.

Then there was Sales. As the season wore on, she was only getting better. In her last three games coming into Knoxville, she had scored twenty-two, twenty-six, and twenty-eight points respectively—and she had hung a stunning forty-six points on the board against Stanford.

There was perhaps no bigger or more important matchup all season than Tennessee–Connecticut. The peculiar thing about it was that it was a young rivalry; it had grown up overnight with the rapidity of a brushfire. There were other teams with whom we had much older animosities: Old Dominion, Louisiana Tech, Stanford, and Vanderbilt, to name just a few. But Tennessee–Connecticut had a magnitude and an intensity I had seldom encountered. Whenever we played, it seemed to mean so much to both sides.

It all started in 1995, when we were ranked No.1 and UConn upset us in Storrs. Then, at the end of the season, Jennifer Rizzoti got a steal and a layup to beat us for the national championship.

The Huskies, starring Rebecca Lobo, were undefeated at 35–0 that year, setting an NCAA record for victories. They added insult to injury by beating us twice more, winning regular season meetings in 1996 and 1997. Rarely had a team dominated us that way. But if they owned us for a while, we avenged ourselves in the playoffs.

We upset them twice in the postseason en route to claiming back-to-back national championships in '96 and '97. Our last meeting had come in the '97 tournament. The Huskies were undefeated and the unanimous favorite to win it all, until our Cinderella team with ten losses stunned them in the regional finals, and went on to claim the title.

We vied off the court, too, for media attention and for prized recruits. UConn was coached by an articulate, persuasive recruiter, Geno Auriemma, who had made the Huskies the darlings of the east coast media. If we won the battle over Semeka Randall, the Huskies won Sauer, after we had heavily courted her.

As much as the rivalry pained us sometimes, we all enjoyed it. Geno and I respected each other and we understood that our seesaw battle for preeminence was great for the game.

We loved our showdowns with Connecticut. The bigger and more important the occasion, the better. A game against UConn was a way of saying, "Just how good are we?"

> > >

THE NATURAL PLAYER to put on Sales was her counterpart for us, Chamique Holdsclaw. But we had a problem. Holdsclaw's defense had been iffy all season.

The more I thought about Chamique's defense, the more irritated I got. I studied film on Chamique, and decided her effort on the defensive end of the floor was just plain lackadaisical. Chamique had it in her to be a great defensive player, but she just didn't commit to it, because she was always thinking "score" instead of "defend." I had suppressed my feelings on the subject, because we asked so much of her as a shotmaker and rebounder. But now I realized there was no excuse for it—it was time for her to be a more complete player. I decided to call her in for a conversation.

Just talking about defense wasn't enough. I wanted to show Chamique exactly what I meant. We traveled with five video machines on the road, and we even taped our practices every day, just for occasions like this. When I wanted to make a point to a player, all I had to do was go to the tape. I decided to give Chamique a multimedia presentation, in stereo.

I did a number on her.

I admit, it was a little unfair. But we needed to take drastic measures if we wanted to stop Sales.

I went to Al Brown, and told him my idea. I wanted him to put together a special highlight tape, something that would make a lasting impression on Chamique. He grinned.

"Oh yeah, I can do that," he said.

Al spent the rest of the afternoon happily cutting together a tape of Chamique's worst bloopers and blunders. It was twelve minutes long, a parade of one defensive breakdown after another.

Al brought me the tape. I took one look at it, and said, "Perfect."

Then I called Chamique into my office for a meeting.

"Who's going to guard Nykesha Sales?" I asked.

Chamique said, "I guess I am."

I said, "Well, we've got a matchup problem."

Chamique looked at me uncertainly.

"Everyone's always talking about how you're the best offensive player in America," I said. "But when they talk about defensive players, you don't even come to mind. No one has ever talked about your defense. If you want to be the best player in America you've got to have a total game.

It would be nice, just one time, to pick up the newspaper and read about Chamique Holdsclaw's defense."

Chamique said, "But I've improved. My defense has improved."

I said, "Really?"

She said, "Really."

"Well, I asked Al to put together a tape," I said. "And I think you could benefit from watching it."

She said, "Okay."

I started the tape up.

Frame after frame showed Chamique resting on defense, or making token attempts to stop the opponent. She stood around, her hands low, while player after player fired off uncontested shots. She got beat to the baseline. She got beat to the middle. She got beat in transition. Al had made it look as though she got beat in every possible way.

Every now and then, I'd back the tape up, and play it again.

I didn't say a word.

Finally, we reached the end of the tape. Chamique was silent for a moment.

Then she said, "I got you, Coach Summitt."

After the meeting, I stuck my head in Al's office.

"Great footage!" I said.

"She actually played some pretty good defensive series," Al said. "It took me a while to find twelve minutes' worth of that stuff. But you said that's what you wanted."

I said, "That's exactly what I wanted."

> > >

THE NIGHT BEFORE the UConn game, I had the whole team over for dinner, and told them I would fix whatever they wanted.

Big mistake. We had eight steaks, three chicken dinners, fried shrimp for all, and lots of home style vegetables. My mother even made Chamique a sweet potato pie. Was I spoiling them? Maybe. Or maybe I was just getting them ready for the Huskies.

My parents had come in from Henrietta for the game, and so had friends like Billie Moore, my old Olympic coach, and Nell Fortner, the current Olympic coach. There must have been twenty-five people in the house. My father provided the entertainment. Richard Head has always been demanding, as anyone who read *Reach for the Summit* knows. He loves to tell me what I *can't* do, because he knows how crazy it makes me.

So what did he do?

He bet Billie Moore aloud that UConn would beat us.

"Ten bucks says UConn wins," he said.

The following night, we walked on to the floor of Thompson-Boling Arena to roars from a sellout audience of 24,597. It was the single largest crowd ever to see a women's collegiate basketball game. The stadium was packed to capacity, with people standing in the eaves.

As we walked on to the floor of the arena that night, I experienced one of the most profoundly gratifying moments of my career. I stared upwards at the rafters, in wonder, thinking that in a sense both teams had already won.

For years, we had worked in a sport no one else seemed to care about. We loved what we were doing, but there were times when we despaired of ever filling a stadium. I could remember hoping five thousand people would show up, and praying for ten thousand. This team, it occurred to me, was doing more than winning ball games. They were helping the sport to grow in front of our very eyes, proving that it could be big box office. We had a sellout crowd, the *New York Times* on press row, and a battery of CBS cameras at courtside, broadcasting the game nationally.

I simply wasn't prepared for the seething mass of sound that greeted me. It was so loud and sustained that it seemed to have physical properties; it was a force field. I felt almost inside of the noise, or way down at the bottom of it. It was a vibration that at once surrounded me, and yet reached inside, into the center of my bones. When I walked out to meet Geno for the usual pregame handshake, all I could hear was my own heartbeat in my ears. I looked down at my forearms, and saw gooseflesh rising.

I met him at courtside, and we shook hands. I yelled into Geno's ear, "This is a compliment to both programs." He nodded his head in agreement, beaming.

As our players warmed up, they couldn't hear themselves talk. We were all giddy.

"It's like walking into a rock concert," Kellie Jolly said, exultantly.

But there was one uninvited guest among the throngs in the arena that night.

Kyra Elzy's stalker.

➤ ➤ ➤

KYRA RECEIVED her first letter in November of her freshman year. Initially, it seemed like a harmless note from someone with a crush. Our players got missives from amorous admirers all the time.

"I love you, you're my sweet cake," he wrote. "You're the one for me. I see you on TV, and you're pretty as candy."

Kyra laughed it off. To her roommates, LaShonda and Niya, it was a source of hilarity. "Sweet cake," they would say, giggling.

But this guy didn't go away. Kyra began hearing from him regularly. Then he started composing proposals. "I love you. I want to marry you," he wrote. He sent her cassette tapes full of love songs.

"Y'all, this is crazy," Kyra said.

But LaShonda and Niya refused to take it seriously. They teased Kyra about the identity of her admirer. "I think he's a girl," Niya said. They cracked up. "Think about it," Niya said. "He never sends a picture. He's a girl."

Then the letters began arriving daily. All through the spring, Kyra would collect her mail, and every single day there would be another note or card. "Thinking of you today."

Niya would just wave her hand and say, "He's a girl."

In the summer, Kyra had a respite. She toured with the USA junior national team, and went home to LaGrange to visit Sheryl and her aunts and uncles. Eventually it was August and time to report back to campus. No sooner was Kyra back in Knoxville than she got another card.

"Missing you while we're apart," he wrote.

By now Kyra was growing leery. A situation that had seemed harmless was now escalating.

Shortly before the season started, we played an exhibition against an Armed Forces team. The day after the game, Kyra got a truly disturbing note.

"I saw you walk out of the arena," he wrote, "but I didn't want to bother you."

A day or so later, yet another note arrived. "I watched you walk out of the library," he wrote. "And I liked what you had on."

Okay, this isn't funny anymore, Kyra thought. *I've let it go on too long.*

He had been writing for months now, and she regretted having kept it a secret from the coaching staff. Kyra decided it was time to tell Mickie; she would know what to do. It was interesting to see which staffers the various players chose to go to for comfort and advice, and it was largely a matter of personal style. Some preferred Al's analytical bent, some Holly's compassion, and some my directness. Mickie, easygoing and sensible, was the coach in whom Kyra most often confided.

Kyra took the note to Mickie, along with some of the other letters he had sent. Mickie read them with concern. If it happened again, she decided, we would go right to the police.

Meanwhile, back at the dorm, Niya and LaShonda kept up a steady stream of friendly taunting. "You must be pretty important to have a stalker," Niya said.

. That was the last Kyra heard from the stalker for a while. A month went by, with no letters or cards. Kyra had almost forgotten about it, and so had Mickie.

Until the night of the UConn game.

Kyra bobbed around the floor during the pregame warmup, loosening up and taking a few jumpers. She jogged to the bench for a drink. As she stood on the sidelines, an usher came down the aisles and handed her a note.

"Your cousin said to give you this note, and to tell you good luck," the usher said.

He handed Kyra a piece of torn paper, with scribbling on it.

Kyra unfolded it.

"I'm here to watch my baby play," the note read. "I'll be sitting in the third row of section 109."

Kyra felt sick. She refused to turn around and look into the stands.

"Niya, Niya, come here!" she said.

Kyra showed Niya the note. Niya immediately scanned the stands, and spotted him: a large man wearing dark shades. There was something inherently frightening about someone who wore sunglasses indoors, Niya decided.

Niya said, "He's scary looking."

Kyra didn't want to turn around. Instead, she bolted straight into the locker room and found Mickie. Kyra showed Mickie the note. There wasn't much anybody could do at this point, Mickie realized. She didn't want to upset Kyra any more than she already was. Mickie assured Kyra that arena security would keep this guy away from her. Kyra spent the rest of pregame warmup in the locker room, trying to rid herself of her creepy feeling.

Mickie returned to floor, mulling it over. There was still a chance he was just another obsessed letter writer. We got all kinds of mail and calls from admirers. Mickie debated whether or not to tell me what was going on. Mickie decided to wait until after the game was over. Knowing me, I might just go up into the stands after him.

➤ ➤ ➤

BUOYED BY THE CROWD and the rock concert atmosphere, the Lady Vols came out flying.

Our performance seemed heightened. Was it my imagination, or did we elevate more than usual, and did our shots ripple through the net with unusual crispness? We scored the first ten points of the game unanswered, and built a seventeen-point lead.

Of all people, Kyra Elzy was the one who fired the run for us. She shook off her fright to score nine points in the first half. At halftime, we went in the locker room leading 42–28.

I was pleased. We almost never dominated Connecticut this way. What's more, our challenge to Chamique had worked: she was putting the manacles on Sales and had held her to just six points.

But I also knew it couldn't last. I had too much respect for Geno and the Huskies to believe that we would get out of this game so easily. We were in for at least one big scare.

"It's a forty-minute game," I told the team. "*Believe* me, they will make a run."

I was right. In the second half, UConn turned it up, and we suddenly lost our heat. In one cold five-minute stretch, we scored just two points.

Connecticut cut the lead to one, 49–48, with 12:34 left in the game.

We were containing Sales and Sauer, but we hadn't reckoned on a surprising new source of points, the Russian Abrosimova. She was banking in shots from everywhere.

During a time-out, I tried to calm down the Lady Vols. The noise was deafening. "Come in close," I shouted over the din. "We quit playing defense," I yelled. "We're taking good shots, but they aren't falling. So you've got to make it up on the defensive end. Turn up the intensity, and turn it up *now*."

We pressed.

Instantly, Semeka Randall forced a turnover. She slapped the ball away, retrieved it, and flipped it to Kellie Jolly. Kellie had struggled offensively all night—she was zero for five from three point range, her shots bouncing harmlessly off the rim. But Kellie paused again at the three point line, and dipped the toe of her sneaker out.

And drained the three pointer.

Next, Holdsclaw threw in a couple of her patented double clutch lay-ins. With barely a rustle, like a twist of silk, she put the ball in the net. Suddenly, we had an eight point lead again.

Randall kept up the pressure. She whirled, she jitterbugged, she drove—and scored sixteen points in the final ten minutes.

We won going away, 84–69.

For the night, Holdsclaw had six steals, and held Sales to twelve points.

In the aftermath of the game, as usual, everyone would talk about the Meeks and our offense. But in the locker room, we knew better. It wasn't our offense that won the game. It was our defense, and Kellie Jolly. As a team, we forced twenty-seven turnovers from Connecticut, fifteen of them on steals. Meanwhile, Kellie, who went all but unnoticed, had *zero turnovers*. It was one of those itemized details in a box score that few would understand the critical impact of—but to me, it was the difference in the game.

Afterwards, Geno was gracious. "Tennessee is certainly everything it's advertised to be," he said. "There just seems to be little you can do, because they put so much pressure on you. And they had a lot of assistant coaches up in the stands, too."

Unfortunately, the good manners on both sides deteriorated the morning after the game. Semeka Randall, euphoric as she came off the court, made an ill-considered comment on a postgame radio show. When asked whether the crowd had been a factor, she said, trying to compliment our fans, "Oh, yeah, I think Connecticut about ran off the floor, they were so scared."

The quote hit the morning papers and was taken out of context. A day later, according to the east coast press, Geno made some unkind remarks in response to Semeka's comment, including a slighting reference to the way our team lost the 1995 championship game to UConn.

A controversy was born. Semeka's comments and Geno's retort roiled through the media in the northeast. My phone rang off the hook, seeking comment. I declined to throw fuel on the fire.

A day later, we drove to South Carolina to begin a four-game road swing. Before practice, I gathered our team in a circle and told them I wasn't crazy about the comments made on either side. I realized Semeka was only a college freshman, but this was an opportunity for the entire team to learn from the situation, I said.

One thing was clear: no women's team had gotten this much media attention before. We were receiving daily calls from the national press and cameras and microphones were at courtside every night.

"All eyes are on this team," I told the Lady Vols. "You have to handle success. We win with class."

➤ ➤ ➤

KYRA'S STALKER started appearing at road games. We would look up, and there he was.

There was a rhythm to January. We practiced and played, practiced and played, the steady beat of a regular season. We rode the bus, we napped, we studied, and the victory total steadily mounted. But every so often, the rhythm was broken by a crisis. If January was a month of win after win, it was also a month marked by a couple of frightening episodes. Stalkers and stitches—that's how I thought of it.

Mickie and Kyra told me about him right before our game against South Carolina in Columbia on January 6.

Once again, Kyra jogged through her pregame ritual, limbering up and taking a few casual jumpers. Then she turned around—and there he was, sitting in a section close to the floor. So now he was following her on the road, too.

Kyra drifted to Mickie and said, "He's here."

Mickie said, "You're kidding?"

Kyra pointed him out.

Mickie said, grimly, "It's time to tell Pat."

They found me in the locker room, where I was making some notes for a chalk talk. They recited the whole disturbing story.

I was angry. But more than anything, I was determined to get this guy off of Kyra's back. Nothing made me more furious than an unwanted overture to our players. We had dealt with obscene callers and amorous letter writers plenty of times before. But I had never gotten used to it.

Parents sent their daughters to me for safekeeping. They chose Tennessee in part because we were a disciplined, structured program, and promised to look after their children. In fact, players sometimes complained I knew too much about their business. But it was my responsibility to know where they were and what they were doing, within reason, because I would have to answer to their parents.

Ace had already dealt with two obscene callers earlier in the season. I was so mad I called one of them up myself. He had been enough of a yahoo to have given Ace his name and home phone number. So I dialed it.

"Buddy," I said. "This is Pat Summitt. If you ever call one of our players again, I'll have you arrested. I've got your name, and your number, and your address. Do we understand each other?" Then I hung up.

But this was far more serious. We had never dealt with someone who was so persistent, and who actually came out of the shadows and appeared in person. We notified security. After the South Carolina game, we were scheduled to bus right back to Knoxville that night. We intended to notify the campus and Knoxville police as soon as we got home.

Mickie said, "When we go out on the court, I'll show you where he is."

We took our seats on the bench with about three minutes remaining before tip-off.

Mickie murmured, "He's directly across from us." As our team took their places on the floor for the opening jump ball, I scanned the stands. There he was.

He had black shades pulled halfway down his nose—and he was staring right at Kyra.

With every move she made, his eyes followed her. He watched her run the floor, he watched her come to the bench, he watched her towel off.

I didn't like it. I didn't like it at all.

His presence ruined the whole night for me. And that was too bad, because the game represented a triumphant homecoming for Tree Geter. Signs waved all over the arena welcoming Tree back. Her dad, Robert, had bought two hundred tickets to the game and handed them out to everyone he knew in town. Her mom, Joanne, was there, the first chance she had had to see her daughter play a collegiate game.

We won, 94–52, after leading by as many as forty-four points in the second half. Tree put on a show with nine points, a team-high ten rebounds, four assists, and three blocked shots.

But throughout the game, I kept one eye on Kyra's man.

On the bus back that night, the Lady Vols watched the Wes Craven movie *Scream.* Much as I liked this team, there were some things I would never understand about them, like how they could watch a slasher movie. I kept my head down and tried not to listen to the sounds of cinematic mayhem.

As soon as we got home, I called Donna Thomas, our associate athletics director in charge of compliance and operations, and told her we had a stalker on our hands. "We've got to do something," I said. To me, there was no such thing as a false alarm in a situation like this. Donna immediately notified the security force in Thompson-Boling Arena, and then called the campuses we would be visiting.

Next, I called the chief of our campus police, Ed Yovella. He immediately posted extra security behind our bench, and assigned a detective to walk Kyra to her car after home games. He informed the Knoxville police and the F.B.I. Everyone was very much aware of and on top of the situation. We would all keep a close eye on Kyra, and make sure he wouldn't come any closer to her.

I sat her down for a talk.

"You don't walk anywhere alone," I said, "and you keep your doors locked. I'm not trying to make you paranoid, but I don't want to act like this is nothing, either."

I called Kyra's mother, Sheryl, too. I reassured her as best I could, but I wanted to reiterate that Kyra should be cautious. "Security is on top of it," I said. "Sheryl, we're going to take care of her."

But for the next three games, he appeared in the stands.

He was in Thompson-Boling on January 10, when a Florida team ranked twelfth in the country came to visit. A crowd of more than 15,000 showed up for what was a routine conference game—and we rewarded them by playing our single best game of the season up to that point. We led at the half by the staggering score of 57–18. But I couldn't enjoy it. Not with him there.

Something else intruded on my peace of mind, too. This team played so hard and so heedlessly that they were in constant danger of injury. Right before the half, Tamika Catchings went for a steal above the three point circle. All of a sudden an arm came out of nowhere, smacking her in the face. She took the blow squarely in her right eye. Tamika fell like a stone.

She thought her eyeball had come out.

Tamika curled up on the floor, with her hands wrapped tightly around her face. She thought that if she could just hold her eye in her head, she'd be all right.

I got to her, and kneeled down.

"Let me see," I said. "Let me see."

Tamika wouldn't take her hand away from her face.

"We have to check you," I said, gently. "You have to let me see."

Tamika peeled her hand away.

There was blood everywhere.

She had a cut over her eye that was pouring blood, and another under her eye. Jenny wiped the blood from Tamika's face and assured her that she was okay, that it was just a deep cut. I turned away from all the blood, and Jenny helped her to the locker room.

We won, 99–60. But Tamika took five stitches.

Next, we traveled to Georgia, on January 14. Once again, just before tip-off, Mickie said to me, "Kyra's man is here."

I decided that I was about over him.

It was a bad start to a cranky night for me. The Lady Bulldogs outrebounded us, which didn't do anything for my mood, and poor Catchings looked like she had taken a crowbar in the face. So I didn't need much of an excuse to get all over Holdsclaw. She was below average against Georgia, and in the second half, when the Lady Bulldogs made a run, I took her out of the game.

As soon as Chamique came out, she sat in my chair, as usual. It was a kind of a thing between us. When Chamique took a breather, she liked to do it in my chair, between Mickie and Holly, so she could confer with them. Sometimes, when a game was out of reach, I'd turn to her and say, "What do you want to run?" I'd let Chamique pick out a play. Chamique called it, "sitting in Big Mama's chair." It made her feel rewarded.

But I didn't intend to reward her on this night.

When I turned around and saw Chamique sitting in my chair, I flared up like I had been shot out of a gun.

"Get out of my chair!" I said. "You think you can sit there after the way you're playing? You need to sit somewhere else. Like at the end of the bench."

It was the last word I spoke to her for the night.

We won, 96–71, to raise our record to 18–0, the best start in the history of the program. But it didn't improve my mood, which was made even worse by what happened next.

Just after the game, the stalker managed to get Al Brown's attention as he stood around on the sidelines talking to some friends. Al didn't realize who the guy was. The stalker said to him, "Could you give this to Kyra for me?"

He handed Al an envelope. Al unthinkingly passed it to Kyra, who stuck it in her bag.

Later that evening, as we were traveling home on a charter flight, Kyra opened the envelope.

There was a hundred dollar bill inside.

Kyra, horrified, stuck it back in the envelope and took it to Mickie. For a player to accept cash from a booster or a fan would be an NCAA violation. Mickie grabbed the envelope like it was a hot brick, and marched Kyra over to me.

Kyra said, "We have to tell you something," and she showed me the bill.

My heart almost stopped. I snatched it out of her hand.

I said, "You cannot keep that. I'll return it."

I stuck the bill in my pocket.

At practice the next day, I was still in a rotten frame of mind. I let them all have it.

"Okay, our post game stinks," I said. "Tell the truth, Tree Geter. You're lazy. And you only get up for big games. I'm not going to lie. In twenty-four years, this is the softest we've been in the paint."

We finished a swing through the southeast with a trip to Kentucky. On the bus ride down, the team watched *Soul Food*—another movie I was taken aback by. I looked up from my work right in the middle of an explicit sex scene. I realized my son, Tyler, was in the back of the bus.

I yelled to the back, "Somebody cover Tyler's eyes!" I turned around. Chamique had already put her hands over his face.

The Kentucky game was a homecoming for Kyra. Her mom, Sheryl, drove over from LaGrange, along with assorted other Elzys. But someone else had driven over to see Kyra, too.

The stalker.

Once again, Kyra took the floor for the pregame shootaround. She scanned the stands, and found her family. Then she turned—and saw that he was sitting right behind our bench.

Kyra went over to Mickie, and said, mournfully, "Mickie, he's here again."

Mickie said, "That's it."

Mickie strode over to me, furious.

"Kyra's man is here *again*," she said.

I spotted him behind the railing that separated the crowd from the bench area. I thought, coldly, we had some business to settle, him and me.

We beat Kentucky, 93–65, for our nineteenth straight victory. Five different Lady Vols scored in double figures, including Kyra. The Meeks led the show with thirty-one of our forty-five points in the second half.

But I was too preoccupied to fully enjoy the action. The game wasn't even over when I decided I couldn't wait to take care of that unfinished business with Kyra's stalker.

I turned around to our team administrative assistant, Kelly Sahner, and said, "I need that hundred bucks, right now." Kelly fished the money out and handed it to me.

I walked over to the railing, and I looked Kyra's stalker right in the eye. Or shades, rather. I said, "I want to talk to you."

He stared at me.

"You need to take this back." I said, shoving the money at him.

He took the money.

I said, "Don't ever do anything like that again."

He started stammering. He said, "I didn't mean anything by it."

I said, "I don't want any trouble, and I don't think you do either. I think you know what we're trying to accomplish with this team."

He said, "I just wanted to give her some spending money. I don't want any trouble."

I said, "Fine. Then you stay away from Kyra and you stay away from this team. Don't you contact her again. Do we understand each other?"

I turned on my heel and walked back to the bench. But in the meantime, Kyra told her mother, Sheryl, that her stalker was in the stands.

Sheryl went crazy. She and her family took pictures of him, and then they surrounded him. As they confronted him, he made it clear that in his mind, he and Kyra were meant to be together. He was convinced that people were trying to keep them apart.

Sheryl is a strong, tall woman, with a presence. She told him in no uncertain terms she would take him outside and hurt him seriously if he bothered Kyra again.

She got in the guy's face, hollering. "You leave my daughter alone!! Do you understand me? That's my *baby*. My child, do you understand? If you go near my baby again, I'm going to come after you."

Afterwards, Sheryl and I talked. Sheryl didn't like getting upset, and neither did I, but the man was fooling with some serious emotions.

"Pat, she's all I have," Sheryl said. "He's messing with my baby."

We found out later that on his way out of the building, he tried to slip another letter and $100 to Kyra's real cousin. He still didn't get it.

But he quit writing, for the time being, and we didn't hear from him again—for a while.

➤ ➤ ➤

FINALLY, after so many disturbing events, something good happened for us off the court.

We met Michael Jordan.

After the Kentucky game, we flew to Chicago to play DePaul. The night before the game, we took the team to eat at Jordan's restaurant. I hoped the team might be able to meet Jordan, the Chicago Bulls star whom I'd known since the 1984 Olympics in Los Angeles, when I was a coach and he was a player for the U.S.

Jordan, as everyone knew, was an acute businessman, and an increasingly interested fan of the women's game. What's more, he was preparing to launch a line of women's athletic gear for Nike, including a sneaker. Meanwhile, Chamique's stature was growing daily, and Michael was interested in meeting her. Michael and I spoke. The whole team, I suggested, would love to meet him.

Michael agreed. So the next afternoon, we all traipsed over to Michael's headquarters in downtown Chicago. We walked into a suite of offices, and there he was, sitting behind his desk. He had on a muscle shirt and sweats, and looked just like a poster. Then he stood up.

Kellie Jolly just stared at him, open-mouthed. I won't forget the look on her face. She, Semeka, and LaShonda were bashful to the point of speechlessness, but Ace, Kyra, and Niya descended on him. Niya sat in his chair. Ace put her arms around him. They besieged him with photos and T-shirts to sign. Then Michael saw Chamique, sort of hanging back.

"Hey, Chamique!" he said. "I heard about you. How you doing? You and me need to play some one-on-one."

What do you say when the most recognizable man on the planet recognizes *you?*

Chamique opened her mouth and then closed it again. She was "Michaeled."

He started in again. "I mean it," he said. "You and me need to play."

Chamique finally found her voice. "You got a court in here?" she said.

He laughed.

As we got ready to go, Michael said again to Chamique, "When are we going to play?"

Chamique said, teasingly, "One of these days."

Outside, Chamique tried to regain her composure. "He knew my name," she giggled, whooping. "Oh, my goodness."

That night, we beat DePaul by 125–46. It was the second-highest point total in Tennessee history. The four freshmen combined to score 82 of our points. Catchings still had a scar over her eye, but she threw in a UT rookie record 35 points. Typical, I thought. What a bunch of fearless exhibitionists; you introduced them to Michael Jordan, and how did they respond? They hung 125 on the board. Funny thing was, Chamique only had 8 of our points. I think she was still Michaeled.

By late January, there was only one thing bothering me. Chamique was chafing at the restrictions of college life. Rumors were rife that she was seriously considering turning pro. Despite all of her protests to me personally, when it came to talking to the press, she still refused to reject the possibility outright.

Plus, we got a call from a sneaker company representative who was worried; the rep had heard that Chamique was being pursued by an unsavory agent. I had to deal with this once and for all. I called her in.

I said, "Chamique, I wanted you to be the first to know. I'm seriously considering taking a pro job at the end of this year."

Chamique stared at me, in shock.

"Are you serious?" she said.

"No," I said. "But now you know how all the rumors and speculation over you turning pro could affect this team."

Chamique nodded. She got my point.

Then I laid it on the line. "You've left the door open, and we need to close it," I said.

If, at the end of the season, she wanted to consider turning pro, that was her decision, I said. When the time came, I would even assist her in finding a reputable agent. But until then, I didn't want to hear another word about it. What's more, I said, if I ever heard she had anything to do with a disreputable agent, I would wash my hands of her. It would be the hardest thing I ever had to do, but I'd do it, I said.

"I'll leave you to the sleazeballs who want to take all your money," I said.

I think we understood each other.

We sped through the rest of January, racking up win after win. Towards the end of the month, Georgia came to town. Anyone who knew about the Tennessee-Georgia rivalry knew there was no love lost between the two programs. Before the game, our promotions department gave out ten thousand mask replicas of my face. Right before tip-off I went by the Georgia bench. "This must be your worst nightmare," I said to Georgia coach Andy Landers. "There's not just one of me. There's ten thousand." We both laughed.

We won by fifty-nine, 102–43.

At the end of the month, we were 20–0. All I thought about now, all I breathed, was this team.

One afternoon, some reporters asked me who I favored in the Super Bowl.

"Well, fellas, let me ask you a question," I said.

I paused.

"Who's playing in it?"

Q & A with Semeka Randall (Freshman guard)

What did the song "No-Limit Soldier" mean to you?

It was about going to war. And that's what we felt like, every game. Pat said she had never heard it. And I said, "You don't want to."

You were still struggling with Pat, right?

The coaches told me, if they stop yelling at me, that means they don't care.

And?

Evidently, Pat cares about me a lot.

CHAPTER EIGHT

February, Full Body Sacrifice, and the Third Meek

FEBRUARY WAS THE LONGEST MONTH. It was gray, and sad, and seemingly endless. In February, the Lady Vols played on sheer integrity and motive, because their legs and minds were too fatigued to cooperate. They wore ice bags and had discolored marks all over their bodies, and they walked hunched over, like arthritics. Our trainer, Jenny Moshak, spent so much time working on the players she even named her dog Rehab.

All season, I had been haunted by the possibility of injury. This team played so heedlessly that I couldn't help worrying about them. Game in and game out, they committed full body sacrifice, until I wondered exactly how far they would go, to what utter, absolute extremes they intended to take this thing called an undefeated season we were all involved in. It was my job to push them, because I was a coach and it was February, and that was what you did in February, you pushed. But it killed you to do it, because what you really wanted to do, all you wanted to do, was just take care of them.

On February 1, Kyra Elzy blew out her knee.

That's how the month started.

I knew right away what had happened. Before she even hit the floor, I knew. And I buried my head in my arms.

We were in a tight first half of play against Alabama, when Kyra went up to retrieve the ball for what should have been a simple layup. Tamika lobbed an alley oop pass to her under the 'Bama basket. Kyra hung in the air. But as she hovered above ground, the Alabama defense shifted over—and suddenly, there was no room for her to come down. Kyra tried to alter her direction in midair, but there was no time. She landed at an angle, and her right knee bent the wrong way. Right then, I knew it was gone.

Kyra crumpled to the floor. For a long second there was no sound from her. It was one of those hurts that was too deep to express in sound. But then her mouth opened, and she screamed.

A torn ACL in February was a season-ender—and there had been a time when it was a career-ender.

The anterior cruciate ligament stabilizes the joint and allows it to flex and recover. When you tear it, it snaps like a rubber band breaking, and the knee is without muscular control or support—it flops helplessly. And if your knee won't work, the rest of your leg won't either. Your whole body becomes a collapsed house of cards.

Fortunately for Kyra, it was no longer such a catastrophic wound. These days, people recovered from ACL injuries—but it was still a long, hard rehabilitation.

I knew how it felt.

It felt like her kneecap was on the back of her leg.

It felt like someone had sunk an axe into her knee. It was a hot strike of pain, the chop of a sharp blade.

I tore mine in 1974, early in my senior year. The surgery left a curling, S-shaped, twelve-inch scar running down the inside of my leg, and took well over a year to recover from. Watching Kyra, I remembered lying in a hospital bed, trying not to sob, as a doctor told me I would never play basketball again. Most *men* didn't return to the court from ACL tears, he said, much less a woman. I had my heart set on playing in the 1976 Olympics in Montreal.

My father stared the doctor down, and said, "Play? She's going to make the Olympic team. So you fix it, and fix it right."

In those days, rehab wasn't very sophisticated. I would strengthen my knee by hanging a sackful of bricks from my foot and lifting it up and down. So I knew all about knee injuries.

Kyra screamed. And screamed, and screamed.

I bolted on to the floor. Jenny and Holly were already ahead of me. In fact, they were up off the bench even before Kyra landed.

As I ran towards Kyra, I realized the gym had fallen completely silent. I could hear my heels clicking across the hard wood floor. I saw Alabama coach Rick Moody out of the corner of my eye. He had his face in his hands.

Kyra lay on the court, crying. "Pat!" she cried. "Pat, Pat!"

I said, "I'm here, Kyra. I'm here."

I took her hand.

Holly said, "It's okay, baby doll. It's going to be all right. You've got to calm down so they can check you."

Kyra said, crying, "Oh, Pat it's torn! I know it's torn!"

"We're going to take care of you," I said.

We got Kyra calmed down. She finally uncurled and turned on her back so Jenny could examine her. Slowly, Jenny and the medical staff worked on Kyra. But every time they moved her, she wailed in pain. Finally, they got Kyra up and carried her into the locker room, where they stretched her out on a training table. Kyra lay on the table, her breath coming in hitches, praying, "Please let it be something else, please let it be something else." But every time they moved her leg, the pain was unbearable. Kyra would say, "Oh, Jenny, it's torn."

"Maybe not," Jenny said.

Our orthopedic surgeon, Dr. Bill Youmans, gently probed her knee. Finally he said, solemnly, "Well, Kyra, you've done what a lot of women athletes do. You've torn your anterior cruciate ligament."

Female athletes, especially basketball players, are disturbingly prone to tearing their ACLs, and we don't know quite why. It may be that weight training and fitness methods have not yet caught up to what women are trying to do with their bodies. Some studies suggest that because the female pelvis is wider, we therefore hyperextend our knees more easily. Also, the game is now being played at an increasingly fast pace. We know this much: the injury is haunting our sport.

Kyra just lay there, with tears running down her face. She pulled a towel up over her head, and sobbed.

Back out on the floor, we were all heartsick. We had to find a way to get through the rest of the half. Tree Geter helped, by blocking four shots in a six-minute span. But our minds weren't on the game. We trailed by six points before we recovered to lead at the half, 39–26. Alabama made things difficult by bumping us around and forcing us to play a slowly paced, physical game.

At halftime, we ordinarily filed into the locker and our team took their assigned stools in front of the chalkboard. But this time when the team came in, they ran straight past me, and into the training room to see Kyra.

Kyra was still on the table with the cover drawn over her head. Ace, Kellie, and Tree surrounded her.

"We're going to do this for you," Ace said.

Kellie Jolly was quietly distraught. Kellie had torn her ACL—twice. She blew it the first time in high school. Then she suffered another blowout in a pickup game just before our '96–97 season started. She had spent much of the season in rehab, recovering just in time for the NCAA tournament. The thing was, when Kellie blew her knee, Kyra had cried almost as hard as Kellie. Now, Kellie was trying to comfort Kyra.

Kellie said, "You'll be all right, I promise. We're going to get you through this."

We spent the remainder of halftime trying to figure out how to survive Alabama without Kyra. We had just lost a starting guard and our single most experienced defensive player. We called Kyra our "stopper"—she was the leader of the press, and the player most responsible for shutting down the other team's biggest offensive threat.

But just as important, Kyra had become one of our *emotional* leaders. She commanded an unusual level of respect for a sophomore. That was because everyone knew that for a season and a half, Kyra had been ridden harder by me than any other player—and she had fought off every obstacle and bit of scorn I threw at her to become a starter.

➤ ➤ ➤

IT HAD BEEN A LONG HAUL for Kyra at Tennessee. During her freshman year, she had thought more than once about quitting the program and going home. I challenged her constantly, because I thought she was an underachiever who had more talent than she realized. Kyra couldn't understand why I stayed on her so.

Mickie would tell Kyra, "Just remember, you must be awfully special for Pat to say your name so often."

Kyra cried and wanted to go back to LaGrange. But I had called Sheryl in advance of Kyra's freshman season to warn her that Kyra might try to leave school. "I'm going to get on her, and she's going to want to come home," I said. "But I'm asking you now, don't let her." Sheryl listened to Kyra cry on the phone night after night, but she refused to give in to her.

Sheryl asked Kyra, "Do you want to work hard for four years, or for the next thirty-five years?"

So Kyra stayed, and I kept after her. I challenged her, coaxed her, even insulted her. I told her I liked her, but I didn't respect her. I told her I would take her to lunch but not to war. I said we were a two-guard away from winning a championship. I think I even threatened to fire her. But she responded.

Kyra was instrumental in our victory over Old Dominion in the 1997 national championship game as a freshman. She forced All-American Ticha Penichiero, a junior, into eleven turnovers. Now, as a sophomore, she had become a wonderful example of a selfless role player. If Kyra could handle what I dished out, our team seemed to decide, then they could, too. Kyra cheerfully assumed roles that weren't fun, like her defensive stopper responsibility, while others got the offensive glory. Even more importantly, she had become a mother figure to the four freshmen, talking them through the emotional transitions they had to make in becoming college players.

Kyra and I were finally reaching an understanding. It was an affront to fairness and to her hard work that now, after all she had been through, including the stalker, she had to cope with injury, too.

It was time to start the second half against Alabama, but I went back to the training room to see Kyra once more before we took the court.

"Kyra," I said, "I'm sorry this had to happen to you. Now listen. You have an athletic body. You're in great shape. If this old lady can come back from an ACL, you can, too."

Kyra tried to smile. But nothing was funny to her.

The players began filing out of the locker room. I hugged Kyra, and joined the team.

We were in no mood to finish a basketball game. All any of us could think about was Kyra, lying in the locker room with the sheet pulled over her head, crying. Kellie put it best. She said, "It was like we felt guilty, and that somehow winning the game would be an insult to Kyra. We didn't want to play without her."

I kept calling time-outs and saying, "You have to do this. You have to do this for Kyra. You've got to get your heads in the game. You think she wants us to lose?"

But I was no better than they were. I said to our assistants, "You have to help me. I don't know if I can coach the rest of the game."

We clawed to a 73–66 victory. But to me, it was a loss.

Kyra spent the better part of the night in the training room, where Jenny tried to keep the swelling in her knee down. Late in the evening, I called Kyra in the training room.

I wanted to see how she was. And I wanted to tell her how I felt. In the past, I had let our players figure me out for themselves. It was up to them to realize how much I cared about them, to understand that the reason I put so much work into them, the reason I expended so much emotion on them was this: because I thought they were so worth it.

But that wasn't good enough for me any more. I wanted Kyra to know how much I cared, and I wanted her to know it for sure, not just to suspect it. I hung on the phone for a moment.

Then I said, "I love you, kid."

It just slipped out.

It wasn't what Kyra expected me to say. On the other end of the phone, Kyra was speechless. She mumbled a thank you. We said good night, and she put down the phone. For a moment she stared at our trainer, Jenny Moshak.

"Oh my goodness, Jenny," Kyra said, in a tone of pure amazement. "I think it's going to storm outside."

Jenny said, "What?"

Kyra said, "Pat Summitt just told me she *loved* me."

Jenny smiled. Then they both burst out laughing.

That night, Kyra vowed that she would be back in time for the NCAA tournament. A year earlier, Kellie Jolly had come back from her ACL in just eight weeks. Kellie not only played in the tournament, we couldn't have won it without her. But Kyra's case was different. It was already February, and the tournament was only four weeks away. It just wasn't possible, and we all knew it. But I didn't say it aloud, because Kyra needed to believe that she could get back on the court in time.

A few days later, after Kyra had arthroscopic surgery, I got a note from her. She thanked me for helping her through a difficult time. She closed by saying, "I love you, too."

Almost as soon as Kyra woke up from surgery, she started back to work. She rode a stationary bike on the sidelines while we practiced. She limped in and out of the locker room for her treatments, while we had meetings. She remained as much a part of the team as if she were playing. If anyone could make it back by March, I thought as I watched her work, Kyra could.

Kyra had her disheartened moments. Sometimes, Niya or LaShonda would turn around and Kyra would be crying.

But she never cried aloud. The tears slid noiselessly down her cheeks.

➤ ➤ ➤

WE NEEDED another Meek.

Without Kyra, we would have to depend more heavily than ever on our freshmen. From here on in, they would have to act like and play like veterans. Semeka Randall would have to become a starter. It was time for the third Meek to step up.

On the morning after the Alabama game, we had an early practice starting at 7:30. I treated the game just like a loss. I was miserable to the whole team. Alabama had given us a boot in our butts, I snarled. I just didn't know if we were a good enough team to win without Kyra—not the way some of our freshmen were playing. I ripped into them.

I got to Ace Clement first. "You're soft and you're a sissy," I said. "Now, what have you learned?"

"I'm soft," she said.

"Prove me wrong." I said.

Ace lifted her chin and looked me straight in the eye.

She said, "Okay. I will."

Next, I laid into Semeka. I got to her at 7:35 A.M.

"I'm not spending the next four years coaching a brat," I said. "Straighten up, or you're out of here."

Afterwards, Holdsclaw couldn't help teasing me a little on her way out of the gym.

"Coach, I really like these morning practices," she said.

I said, "Why?"

She said, "Because we're finished at nine, and I don't have to see you for the whole rest of the day."

There was more to my mood than just early morning testiness. On February 7, we would meet third-ranked Old Dominion, the team we had faced in the national championship game a year before. The Lady

Monarchs not only had Ticha Penichiero, but a powerful post player in Nyree Roberts. I meant what I had said; I wasn't sure we were a good enough team to win without Kyra. And I was having difficulty communicating with the one player who would now be crucial for us: Semeka Randall.

The third Meek and I had been at loggerheads off and on all year. In fact, shortly before Kyra got hurt against Alabama, I had grown privately furious with Semeka. She spent most of the first half of that game on the bench. She cut a pouting figure, slumped in a chair separate from the other players, staring at the floor.

Semeka was critical for us for a couple of reasons. She had the physical presence of a jackhammer. She had muscles in places I had never seen before, and the conviction that she could power through any obstacle or problem. She was perhaps our most crowd-pleasing player, and she was our social chairwoman, a ringleader of dancing and singing circles in the back of the bus. Even Tyler joined in, trying to catch a beat.

But she could be a temperamental young person, too. Semeka had to learn to play with four other people, she had to learn better shot selection, and she had to learn to share playing time.

My main problem with her, however, was that she was too easily frustrated, particularly when she sat on the bench for too long without getting in the game. If she had to sit still for longer than six or seven minutes, she would begin to brood. It was a bad habit, and I intended to break it. On a championship team with as much talent as ours, I wasn't going to let anyone mope about playing time. With a freshman, especially, I felt you had to break the habit early. Otherwise it could be a fouryear problem.

What Semeka didn't understand was that she was invaluable coming off the bench; she had the effect of a detonator, who could lift our whole team to another level. In combination with Kyra, she gave us a devastating one-two defensive punch. Kyra would clamp down. Then Semeka would enter the game. She would bring the same intensity as Kyra, and if anything, she was more physical. Semeka called playing defense "putting the glove on 'em."

But when Semeka brooded and got too caught up in her emotions, she play recklessly. She gave unflagging effort, but she needed to play with better control. And like most great talents, she was stubborn and sensitive to criticism; she couldn't understand it when I criticized her. Her attitude was "But I'm trying."

On the sidelines during the Alabama game, I wandered down and took a seat next to her. I wanted to talk. But she ignored me. That was Semeka's favorite tactic; she would stare off into space, and give you a perfunctory nod of the head.

Now, if there was one thing I refused to tolerate from a player, it was lack of eye contact—and Semeka knew that. I wanted to lock eyes with a player, to be sure they had heard and understood me. But Semeka would purposely duck or turn her head as I was speaking. To me, it was disrespectful. It meant Semeka was going to do things her way.

Or so she thought.

Actually, she was going to do them my way.

After the Alabama game, Semeka knew she was going to catch it from me. She just didn't know when. As she walked into the locker room, I followed her. Semeka wound her way to the back, where we kept a cooler full of sodas. Just as Semeka grabbed a Sprite, she heard my footsteps coming after her. I stepped in front of her.

"Now you listen here," I said. "We cannot win basketball games with you acting like this."

This time, Semeka made eye contact. "You're being selfish and stubborn," I said. "You're acting like a brat. Is that who you really are?"

Semeka apologized, and said it wouldn't happen again.

But I knew it would. My Alabama confrontation with Semeka was just a beginning. Most freshmen reached a reckoning point with me, and Semeka's was still to come.

But in the end, I hoped we would be able to count on her. I understood the most important thing about Semeka: she had an inherited talent for making good things grow out of bad.

> > >

BERTHA RANDALL WAS RENOWNED for her garden. It bloomed in the midst of inner city Cleveland, a splendid surprise in the back of the house on Farringdon Avenue. Bertha planted and pruned until greenery, petunias, and impatiens waved over the decks and flowerbeds. Neighbors told her it belonged in *House and Garden.*

Farringdon Avenue was a haven, a stretch of family-owned homes with very little turnover and watchful neighbors. Bertha had owned the Farringdon Avenue house for twenty years—and that made her a new-comer. The whole street practically helped raise Semeka, while Bertha worked long hours as a counselor for abused children.

Bertha separated from Semeka's father, Lee Johnson, a Baptist minister, when Semeka was a small child. For a while, according to Semeka, her father lived in Sandusky, Ohio, and she saw him regularly. But when she was still in grade school, he moved to North Carolina and started a second family, and after that, Semeka's visits were restricted to vacations. She would go down to see him and spend whole days in church, from 7 A.M. to 3 P.M., waiting for the cookies and punch breaks.

The result was a devout Baptist child—but a somewhat angry one, too. Semeka didn't see her father much during the rest of the year, and gradually, they grew apart. Semeka says that as she got older and watched Bertha struggle to get by, living from payday to payday, she cooled on her father. He came to her graduation from Trinity High School in Cleveland, but Semeka kept an emotional distance. She felt that she and Bertha had made the long, hard pull largely by themselves—with the help of a couple of basketball coaches.

Who can explain why a small child is drawn to a ball? Maybe the future simply enters into them. From the time Semeka was six, she had a basketball fixation. A lot of the driveways up and down Farringdon Avenue in Cleveland had basketball hoops, and Semeka would leave her house at 3:00 in the afternoon, and work her way down the street, playing ball with the boys.

Bertha didn't approve. She thought basketball was too rough for her little girl. She would buy Semeka baby dolls and Barbies. After a while, Bertha noticed that the dolls kept disappearing.

Bertha would find them thrown under the bed.

Finally, Bertha forbade Semeka to play ball. But there was no keeping her out of the driveways. Bertha would send Semeka to the store for butter, and Semeka would disappear for hours. Bertha would come marching down the street, and say, "Have you been playing basketball again?" Semeka would say, "No ma'am," with the sweat pouring off her.

Bertha would wait to catch Semeka red-handed. She'd stride down the street with a switch in her hand and find the groceries lying in the grass, and Semeka playing ball. She would chase Semeka all the way home. So Semeka worked out a system. They would post one boy as a lookout for Bertha, while Semeka played—and when Bertha came down the street, he would whistle in warning.

Bertha tried to explain the facts of life to Semeka. Girls were *supposed* to play with baby dolls, she would tell her. That's how the world worked: boys played basketball, and girls played with baby dolls.

"You are not a boy!" Bertha would say. "God made you a girl. You are a female! You have female things!"

Nothing worked. Semeka would throw her baby doll across the room, and run down to join the pickup games. Her mother would haul her back home, and stick another baby doll in her arms. They would start the whole stubborn war all over again.

One day Semeka decided to solve the problem for good.

She broke one of the baby dolls in half.

Then she picked up another. And broke that one, too.

When Semeka got to junior high school, Bertha finally agreed to come watch her daughter play in a game. The first time Semeka stole the ball, Bertha yelled at her.

"Semeka!" she said, "You know it's not nice to steal! You give that back to her! I taught you better than that!"

A security guard explained to Bertha that it was all right. "It's part of the game," he said.

Bertha said, "Oh, is it?"

By then Semeka was scoring thirty and forty points at a clip for her junior high school, and making the local papers. Semeka's coach and math teacher, James Wallace, explained to Bertha that the game could mean a college education for her daughter. Mr. Wallace, as Semeka called him, recognized that Semeka was a handful, and he kicked her out of the gym one day for acting up. "You have talent, but you need discipline," he said. Semeka decided she liked him for it and enrolled in all of his classes.

Mr. Wallace told Bertha and Semeka about Trinity, a noted Catholic school with one of the best high school girls' programs in the country, coached by the highly regarded Pat Diulus. If Semeka went to Trinity and played for Coach Diulus, and kept her grades up, there was a good chance she would be recruited by some of the major colleges.

The only problem was money. Trinity was a private school, with tuition of a couple thousand dollars a year. Bertha didn't know where she would find such a sum. She took a second job as an officer in a juvenile detention center, working nights, and she made sacrifices.

If she put a full tank of gas in the car, would she have enough money to buy food for the rest of the week? No.

The sink in the bathroom was stopped up. There was a problem with the pipes that needed some major plumbing. Could she afford to get it fixed?

No. They brushed their teeth using the bathtub faucet.

But there was never a complaint in the Randall house. Bertha worked with too many people who were more unfortunate than they were. She counseled children who were physically and sexually abused. At the detention center, she worked with kids who were involved in drug trafficking and gangs. Struggle, Bertha told Semeka, made you strong. "There's no reason to hang your head," Bertha would say. It was a precarious business raising a child in the city, a tightwire act. Although their block was solid enough, it seemed like there was potential trouble on all sides. They lived on a fault line, between gangsta territories of the Crips, the Bloods, and the Viceroys. Once, a girlfriend of Semeka's tied the wrong color bandana on her head, and a car tried to run them both down for it.

But it seemed to Bertha that there were just as many people willing to help Semeka. Her daughter had a natural ability to win benefactors. There was nothing magical about it: people wanted to help Semeka because she worked so hard. You could see the sweat in everything she did.

There was Semeka's godfather, Mr. Ted Alexander, a neighborhood acquaintance who made it his business to spot promising young athletes and aid them financially. There was her godmother, Mildred Jackson, who bought her first pair of shoes. There was Pat Diulus, and his daughter and assistant coach, Michelle, who checked up on Semeka every day. The members of the parish, Greater Tabernacle Baptist Church, kept an eye on Semeka, and so did everyone at the 131st St. Boys and Girls Club, where Semeka could spend the afternoon for the price of $2 admission. Sending a child to college was the highest achievement in the neighborhood. Everyone celebrated an educated child as if it were their own.

But no one looked after Semeka more dedicatedly than the nuns at Trinity. They tutored her as she wrestled tirelessly with the adjustment to a rigorous private school. Semeka was behind the other students academically, but she took on classes the way she took on the opposition, as if she could muscle her way through them. The nuns even fed Semeka. They would tutor her, and then make her stay for dinner. The sisters would call up Bertha and say, "How does Semeka like her corn?"

Semeka took the college entrance exam over and over. She took it several times, and on each occasion, she raised her scores a little more.

Semeka was becoming less like a child and more like a friend to Bertha. She seemed to understand how hard her mother was trying to be a complete parent. Semeka could be strangely adult. "Mom, don't ever be narrow-minded," Semeka would say. "When you're narrow-minded, nothing can come in, and nothing can get out."

It was no wonder that on the night Semeka left for college, the whole neighborhood went sleepless. Every now and then a police cruiser would come by and nose through the crowd in the street, but even the cops knew what was going on. Bertha Randall's daughter had made it. She was going to college.

Over the next few months, Bertha seized on any excuse to visit Semeka at school. She would make the sixteen-hour drive just to see a single ball game. Between working two jobs, she still found time to cook a huge Thanksgiving meal and drive it to Knoxville. Bertha was determined that the team have a conventional Thanksgiving meal, so she roasted a turkey with all the trimmings and baked a dozen pies, and packed it in the car. The freshmen kept the leftovers at Chamique's apartment, since she had a refrigerator big enough for all that food. They ate well for days. Bertha was so exhausted the next week at work, she thought she might pass out.

Bertha might have been tired of driving, but she never got tired of seeing her daughter in college. She would gaze at Semeka, studying in her spectacles. She would say, "My goodness, you look so studious and smart."

And every Sunday the Greater Tabernacle Baptist Church in Cleveland, Ohio, offered a public prayer for Semeka Randall and the Tennessee Lady Vols.

➤ ➤ ➤

IT WAS SEMEKA'S nineteenth birthday, and as she warmed up on the floor, she couldn't help thinking that it was a swell party. Another sellout crowd was on hand in Thompson-Boling Arena, and Semeka intended to have her coming of age against Old Dominion.

Once again, we were on national television. Everything we had worked for was coming to pass: national coverage, sellout crowds, and a team that played like they had wings. There was something almost celebratory in the air, despite the tension.

There was just one thing wrong with the occasion: Kyra was devastated that she couldn't play. In fact, she couldn't even bear to watch the team in their pregame warm-up. She sat in the training room, crying. Finally, she made herself hobble out of the locker room and join the

Lady Vols on the floor. Then something happened that startled her out of her misery.

Kyra stood on the floor next to Holly, gazing around the filled-to-capacity arena. Suddenly, she said slowly, "Oh . . . my . . . goodness."

"What?" Holly said.

Kyra said, "I think that's my dad."

Kyra had seen Bobby just a handful of times since she was a baby. Now here he was, jogging down the aisle.

"Kyra, Kyra!" he called.

Bobby Jones waved to the daughter he had really never known.

"I just wanted to tell you I was here and wish you luck," he said.

Kyra nodded and sort of smiled. But inside, she said later, she felt a peculiar sense of . . . nothing. It was just one more odd twist to the year, she decided.

We gathered in the locker room for my usual pregame chalk talk. I was concerned about how our post game would hold up against ODU's physical inside game, led by Nyree Roberts and a combative forward, Mery Andrade. I said everything I could think of to get LaShonda and Tree to hold their ground. I promised to give the team the newest model of Adidas sneakers if only someone would take a charge.

I still hated it that we were a finesse team. It gnawed at me that we had to go into a game not knowing whether we would have a big presence in the middle.

"Tree Geter," I yelled across the locker room, "if you don't take a charge today, don't you come in here looking for a pair of sneakers."

Holly jumped in. "Geter," she blared, "you'd better eat you some raw meat. Some steak."

For all of that, we started slow. It took us three full minutes to score a basket.

LaShonda picked up two quick fouls, and I subbed her out with Geter. As LaShonda came to the bench, I was livid. I was afraid to open my mouth for fear of what I might say to her, so when LaShonda sat down and grabbed her towel, I scribbled furiously on my clipboard in huge block letters, so big you could see them in the eleventh row. Then I handed it to her. "PLAY SMART!" it said.

Finally, we caught fire—thanks to Randall, who hounded ODU into turnover after turnover. With each steal, we built a lead. Catchings got a fast break that put us up by six. By halftime we had widened the lead to twelve, 37–25.

In the locker room, I gathered the team around. "You can't run enough for me," I said.

Was that me talking? The queen of the half court game? The coach who insisted on being in control?

"I want you to run, and run, and run, and run some more," I said. "I don't want you to come back in here with anything left. Nothing. Not a breath. Leave it all on the court. Don't you come back in here with anything."

On the floor again, we ran the lead up to eighteen. But ODU didn't lay down. The Lady Monarchs fought back, five different times cutting the lead back to single digits.

But each time they did, Chamique would settle in one of those soft jumpers. She had twenty-four of her thirty-three points in the second half, and pulled down a dozen rebounds. But here was the best part. Tree Geter took a charge. I high-fived her as she came to the bench.

We pulled away. The final score was 85–71, but that wasn't the most important statistic as far as I was concerned. It was this: we had eighteen steals—seven of them from Randall, a freshman working against an All-American senior in Penichiero. Randall also had eighteen points. She was jubilant afterwards.

"I put the glove on 'em," she howled.

➤ ➤ ➤

I WAS OVER being sympathetic to Ace Clement.

It was February 11, time enough for her to recover the form she showed in preseason. Ace had to become a player for us again, a viable factor, if we were to make a successful postseason run. I decided to try a shock tactic. On a road trip to play Memphis, I met with her in our team conference room at the hotel.

"If Kellie Jolly fouls out of a game or goes down, are you ready to lead this team to a championship?" I asked.

Ace wasn't sure how to answer me. I explained that if we were going all the way, we needed every healthy player at her best, starting with her. Then I showed her, live on tape, what her lack of focus looked like on the floor. A sequence of turnovers and broken plays reflected her muddled decision making and sloppiness with the ball.

"You don't want to be thought of as the biggest disappointment of the freshman class," I said, straight out.

She looked stunned.

"I don't know where your head is," I continued. "You're just going through the motions. Frankly, I don't know if we can win a championship with you playing this way. What's more, you're a liability on defense. You aren't acting like the player I recruited."

Ace just sat there and nodded her head bravely, her ponytail bobbing. Finally, I wound down.

"Now, if you're the person I think you are, you'll take this as a challenge," I said. "You'll show me I'm wrong."

"I'll show you," she said.

"When?" I said.

She said, "Today. I'll show you today."

➤ ➤ ➤

THAT NIGHT, Memphis played out of its mind, and kept the game in doubt until the last twelve minutes. It wasn't entirely unexpected; Memphis always gave us fits. The gym was packed with three-thousand-odd Memphis fanatics, including one old nemesis. Every year a large-voiced man delighted in hurling abuse at us from his seat behind our bench. He abused our appearance, our hair, our clothes.

Over the years, we had developed a sort of rivalry with him. At first we called him Big Man, but as we got increasingly irritated, it had evolved into Fat Boy. Once, our former men's coach, Kevin O'Neill, tried to shut him up by sending him two hot dogs and a plate of nachos.

Another time, I caught him hanging out by our bus, waiting to scream at us. I said, "Excuse me. We're starved and I figured you'd know the best place in town to eat." He looked all hurt. So I said, "Look, you can be a fan without being cruel." From then on, our relationship was almost friendly—in a barbed kind of way.

I just knew Big Man would be there again, dogging us out. I was right. After the pregame warmup, some of our players came jogging into the locker room, and said, "He's here. He's out there riding Holdsclaw."

I was in the middle of my usual pregame ritual, writing our keys to victory on the drawing board. On this night, I decided, there were five keys to winning the ball game.

"No.5," I wrote. "Shut Up Fat Boy."

But it didn't help. We came out flat. As we took the floor, I looked up at Big Man, and we gave each other a thumbs up. It was the last nice thing that happened. From then on, it was ugly. With 1:47 to go in the first half, Memphis led us by seven points.

I called a time-out. I clenched my teeth and curled my lips and said, "Get the ball in the damn paint!" Now, I rarely if ever swear. They looked shocked.

"You heard me," I said. "Get the ball in the damn paint!"

The Lady Vols went back out, and clawed to a halftime lead, 42–40.

I started Ace Clement in the second half—hoping she would make good on the promise she had made that afternoon. Instead, she immediately gave up back-to-back turnovers. I dropped my head into my hands. Memphis was only down by a point with slightly over twelve minutes to go, and I was beside myself.

But in the next two minutes we ran off ten unanswered points, most of them on a flurry of jumpers from Holdsclaw that effectively ended the game. The final score was 91–65, but it was deceiving. Things were never that comfortable.

The next day, I lit into all of them, but especially Ace.

"Should I ever have to ask you to play defense?" I said. "Especially as much as you turn the ball over? You *know* it drives me crazy."

Ace made a frantic little nodding motion.

I turned to Kellie Jolly. "How many assists did you have?" I asked.

Kellie murmured that she wasn't sure. Actually, she was just protecting Ace.

"You had seven," I said. "Seven assists. And how many turnovers? Just one."

I wheeled back to Ace. "You had three assists—and four turnovers. Does that tell you anything?"

Ace was silent, staring at her shoetops.

"Figure it out," I barked.

➤ ➤ ➤

A NIGHT LATER, Semeka Randall was in the doghouse. We were playing Auburn in Thompson-Boling Arena on February 14, on only a day's rest—and once again, we were struggling.

When Semeka got moody, I decided it was time for a showdown. Early in the game, she got that look on her face, a hard, implacable expression that meant she was unhappy with herself and on the verge of going into the tank. Her shot wasn't falling, and she responded by playing lazy defense. Now, that drives me to the brink. Anyone can have an off night shooting the ball, but there is no excuse for letting it affect your defensive effort. Defense is within your control, it's all a matter of attitude. But Semeka hadn't heard a word I'd said to her. So I yanked her.

"Get Randall out of there," I said to Mickie.

Semeka came to the bench clearly furious. "You're letting your offense affect your defense," I said as she walked by me.

Semeka ignored me.

I said, "Did you hear me?"

She wouldn't even look at me.

"Randall!" I snapped. "Look at me! Did you hear me?"

Semeka said, all sulky, "Yeah."

Well, that was it. "You don't want to play, you get your little butt to the end of the bench," I ordered. "I don't want to see you again tonight."

Everybody knew Randall was really in trouble this time. Kyra went down and sat next to her for a few minutes, talking to her. Then Mickie went down and sat with her. Semeka grew apprehensive—she knew I wasn't finished with her.

"What should I do?" Semeka asked.

Mickie counseled her, "You need to make eye contact, and just agree with whatever Pat says. No matter what she says, don't disagree with it. You hear me?"

Randall nodded.

Mickie came back to me and tried to talk me into putting Semeka in the game again, but I wouldn't hear of it. I didn't play her for the rest of the half. I told the staff, "I'm too mad to coach."

Meanwhile, the rest of the team struggled to play consistently. We ran up a 32–16 lead, and then we blew it. Just before halftime, Auburn outscored us 17–6, to go into the locker room only trailing by five.

Semeka approached me. "Can I see you please?" she said. We went into the coaches' room.

"All right, look," she said. "My team is struggling, and I want to play. I'm sorry, or whatever, but right now we need to win as fast as we can."

I said, "No, *you* look here. I'm not going to tolerate your moods any more. You want to play, you play hard, you hear me? Or I'll sit you for the rest of the season."

Semeka agreed. She went back out and had a decent second half, and we eventually won, 79–63. But the real difference for us was Holdsclaw. She scored almost exactly half of our points, with a career high thirty-nine.

I decided to let matters rest with Semeka for a while. We were all tired and short on patience, I realized. The very next morning we had to pack up and travel to Nashville to play Vanderbilt. It would be our fifth game in the space of just ten days. That night, after the Auburn game,

Tamika Catchings sat in front of her locker, and said, "I just want to go home and sleep."

I was desperate for ways to keep us going—we had just one more week left in the regular season, but it seemed like a month. After the game, the coaches discussed how we could give the team some extra incentive to push them past their exhaustion in these last few days.

Al Brown had an idea. We were also looking for a way to keep Kyra Elzy as involved in the team as possible. Al suggested we establish an award named after Kyra, to go to the player with the biggest rebounding margin above their average each night—in other words, the player who went above and beyond her everyday performance.

I went home and raided my son's room. I sorted through the world's largest collection of Ty Beanie Babies, until I came across a small stuffed kangaroo.

"Tyler, would you mind if I borrowed this?" I said.

It was a small, silly little toy. But it signified something bigger and it would have an impact on our team.

For the three-hour bus trip to Nashville to meet Vanderbilt, I issued an executive order. Normally we would watch a scouting tape, but I didn't want our players to even look at a basketball. "No basketball tapes, no basketball talk," I said. We rented a stack of movies instead. But they were too tired to even do that.

They napped for the entire ride, only rousing themselves as we pulled up to Vanderbilt's Memorial Gymnasium. We struggled off the bus and into the gym for a brief practice. I gathered them in a circle on the floor, and told them to sit down on the court. I knew their legs were tired, and their brains were fried.

"I'm to blame for this schedule," I said. "I did it by design. Now, why would I do something like that?"

Catchings said, "To see if we could handle it."

I said, "Correct."

I presented Tyler's floppy little Beanie Baby to the team. "This is KK," I said. "KK, for Kyra Kangaroo," I said. Kyra giggled, delighted. "KK goes to biggest rebounder each night."

But that night, we came out slow as molasses. We just couldn't get our legs going. I felt for the Lady Vols. They were so tired they could barely elevate off the floor. Midway through the first half, we trailed by 16–7, and we had given up more turnovers, eight, than we had scored points. I called a time-out, and made it clear that fatigue was no excuse for not taking care of the ball. "Take pride in every possession!" I said.

We burst back on to the floor to go 17–0 over the next six minutes, led by the Three Meeks. At the break, we were up by 32–23 — and the Meeks had scored all of our points.

In the locker room, I asked just one thing of them. "I want you to send them a big message when we open the second half," I said. "Don't let them back in it."

We sent the message. We jumped on Vanderbilt from the outset and built a thirty-one-point lead. Once again, the Meeks led the charge — through twenty-six minutes of action, the trio had outscored the Vanderbilt team by thirteen points.

Final score: 91–60. And the Meeks ended up with seventy-three of our points.

Afterwards, I finally allowed myself to think it. For the first time, I let the words consciously form in my mind: *this team just might go undefeated.*

➤ ➤ ➤

WE HAD JUST ONE game left in the regular season. But the pace at which we were playing, and the rough schedule, was taking its toll. Everyone was sick.

Tyler and R.B. had bronchitis.

My secretary, Katie Wynn, had the flu.

So did Ace Clement.

Our volunteer assistant, Sherry Dihel, was at home throwing up.

Mickie was having dizzy spells from an inner ear infection.

I was the only one who wasn't sick. I was moving too fast for germs.

We went through twenty ice bags after every practice. The whole team was banged up. Chamique's hands were cut and swollen, and her arms had claw marks all over them.

Then Tamika Catchings broke her nose.

It happened in practice. Catch was driving to the basket against one of our male practice players, going full speed, as usual. She went up, and they banged heads. She dropped to the floor with her hands over her face.

Holly was the first one to her, and she peeled Tamika's hands back from her face. Holly isn't squeamish, but what she saw made her want to turn away. Tamika's nose looked like it had moved under her left eye.

Jenny iced Tamika down and got her to a doctor. Later that night, we learned she would need surgery. I called her mother and father and assured them it was a minor procedure, called a closed nose reduction. Basically, the doctor had to pop her nose back into place.

It went without a hitch. Afterwards, I talked to Harvey about how to protect Tamika. We were all concerned about her getting hit again, because she was such an active player.

"Harvey, it's almost inevitable," I said. "No one plays harder than she does. She's always in traffic. When she takes a lick, it's going to be a hard one."

Somehow, we had to crawl through one more regular season game, even if it was on our hands and knees. Louisiana State was due in Thompson-Boling Arena on February 22. Then we would have three blissful days off, before we had to play in the Southeastern Conference Tournament. I felt like I had wrinkles down to my chin.

But I stayed after them. Ace Clement was still my target. I picked on her the day before the LSU game. I informed Ace that I was recruiting a great young high school point guard. "And she outworks you two to one." Ace just coughed and nodded.

Then Ace and Tree went out in practice and turned the ball over four times against the press. I called the workout to a halt.

"I know you don't feel good today," I said to Ace, sympathetically. She looked at me, hopefully.

"So what's your excuse for the other three months?" I added.

After practice, Bob Kessling, the sports director from Knoxville's Channel 10, wandered over. "Well, have you gotten some rest?" he said.

I looked at him like he was crazy.

"Do you need glasses, Bubba?" I said.

But the next afternoon, all of the fatigue evaporated when the Lady Vols hit the floor against LSU. Our crowd was roaring, and it was Senior Day. I started Laurie Milligan, our senior guard who had sat on the bench all year with arthritic knees. It was only Laurie's second appearance of the season—but it was her last chance to stand on our home court for a Tennessee tip-off. I had promised Laurie that if she worked at her rehab, I would find a way to play her in postseason. I wanted her to be the first player in NCAA history to go to four straight Final Fours. And who knew—with Kyra hurt, we might just need her.

Laurie stepped on the court, radiant. Her smile seemed to suffuse the whole team. We came out scorching, and hit thirteen of our first sixteen shots. Everything we aimed at the basket fell in. When we weren't sinking shots, we were stripping LSU of the ball—we forced fifteen turnovers in the opening eight minutes.

We took a 54–23 lead to the locker room at the half, and things only got better in the second half. The four freshmen put on a show, racking up sixty-five points between them. Catchings had twenty-one, Randall twenty, Geter had sixteen, and Clement had eight. Final score: 90–58.

On March 1, we won the SEC Tournament in Columbus, Georgia. We had defeated Mississippi State, Vanderbilt, and Alabama, in that order.

Our rematch with Alabama in the SEC title game was another slow-paced, brutally physical game. But we eked it out, 67–63, and no one got hurt. It wasn't an especially convincing victory. Alabama had given the rest of the country a blueprint for staying with us. They outrebounded us, outmuscled us, and proved that a very physical style of play could affect our offense.

But the good news was that Ace Clement was finally with us again. She gave us her best and most consistent play of the season—which was exactly what we needed to make a run in March. She was intense, vocal, and a defensive presence. I congratulated her—she finally got her game back.

All that remained now was the NCAA tournament. We had several days off to recover physically, and to consider what we had accomplished:

We were a perfect 33–0, still on pace to become the first undefeated team in school history.

➤ ➤ ➤

In February, our team became something more than just a roster or a photograph, a one-dimensional image of faces and numerals in a row. The word "team" didn't do justice to us, in the wake of the injuries and the stalker and the victories. It rose above a mere word into pure feeling. We were a family.

There was just one piece of unfinished business: Semeka's relationship with me. Her lack of response to criticism and her body language still bothered me. I felt that Semeka had to get a grip on her emotions before the NCAA tournament. She was the one remaining loose thread that could unravel us. Otherwise, we might not make it through.

Our emotions as a team tended to mirror Semeka's own. She was so charismatic, such a powerful conveyor of energy for us, that we couldn't afford any sharp swings from her. When she was jacked, the team followed her. When she was low and hung her head, she could drag us all down.

After the SEC Tournament, I called Semeka's high school coach back in Cleveland, Pat Diulus. They had been extremely close ever since she played at Trinity, and he understood her. I explained my problem with Semeka to him.

"Why is she fighting me?" I asked.

"Pat," he said, "you've got to hug that kid."

He explained that Semeka thrived on a close relationship with her coach, someone to whom she could give her all. Semeka's answer to every problem was to just try harder. She thought she could physically force her way through any difficulty. She worked so tirelessly and was so hard on herself that it was easy for her to feel resentful if her effort wasn't fully appreciated. She needed reassurance.

So Semeka needed a lot of caring. And I needed a player who would talk to me.

After we spoke, Coach Diulus called Semeka. "You have to talk to Pat," he said. "I can't fly down there and do it for you. When we had problems, you came and told me. You've got to do the same with her."

Semeka said, "That was easy. It's not so simple with her."

Finally, I called Semeka and asked her to come in and meet with me. She sat on my couch. "Semeka, I have wanted to be your coach since I first saw you play in the ninth grade," I said.

She needed to learn the most important thing about this game, I told her: the beauty of it is that you don't have to do it alone.

I said, "You need to communicate with me, and you need to trust me."

Semeka was quiet. Inside, she said later, she was thinking, *Trust? I don't trust anybody.*

"I can't keep coming to you," I said. "If I do, the other players would think I was showing favoritism."

Semeka said, "I'm not looking for that."

"Then what are you looking for?" I said. "I'll do whatever I can to make this work."

Semeka said, "I don't know."

"All right," I said. "How about this. I won't ask you to trust me. Instead, *I'm* going to trust *you*. I'm going to trust you to be the emotional leader of this team, and to not let us down. We can't win this tournament otherwise. So can you do that?"

She said, "Yes."

"Okay," I said. "Is there anything else you need?"

Semeka said, "Well, I need a hug."

I said, "I'll give you a hug."

And I gave her one.

PART THREE

➤➤➤ Society
Kiss

Q & A with Niya Butts (Sophomore guard)

Why was this team so driven?

It just had that kind of personality. Everyone always wanted to win, they always wanted to be better than the person next to them. Sometimes we knew we could have beaten the other team by more, and so, even though we won, we weren't satisfied. We didn't think it was good enough.

There were games where you weren't satisfied with a win?

Sometimes you asked yourself if you could have done more. We could beat a team by twenty, and most people would say, "Let's go home, I'm done with it." We'd say, "We should have won by thirty."

CHAPTER NINE

Survive and Advance

TOURNAMENT TIME WAS A TRANCE, a caffeine-disturbed pool of unconsciousness. It was a matter of Diet Coke for breakfast and a handful of potato chips for dinner. Sleep wasn't really sleep, it was a temporary blackout, a break in the rhythm of tension, triumph, and superstition. Nothing mattered, nothing counted, but the final score. Our motto was "Survive and Advance."

The last thing I recall putting in my mouth before it all started was a large breakfast I cooked for my family on the weekend prior to the NCAA tournament. I went back for a second helping of eggs and biscuits. When I hesitated, feeling guilty, my husband said, resignedly, "Go on. It's probably the last meal you'll eat until April."

All other responsibilities were suspended. There were no bills due, no appointments to keep, no errands more important than this: making sure that one of the greatest teams anybody ever saw won the championship it deserved.

To an outsider, we must have looked hypnotized.

The NCAA tournament officially began on March 13 and would conclude on March 29, and it was structured this way: sixty-four teams, divided into four regions, competed in a single-elimination format with the winners from each region to meet in

Kemper Arena in Kansas City for the Final Four. We would play six games over two and a half weeks under mounting strain and ever higher expectations.

The team gathered at my house for a live ESPN show to announce the brackets and seedings for the tournament. We sat around, sprawled on the living room floor, as ESPN's studio host Robin Roberts announced the news that Tennessee was seeded No.1 in the Mideast Region. We would open with a two-game home stand, and if we won those, we would advance to the Mideast Regionals in Nashville.

Our first opponent would be Liberty University, a small fundamentalist Christian college in Virginia, founded by Jerry Falwell. Liberty was the only other team in the country besides us to go undefeated in the regular season.

From that day on, the coaching staff entered a phase that was best described as body snatched. We divided up scouting duties. We stared at film, endlessly. We became obsessively superstitious. If we entered a room through a certain door, we had to be sure to go out the same way. We lifted our feet when we drove over train tracks. We scoured the ground for heads up pennies. No matter what, we didn't kill crickets.

And the staff ate ice cream sundaes with our pregame meals. It was a ritual, regardless of the hour of the day—even if it meant eating it with our eggs and bacon. It had to be the right kind of sundae, too: vanilla ice cream with chocolate syrup. And each time, Mickie had to ask the waiter the same question.

"Now, is this Bluebell ice cream?" she would say.

"I'm not sure," the waiter would reply, predictably.

She would make the waiter go to the kitchen and ask. Then he would return. "No, that's Mayfield's," he would say.

Each time, Mickie would frame the same careful reply. "Why, thank you."

➤ ➤ ➤

THERE IS A REASON it is called March Madness.

March Madness requires that you turn yourself completely and wholeheartedly over to the endeavor. There are no easy games, no margin for error, every team is hungry, and every team a threat. In the regular season, a loss was disappointing, but it wasn't fatal. In the NCAA tournament, a loss meant the season was over. That was it. An upset now would define our whole year as a disappointment: we would be the greatest team *not* to win a title.

This was my twenty-fourth foray into the month of March, and if the madness had never seemed greater, it was because something strange was happening around this team. Our dream state was heightened by a giant crest of publicity. After years of obscurity, we were suddenly the recipients of a society kiss.

On March 9, HBO premiered a documentary on the 1997 Lady Vols, A *Cinderella Season*, at a gala screening and a black-tie party at the Tennessee Theatre in downtown Knoxville. *Sports Illustrated* hit the stands, with a twelve-page cover story on my life and times at Tennessee. The magazine, despite an exceedingly unattractive cover picture, sold out in three hours in Knoxville. My first book, *Reach for the Summit*, appeared in bookstores and was an overnight national bestseller.

We were the subjects of front-page articles in the *New York Times* and the *Washington Post*. We were on MTV and in *Time* magazine, and Adidas decided to release a line of Lady Vol sportswear.

Why now? Why, after twenty-four years, was Tennessee basketball such a sensation?

Perhaps it was simply a case of talent meeting opportunity. The Meeks had come along at the perfect moment, when the networks and national media were willing to give the sport air time and prominent play in their pages. We had won thirty-three games by an average of over twenty points. But I thought it was more than that. Maybe spectators sensed what I knew, that these young women were a fascinating combination of strength and vulnerability. If we weren't the best team ever— that was an argument for the pundits—I was convinced we were one of the most *exciting* teams ever. The relentlessly ambitious tempo at which the Lady Vols played and their showtime athleticism up around the rim was something altogether new for the women's game. We pushed the ball, we threw alley oop passes, we put together runs like our 45–6 tear against Florida, a 32–4 streak against Vanderbilt, and our twenty-two–point comeback against Illinois. But we wore our hearts on the outsides of our jerseys, too. You saw every emotion that crossed our faces.

Whatever the reason, we had won fans in quarters we hadn't reached before. Including some areas of Knoxville, Tennessee.

➢ ➢ ➢

KNOXVILLE IS A LIVELY, historical southern city on the banks of the swirling Tennessee River, with a resurgent downtown area where warehouses have been converted into coffee bars and bistros. The air is full of train whistles and a smoky haze from the mixture of barbecue smoke and humidity rising up off the river. And it is, predictably, football crazed. The social center of town every Saturday afternoon is Neyland Stadium. In the fall, the Volunteers had fallen one game shy of winning a national championship, and quarterback Peyton Manning was a Heisman Trophy runner-up.

But Lady Vol basketball was finally becoming a desirable social event as well, thanks to this team. It was a profoundly gratifying turn of events if you happened, as I did, to remember a time in the early '70s when we had to sell donuts to buy uniforms. Now, at last, we were being accepted by the upper echelons of Tennessee society, the very donors who could help build and support a program for the long term.

Our average attendance at home was 14,969—better than six men's NBA teams. Our players were being increasingly hounded by autograph seekers. We needed a police escort to get from the locker room to the team bus. One afternoon, Chamique and Ace went to a shopping mall. Chamique found herself standing outside of The Gap with a line of autograph seekers stretching through the mall. All she wanted to do was shop for a new pair of blue jeans.

I issued an edict: no more autographs until after the tournament. "Blame it on your coach," I said.

The leading industries and businesses in town were becoming Lady Vol boosters. In the course of the season, ticket sales had tripled, and corporate sponsorship had quadrupled, bringing in excess of $1 million in revenue. Some of the town's wealthier boosters paid a total of $9,000 to attend a sit-down fried green tomato dinner at the Summitt home, cooked by me and our athletics director, Joan Cronan. At a black-tie fundraising dinner, we raised $130,000 in a single night.

We were a happening.

But Joan liked to paraphrase Luke 12:48. "To whom much is given," she said, "much is expected."

> > >

ALL THIS ATTENTION could come with a heavy price tag, if we weren't careful. The first order of business was to make sure the Lady Vols had our attitudes right. It would all end in a second if we allowed ourselves to be distracted, or caught up in our own limelight.

In the days prior to the NCAA tournament, we fine-tuned the team emotionally, in ways both pleasant and unpleasant. It was a time for attitude adjustments.

On the pleasant side, I wrote each player a personal note. They didn't say anything earth shattering. They consisted of a couple of sentences telling them how much I loved being their coach, and what we needed from them in the tournament.

"Dear Chamique," I wrote. "Congrats on all of your honors. You deserve them. . . . Now, you and Kellie will have to lead this team during the playoffs. They will need you and *you will need them*. So be ready to communicate and direct them. Let's enjoy the process. I'm here to help you do what no player or team has ever done. Pat."

"Dear Teresa," I wrote. "I'm writing sideways to get your attention. Tree, it's very important that you keep working . . . I promise, it will be worth it. Pat."

"Ace, I like your focus and defensive intensity. . . . Work every practice to become a smarter and better player."

"Dear Tamika, I want you to know and believe no one in America can stop you. Stay focused and confident. Don't hold back in the next six games."

"Dear Kyra, boy, have I missed you. This team has missed you. I'm really impressed with your rehab. Don't get discouraged and keep working daily. We miss your leadership on the court, but I believe you can really play a valuable role on the bench. Be emotional and sensitive to your teammates and what they need. You've been there and know what they are feeling. I'd love for you to inbounds the ball in Kansas City."

But Semeka's letter was different. It was over two full pages long, and it was all about trust and responsibility. I asked her if she would assume Kyra's role as an emotional leader and defensive stopper. "You will need to put the team first," I wrote. "And be a leader when you are struggling, and handle criticism, and communicate with your teammates, and play your heart out. You will need to grow up."

Next, I met with Kellie and Chamique. It would be their job, I believed, to get the freshmen through the tournament. They were our veterans, they knew how to win, and the freshmen revered them. Semeka Randall hung on every word Chamique said, and Ace Clement studied every move Kellie made. The whole team would take their cues from Kellie and Chamique.

"You're both quiet leaders," I said. "And that's fine. But we're going to need an emotional leader, and a vocal one. Semeka is that for us. You guys can encourage her, and Ace, too."

I paused.

"Get 'em in your hip pocket," I said.

There was another matter to attend to. Two of our key players were getting on each other's nerves. It was a time of the year when everyone could be on edge and irritable, so I wasn't surprised. But they were crucial players for us, and they were barely speaking. Ordinarily, I might not have interfered, but it was postseason, and I didn't want anything to unravel us now.

I addressed the issue head on. I reminded them of the rules of playing pickup. In some ways, the NCAA tournament was similar.

"We don't *have* to like each other these next six games," I said. "But we're the ones in this every day. You do have to work together. You win, you keep the court. Make it, take it."

A couple of days later, I made the point even more strongly. Any time we had a few days off, things could get lax; sure enough, I found out that a player hadn't shown up for class. It was the perfect opportunity to do a little team building.

I threatened to put the whole team in study hall. It was the equivalent of tying their feet together with a rope. If one player fell, they all fell.

"One more of these and you're all in study hall twelve hours a week," I said. "So the lesson is, screw up, screw your teammates. Because from now on we're committed to the team."

> > >

AS THE FIRST ROUND GAME with Liberty approached, there was a slow ratcheting up of tension. I, for one, became increasingly manic. I kept returning to the problem of our postgame, almost obsessively. It was like a puddle of acid in the bottom of my stomach. How could we expect to go all the way when we were getting shoved around like we did by Alabama? We *had* to get stronger in the paint.

LaShonda Stephens was the key. But she had been a problematic player for us all season. She was a tall, soft-spoken young woman from Woodstock, Georgia, who had plenty of ability, but was hampered by chronically bad knees. She needed an hour of icing and electronic stimulation treatment after every game, and she even had to resort to pain medication on occasion. All this had hurt her confidence.

LaShonda had spent much of the winter in an offensive slump, and that made things even worse. She was a perfectionist and harsh self-critic. She had a soft shooting touch, but it had deserted her early, and she had averaged just four points per game in the regular season. I told her to forget about scoring and do the other things to help us win, like rebound and play defense. But LaShonda kept grinding and couldn't get any fluidity to her game. As it turned out, the problem was that she felt pressured and rushed by the tempo of our play. LaShonda had a hard time getting up and down the court at the breakneck pace of the others, with the result that she tended to rush her shot. But whenever I tried to talk to her about it, my feeling was that I lowered her confidence. So I would back off. Communication wasn't our strong suit. LaShonda was quiet by nature, and I was intense, and so we always seemed to be tripping over each other's feelings. Mickie communicated better with her than I did; she had patiently talked her through much of the season.

But now we were out of time. We had to have a big presence from LaShonda in the tournament. I knew how sensitive she was, but we had to get a response out of her. Even if it was an angry one.

LaShonda gave me an excuse to confront her when she missed a class to prepare for an exam. Our policy stated that you had to get the professor's permission as well as mine to be excused. But LaShonda was simply too afraid to call me. The situation had to be resolved, I felt, for better or worse.

I caught LaShonda at courtside before practice. Kyra was nearby doing her rehab and heard my voice rising. She said to Jenny, "Oooh, Jenny, my sweet dog is catching it."

I said to LaShonda, "You need to grow your little ass up. What is *wrong* with you?"

"I can't do anything right," she said. And then she started to cry.

"Well that's great," I said. "Have a pity party, why don't you, right before the NCAAs. You know what your problem is? You're scared of me. You can't even have a conversation with me."

"You think I don't try," she said.

"LaShonda," I said. "Have I ever faulted you on effort?"

"No," she said.

"Then *stop* crying."

This was it, I decided. I had to take a chance on hurting her, in order to get the best out of her. It was like lancing a wound: "that which does not kill you makes you stronger." So I ordered LaShonda to run five Big

Threes after practice. A Big Three is a punitive form of wind sprint, a grueling drill that leaves the most iron-lunged players sucking in air. A single one was unpleasant enough.

LaShonda went out and had one of her best practices of the season, trying to work her way back into my good graces. But I wasn't satisfied.

"Okay," I said. "Only three Big Threes. Out of the goodness of my heart."

But then, just so LaShonda wouldn't feel so all alone, I got on Tree Geter.

"I ought to kick your butt up around your shoulders," I said. "I ought to kick it right back over the mountain. You only play when you want to play. Fine. I've got a seat for you. Right next to the water cooler."

I was still on a rampage a day or two later when Ace Clement showed up for practice with her hair highlighted. She never should have done that. I took one look at the streaks of blond in her chestnut hair, and my lip curled.

"Why'd you do that?" I asked.

Ace said, "I wanted to look pretty."

I said, scathingly, "Pretty? We're not here to look *pretty* in March. We're here to look *mean*."

But this time, I had gone too far. I failed to mention to Ace that I always got my nails and hair done before a big game. In fact, it was a superstition that ranked right up there with pennies and ice cream sundaes.

With the Liberty game approaching, I wanted to cancel my usual hair and nails appointment, because I was feeling pressure to get the team ready. But the day before the game, Mickie suddenly noticed my peeling nail polish.

Now, Mickie is as superstitious as I am.

"Pat," she said, "get your nails done."

I said, "I don't have time, I'm going to cancel."

Mickie said, intently, "*Pat*. I'm telling you to get your nails done."

So I did, and my hair, too. Unfortunately, later that day, Ace, Semeka, and Niya came by the office.

Ace was sitting in Mickie's chair, twirling and killing time, when she saw me go by. She took one look at my hair, and smiled a predatory little smile.

"Let me see your nails," she demanded.

I was busted.

I grudgingly held out my nails.

"We're not here to look pretty in March," Ace said. "We're here to look *mean*."

They all whooped and fell around, high-fiving.

➤ ➤ ➤

ON THE NIGHT OF MARCH 14, the NCAA tournament began for us against Liberty University. The Flames had racked up a 28–0 record with a team of sharpshooters. There were lots of jokes by their coaches and players about how if someone had to be thrown to the lions, it might as well be the Christians.

In the locker room beforehand, we kept to the comfort of routine. I wrote on the board in my usual neat block letters, and I stepped into the circle of players.

"This is what you've worked six months for," I said. "Take it one step at a time. Survive and advance. This team is undefeated, just like you are, so they know how to win. You need to be ready to play for forty minutes, or however long it takes. This is your house, and it's up to you to protect your property. They are welcome to visit. But they aren't welcome to the merchandise."

My speech didn't exactly rouse us.

The Flames turned out to be an alarmingly quick team that could score from anywhere. They hit the floor running and took a 7–4 lead. For the next five minutes we seesawed back and forth, thanks to their whippet-like guard, Sharon Wilkerson, who hit on four of seven from the three-point circle. Wilkerson was only 5-feet-6, but she was on her way to racking up twenty points for the half—and she was doing it against our stopper, Semeka Randall. Meanwhile, we made just eight of twenty-three shots from the field in one stone cold stretch.

Finally, we took our first lead, 13–12, at the 14:12 mark.

I sent in Ace to sub out Kellie. I was anxious to see what she would do. Immediately, Ace knocked a ball away for a steal and hit Holdsclaw on a fast break. That got our feet moving. Then, Ace launched a gorgeous three-pointer.

Tree threw in four straight points. Niya followed this with a breakaway layup for a 30–18 lead. We led comfortably the rest of the way, including a 49–30 margin at halftime, and a fifty-point lead midway through the second half.

There was one mini-drama on our sideline. LaShonda was playing like a madwoman. She wrestled down rebounds, she scored on put-backs and tip-ins. Every time she did something, our bench went crazy. Kellie and Kyra were on their feet, swirling towels in the air and screaming. But they really went crazy when I pulled LaShonda from the game with a few minutes remaining, trying not to run up the score.

Chamique said, urgently, "You have to put LaShonda back in." She explained the situation: LaShonda's sister, it seems, had motivated LaShonda in a way that I never could. She had promised LaShonda $100 if she scored a career high against Liberty.

LaShonda had ten points. Two shy of her career high.

I turned, smiling, and told LaShonda to get back in the game.

LaShonda scored a career-high fourteen points.

We led, 100–58, when I finally pulled her from the game with twenty seconds to go. As LaShonda trotted over to the sideline, beaming, the whole bench rose. Kellie, Kyra, Niya, and Chamique leaped and swung their towels. I stood, and applauded her. Then I offered her my hand. LaShonda shook it. I wrapped my arms around her.

Final score: 102–58. All five of our starters were in double figures.

But the statistic that pleased me most was what a factor our bench had been. They were seldom recognized, and no one talked about them much during the regular season. But they were significant contributors, especially on this night. Laurie Milligan, our senior guard, and Niya Butts, whose shins were wrapped all the way to her knees, had combined with the sore-kneed LaShonda for twenty-three points and eight rebounds.

In the locker room, I called for quiet. "Okay, who gets KK?" I said. I paused.

"I'd say LaShonda does," I said, and presented it to her.

➢ ➢ ➢

WE DIDN'T HAVE TIME to celebrate. What few observers realize about March Madness is how quickly it moves. Spectators have a day of leisure between games. But we had to immediately scout and prepare for our next opponent, in this case, Western Kentucky, overnight.

If there was one team we didn't want to meet in an early round game, it was Western Kentucky. They were a major upset threat. They had lost to Louisiana Tech—at Tech—by a single point, and they were seriously underrated, with a 26–8 record. They bore a disturbing resemblence to Alabama, the only team that had come close to beating us all year. And they were plainly unintimidated by us.

The Lady Toppers announced in the papers that they intended to go back to Bowling Green "celebrating."

Steve Small, Western's head coach, was a witty man who, when he was asked how to scout for Tennessee, said, "Hey. There's films on 'em. Documentaries. Books. We don't need to scout 'em. All we've got to do is turn on the TV."

Like Alabama, Western Kentucky had a strong inside presence, and they were led by a pair of fifth-year seniors. Leslie Johnson was a 6-feet-1 forward with thick shoulders and a strong upper body, and no qualms about being physical. She averaged seventeen points and nine rebounds. Their center, Danielle McCulley, was a versatile player of 6-feet-3 who could hurt us both in traffic or from the perimeter.

Mickie, Holly, and Al had dark circles under their eyes from watching tape and preparing the scouting report. We sat in my office and sorted through various strategies for dealing with Leslie Johnson. I chewed my lip, and I said, "I'm worried that Johnson can move Tree and LaShonda out of there. Just shove them out."

Mickie, little 5-feet-nothing Mickie, said, "Heck, *I* can move Tree."

I looked at my watch. I said, "Well, you've got thirty hours to work with them."

And that's what Mickie did.

At three o'clock we practiced. I called the team together and congratulated them on the Liberty game. But I didn't want them to feel too comfortable. "You got what you wanted in the end, but you also did some things that could come back and bite you," I said. "Do you understand what mindset you need? You are not on your heels, you are on your toes. Our philosophy doesn't change in postseason. It *intensifies*. We're coming *after* them."

I turned to Tree and LaShonda. "They got a post player that's an animal," I said. "She's got an attitude as big as this locker room."

They laughed.

"I'm serious," I said. "It's butt kicking time, Tree Geter. They're going to come at you. So be prepared."

Preparing, I believed, was tantamount to winning. That's why I loved practice—because in practice we did all of the things that got us ready to win.

Everyone in the game says they *want* to win, but not everyone has what I call "the will to *prepare* to win," the discipline to do the boring, repetitive tasks that allow you to come out ahead—like practice hard even in the postseason, and scout a little more thoroughly even after you feel you know your opponent.

We walked the players through a series of questions, almost like a classroom drill. Mickie quizzed Tree and LaShonda, especially, on playing good position against Western.

How do you deny that option?

That's *right*. Deny the high post.

What's number 24 going to do there?

That's *right*. She's going to flare.

In the locker room afterwards, we all stayed on Tree and LaShonda.

"Geter, you better eat you some hamburger," Holly said.

"You hear what those Western Kentucky players been saying about Tree Geter?" Mickie said.

Holly said, "Raw meat. With razor blades in it."

Tree said, "All right. We'll see."

There was one player who didn't need teasing. After practice, I quietly asked Semeka to meet with me. Semeka was dispirited. She had played well below her standards against Liberty, and she knew it. In fact, Al Brown was so mad at her that he wasn't speaking to her.

Semeka couldn't bear it when a coach didn't talk to her. *I* knew Al wasn't really that mad at her, he was just trying to provoke her into playing better. But Semeka didn't know that.

Anyone could see Semeka was low. She had made a typical freshman mental error; she played overly cautiously, back on her heels, because it was tournament time. She didn't understand that you couldn't retreat at tournament time—you had to do the opposite. You stepped over the line and attacked.

But how did you get a player to take that step? Sometimes, you did it with a verbal push, with decibels or a harsh tone, as I had with LaShonda. But oftentimes a player was hard enough on herself. As a coach and a teacher, you had to intuit what she needed from moment to moment. On this occasion, a lecture wouldn't help Semeka. She wanted to give us her best, but she needed to be shown how.

Semeka met me in my office, and we pulled two chairs in front of the VCR. As we started the tape, I spoke to her gently. I sounded like a doctor about to give a child a shot with a long needle. It was my "this-hurts-me-more-than-it-hurts-you" voice.

I said, "We're not going to watch much of this, I promise."

On the screen, Semeka visibly backpedaled as Liberty's guard, Wilkerson, blew by her.

I said, softly, "Now, you be the coach and tell me. Who is attacking who there?"

"She's attacking me," Semeka said.

I ran the tape forward. "Are you on your toes, or on your heels?" I asked.

"My heels," she said.

On the screen, Semeka dawdled and Liberty's Wilkerson streaked by her again.

"Help me be your coach," I said. "Do you see why Al is so mad at you?"

"He's still not speaking to me," Semeka said, plaintively.

I ran the tape over and over. Semeka hunched her shoulders, as if she was in pain.

"We're only going to watch a couple more of these, I promise," I said.

Wilkerson buried a three. I backed the tape up.

"You got your little butt whipped there," I said.

I ran it again.

"You've got to come ready to play," I said.

"Okay," Semeka said.

I stopped the tape.

"I'll put the glove on 'em," she said.

➤ ➤ ➤

AND THEN SUDDENLY, it was game day again. We had our usual pregame meal at O'Charleys of chicken, pasta, baked potatoes, and ice cream sundaes for the coaches. I raced home and cooked a massive meal, as usual, for my family, and made myself late again.

My sister Linda called as I was frantically drying my hair. She wanted *me* to calm *her* down.

"Trisha, I'm so nervous," she said. "Tell me we're going to win."

"Now look," I said. "It's going to be tight for a while, so be prepared. But we should pull away."

In the locker room I stepped in front of the circle of players. "Survive and advance, survive and advance," I said. "That's all you have to do.

They are coming at you with an attitude. You know what they've been saying. They're saying they intend to go home celebrating."

I paused. A rash of upsets was sweeping the tournament, and top seeds were dropping like flies. After the Liberty game, our coaching staff had all stayed up until 2 A.M. watching Harvard knock out Stanford, the top seed in the West. If Stanford could go down, so could we. I debated in my head whether or not to mention threat of upset. I decided against it.

We focused on winning, not on losing.

➤ ➤ ➤

AS WE LEFT THE LOCKER ROOM, I could sense Kyra's frustration. She had almost gone to school at Western Kentucky. When she declared for Tennessee, a lot of people in the state had taken it badly. Old friends and players had treated her like a traitor, and told her she would sit on the bench for four years at Tennessee. Kyra was dying to show them what an integral part of Tennessee she had become. Of all the games she had to sit out, this was the hardest.

There was only one piece of good news for Kyra. All of her desperately hard work in rehab was paying off. Earlier that day, she had jogged for the first time, and even done a little rollerblading. As a reward, I let Kyra jog out on the floor with the team in her Tennessee uniform. She joined the shootaround, and actually did a layup.

Kyra came to the bench. I knew how valiantly she was trying to keep a good attitude, and I was so very proud of her. I wandered down the bench and took the chair next to her.

"I *ran*," Kyra said. "Did you see it? I ran, for the first time."

I put my arm around her.

Our victory over Western that night wouldn't go down in any record books. The final score wasn't impressive, and it wasn't a down-to-the-wire thriller. No one but perhaps the coaches understood what a complete performance it was from our team. We played all out, ninety-four feet of ball, for forty minutes.

Once again, it was Ace Clement who jump-started us. In the space of just a minute, she lobbed a no-look pass to Catch for a layup, hit a short jumper, and added a three-pointer as we took a 22–15 lead.

But Western refused to die. Inside, LaShonda locked arms and legs with Johnson and McCulley. Every time I looked in the paint, it seemed like LaShonda was battling for position. In the meantime, Chamique couldn't find her scoring niche. She racked up six early points, and then she fell quiet. We went in at halftime with a 37–25 lead, and the sure knowledge that we were in for another difficult twenty minutes. We had done nothing to disuade them from the idea that they could stay with us.

"All we did was feed their confidence," I said, aggravated. "By not opening the game up, we gave them energy. So we'd better start strong in the second half."

I turned to Chamique. "You're not here to lead this team in assists," I told her. "You're here to score. We're putting the ball in *your* hands."

Back on the floor, we fought over every possession. Ace and Kellie clawed, slapped, and even kicked at the ball, trying to keep it away from Johnson and McCulley, hoping to buy LaShonda a breather inside.

Western gouged away at our lead. They cut it to six points, 43–37, with 17:35 to go—to the intense discomfort of our athletics director, Joan Cronan.

Joan was white-knuckled. She had made a large calculated gamble on the game. Tickets for the regional finals in Nashville had gone on sale a few days earlier, and demand was outstripping the allotment available to us. Joan was worried that there wouldn't be enough tickets to accommodate all of the Tennessee fans.

She had picked up the phone and bought one thousand tickets.

If we lost, she would be stuck with them.

Joan was miserable. We couldn't seem to kick Western loose. They continued to lurk within six, 52–46. In the paint, LaShonda was still duking it out with McCulley and Johnson. All you saw under the basket was an indistinct tangle of arms and legs.

I called a twenty-second time-out, and stamped my foot so hard that it reverberated across the arena.

"We've got to keep running it up their backs," Mickie urged the Lady Vols.

We stared up at the clock and scoreboard. Six points, and still more than ten minutes to play.

"We need to put on the skates," Chamique said, almost casually, to no one in particular.

What happened next was vintage Holdsclaw. It was one of those occasions that defined her in my mind as the greatest player in the game. We returned to the court—and Chamique immediately scored six points in forty-one seconds.

We inbounded the ball, and Chamique drove for a baseline jumper, one of those elegant shots that made a noise like cloth tearing. Next, Kellie stole the ball, jimmying loose an interior pass meant for Leslie Johnson, and slung it to Chamique, who knocked down a twisting layup.

Western Kentucky lost the ball again, and Catchings dove for it. She shoveled it to Chamique, who gathered it in on the run for another layup.

We were up twelve—and as quickly as that, the game was over. Chamique's flurry was the beginning of an eighteen-point scoring burst from her over a ten-minute stretch. We never looked back, and won comfortably, 82–62.

Over on the Western Kentucky bench, Steve Small had just allowed himself to believe Western had the momentum when Chamique killed it. "I was starting to dream the dream," he said later. "I was thinking about what to say about how we beat Tennessee. Then they did what they were supposed to do. They turned up the heat and put the ball in the hands of their All-American." Small still managed to be funny and gracious, although he was weary. "I'll be glad to get out of this state and not hear 'Rocky Top' one more time," he said.

For the night, Chamique had thirty-four points—twenty-two of them in the second half—as well as eleven rebounds, three blocked shots, and four steals.

Catchings had twenty points, fourteen rebounds, six assists, and five steals.

But in the locker room afterwards, we knew something the spectators didn't. As spectacular as Chamique and Catchings had been, the game may really have been won by another player. Every so often, a player performs so thanklessly that it doesn't seem fair. On this night, once again, we owed LaShonda Stephens. She didn't get proper recognition for what she did.

LaShonda went thirty full minutes on her aching knees against Johnson and McCulley. She played brilliant position defense, denying them the ball and muscling them out of the seat of their offense. She scored eight points, including a gorgeous fifteen-footer. And she took three charges, winning the full-body chess match she was forced to play all night long.

❋Afterwards, LaShonda was in pain, as usual. When someone asked her how her knees felt, she said, "I'm kind of sore, but I've learned to live with it. I just ice them and go on."❋

Then she limped off for an hour of treatment.

Up in the stands, Joan Cronan was dealing with ticket requests.

I leaned against a wall in the hallway, talking to the press. A reporter asked me if Tennessee would keep running, or if I had considered slowing the ball down.

I said, "We're either going to win a championship this way, or lose one. I can't see reeling them in now."

➤ ➤ ➤

ON MARCH 18, a headline in the local Knoxville paper read, "Will Meek No. 3 Please Stand Up?"

It was a direct finger jab at Semeka. The Third Meek was still trying to find herself in tournament play. Despite our talk on the afternoon before the Western Kentucky game, Semeka had labored that night. She picked up two quick fouls, and only played seven minutes in the first half, and wound up with ten points.

I tore the article out of the paper. At practice that afternoon, I handed it to her.

"Have you seen this?" I said.

"I heard about it," she said.

I said, "Well, I brought you a copy. I thought you might want to read it."

While I felt for Semeka, we didn't need any Missing Meeks heading into the Sweet 16. It was time for her to find herself again.

We rode a bus to Nashville for the Mideast Regionals, where we would meet Rutgers. With each game came a bigger threat, and a greater reward. I told the team to take it one step at a time. "Survive and advance," I said, over and over. But the steps were beginning to look like leaps.

Rutgers was a brazenly fearless team coached by the legendary Vivian Stringer, a longtime friend of mine. The Scarlet Knights were as young as we were, with four freshmen among their first seven players, and they were learning as they went, with a record of 22–9. But they believed in themselves.

When the Scarlet Knights learned that we would be their regional semifinal opponent, they cheered. They *wanted* to play us. They chanted, "Tennessee, Tennessee!"

The night before the game, all four regional teams—Tennessee, Rutgers, North Carolina, and Illinois—attended a banquet together. It was a chance for the players to socialize before play began. A lot of them knew each other from high school, or from playing in summer leagues. As Chamique and Semeka wandered around the room making conversation with other players, they ran into some of the Scarlet Knights, including Linda Miles, a 6-foot forward with a big left hand. Miles was an old acquaintance of Semeka's from Ohio. They started talking smack.

Miles teased Chamique and Semeka. "You're overrated," she told Chamique, gleefully. Then she turned and pointed to Semeka, "And you're *really* overrated!"

It was the wrong thing to say to Semeka, given that she had been labeled our Missing Meek. Semeka smiled and laughed, and nodded.

But deep down, she seethed. For the next twenty-four hours, she was virtually wordless. She just glared.

Vivian and I couldn't help getting in the spirit of the thing. There weren't too many people in the business I liked as much as Vivian, but we were competitors, too. When it got back to me that Vivian had worn Tennessee orange on the team plane, and even more insolently, was wearing orange warm-ups to her practices, I knew I had to answer her.

I dug up a pair of scarlet sweats; and wore them to practice.

I made as much as I could out of Rutgers' trash talk. Every chance I got, I brought it up.

"They can't help it," I told our team, sarcastically. "They just *want* y'all."

But Rutgers made me tense. They had plenty of talent to back up their words. They were a small, sleek team that loved to take the ball straight to the basket. They revolved around Natasha Pointer, a slashing freshman point guard, and Tomora Young, a junior and a crack shooter, averaging fourteen points each. But every one of them could score including Miles, the cunning lefty, and Usha Gilmore, a 6-foot enforcer type, who, even though she wasn't averaging in double figures, was capable of putting up a big number.

Our coaching staff worked off anxiety by sweating. We wore away hours in a nearby workout center, slogging on treadmills and lifting weights, until we were so sore we could barely raise our arms to click the remote controls on the tape machines. We ran endless laps around the Vanderbilt quadrangles.

The strain finally told on Mickie. As we rode the bus to the arena, she sat slumped in her seat hiding behind a newspaper, trying to hide the fact that she was having terrible stomach pains. She didn't want the players to see it. In a way, it was our job to absorb all of the pressure for the players. No matter how we felt inside, outwardly we always projected confidence and reassurance. We believed in them, and in our preparation, so we were not nervous. But getting to that point, the long, caffeine-drenched nights staring at tape, took it out of us physically.

As our team walked down the arena hall for their pregame warmup, they passed the Rutgers players.

"Get the rope," Miles said, swinging an imaginary noose. "It's hanging time!"

Our players were incredulous. The one thing you didn't want to do to the Lady Vols was taunt us. It was like throwing lighter fluid at us. We had a tendency to flare.

I looked at Randall. She was so intense she was almost glazed. The other players couldn't help laughing at the hard expression on her face. I thought, well, she'll either be great, or awful.

In the hallway on the way to the court, Semeka began to chant the lyrics to the Master P song, "No-Limit Soldier." All year long Semeka had made the song a sort of a battle cry. It was a rough-edged, violent anthem. Not much of it was printable. On this night, Semeka sang one refrain over and over. *"You don't wanna go to war with me!"*

Then Chamique started in. "What time is it?" she hollered. "Game time!" they hollered back.

➤ ➤ ➤

RUTGERS SET THE TEMPO EARLY, staying within three points of us through the first sixteen minutes. It was a taut, combative matchup, and a messy one—but it was dominated by Semeka Randall, who grimly helped force Rutgers into thirteen first-half turnovers.

We went in at halftime leading by only eight, 38–30. But I felt good about how we were playing. Our defense, led by Semeka, wore on people, and I felt we could wear Rutgers down in the second half. "Keep the pressure *on*," I begged them.

That's precisely what we did. Semeka led a defensive fury in the first four minutes of the half, hawking the ball so intensely Rutgers couldn't find an open pass, much less a shot. Reduced to forcing, they made just three of eighteen shots in one stretch—while we turned on the offensive afterburners and pulled away.

Semeka doggedly retrieved her own rebound twice in one sequence, to force in a layup. Chamique followed that with one of her signature finger rolls, for a 46–32 lead.

Rutgers called a time-out. I jumped up and shoved my fist in the air. The game was busted open.

From then on, it was a highlight film. When Catchings made a gorgeous twisting drive to the basket for an 80–50 margin with slightly more than five minutes to go, our bench exploded in celebration. Chamique and Ace, giggling, gave each other elaborate mock Glamour Girl air kisses. ESPN caught it on camera, and would replay it for most of the next day.

I met Vivian for a postgame handshake underneath a scoreboard that read 92–60. "Our kids will understand defense after this," Vivian said. But in fairness to Rutgers, the lopsided margin was largely due to our home-like surroundings playing in Nashville, and partisan crowd. "Fifteen thousand people," Vivian joked, "and they all had the nerve to wear orange."

In the locker room, I congratulated the team, but I was businesslike. As much as the competitor in me wanted to celebrate, we couldn't. We weren't into the Final Four yet. Still, we felt a lot better. Mickie's stomach recovered enough that she was able to put away a plate of enchiladas at Rio Bravo later that night.

"Three to go," I told the team. "You're right where you want to be."

As soon as the team showered, we returned to courtside to scout the other semifinal, between Illinois and North Carolina. Tamika Catchings sat with her mother, Wanda, tensely pulling for Tauja Catchings. Tamika hoped Tauja and the Illini would advance, but she dreaded the prospect of a second meeting with her sister, too. It was a bittersweet night for her. Harvey and Wanda were both present, sitting in the stands. Wanda was worn out from flying back and forth across the country hectically, trying to watch both of her daughters play, and now here they were in the same place.

But then the Illini got beat. North Carolina won a cliffhanger, 80–74, and would be our next opponent. Illinois and Tauja were going home. In a way, they didn't envy North Carolina.

"Imagine," Illinois coach Theresa Grentz said wryly afterwards. "You fight like hell to win this game. And then you get to play Tennessee. There's a reward for you."

Q & A with Chamique Holdsclaw

(Junior forward, All-American)

How did you feel going into the North Carolina game?

I actually wanted a close game. I like the close ones.

What about when you trailed by twelve points with seven minutes to go?

I remember Kyra massaging my shoulders on the bench, saying, "Come on, Meek!" And Semeka was saying, "You've got to pick it up!" I just had this look on my face, like, "I'm trying." It was weird. My body felt sort of like I was in a lake or something, and I didn't understand why the shots weren't falling. I was thinking, "My teammates are depending on me." And I was thinking, if we lost, how was it going to be when I went home? And then I started thinking, "I cannot choke." I don't want to be the kind of player who chokes.

Did you feel pressured to get the freshmen through that game?

The only thing you can do is point them in the right direction. You can't grab them by the hand and pull them all the way through. They have to learn to help themselves, if they're going to achieve great things. And that's what happened. Like, look at Tree. She came up great in that game. If the North Carolina situation doesn't open your eyes to what you're capable of, what does? That's the standard Tree has set now. She knows she can't go back to being inconsistent. You can't give people a taste of something like that, and not accomplish it again.

CHAPTER TEN

The Forty-Minute Game

THERE WERE FISHHOOKS stuck in my eyes.

I was casting with my son on our dock. We dangled fishing rods and watched the muddy Little River swirl by, as blue herons stalked the far shore. We pulled back our rods, and flung the lines. But, somehow, the lines tangled as they whipped through the air. The hooks caught in my eyes, with two sudden, sharp stabs of pain. I stood perfectly still, too frightened to move. I knew if touched the hooks, or tried to remove them, I would lose my sight.

How, I wondered, would I be able to coach the team with fishhooks in my eyes? I called a doctor. He couldn't decide how to remove them. He said, "You'll just have leave them in for now. We'll wait until after the tournament to take them out."

I woke up, wincing. It was the morning of the North Carolina game. That evening we would meet the Tar Heels in the Mideast Regional final for the right to go to the Final Four.

Did I know, on some level, what was in store for us against North Carolina? Was there something I had failed to see? Did I sense that the longest, hardest game any of us had ever been involved in was yet to come?

I was exhausted. I had been dogged by uneasiness throughout the night.

I had awoken for the first time at 3:30 A.M., thinking I heard a knock on the hotel room door. I lay in bed, wondering if I imagined it. I stumbled to the door and opened it. The hallway was empty.

I got back in bed. My son, Tyler, inched over in his sleep, crowding me. I dozed. An hour later, I woke up hanging half off the bed, with Tyler on top of me. I slipped out of bed, jogged around to the other side, and laid down again.

Then I woke up from the fishhook dream. Tyler's feet were in my ribs.

I gave up. It was 6:30 A.M. I left Tyler in the hotel room with our nanny, Latina Dunn, still asleep in the next bed. I wandered into the lobby and scrounged a newspaper and coffee. Back in my room, I slid a tape of North Carolina into the machine, looking for something, anything, we might have overlooked in our scouting.

Eventually, Tyler woke up, and bounced around on the sofa next to me, playing Peter Pan. Recently, he had become obsessed with the J. M. Barrie classic. Everything was pirates. "Blast that Captain Hook!" he would announce in reply to any question.

Ordinarily, Tyler was pretty good at entertaining himself while I worked. But as I advanced the tape, Tyler jounced up and down on the sofa. "Tinkerbell, Tinkerbell," he babbled. I stared at the tape.

"Tinkerbell! Tinkerbell! Tinkerbell!" Tyler shouted at the top of his lungs. I dropped my head into my hands.

"I'll give you a thousand dollars not to do that," I said.

"Tinkerbell!" he screeched. "Tinkerbell! Tinkerbell!"

"Tyler, I cannot take that," I said.

"TINKERBELL!" he thundered.

I made him a deal. If he gave me twenty more minutes of quiet, I'd let him go out to a fast food joint for breakfast. He agreed. He buried his face in a pillow, trembling with supressed energy.

I knew how Tyler felt. He spent a lot of time cooped up in hotel rooms during the NCAAs, just like the rest of us. But it was tougher for him. First of all, the most unnatural thing in the world for a seven-year-old to do is to sit still. Plus, he was attention deprived. R.B. had to work at his bank in Sevierville during the week, and was commuting to Nashville for our games on the university plane. Tyler was cramped into a small hotel suite with me and Latina—and I was focused on the team. So Tyler got cheated.

I reluctantly sent him off to breakfast with Latina. "I guess tournament time is hard on all of us," I said, kissing him good-bye with a pang.

Apprehension hung over me. I decided to work it off. While I watched North Carolina on tape, I grabbed two fifteen-pound weights and did some sets of curls. Then I did lunges up and down the hotel hallway, until my arms and legs trembled and I was covered in sweat. Next, I lay on the floor and did situps until my stomach cramped.

At noon, the team came to the suite for a film session, after which we had a short practice at the arena. As we took the team through their paces, I kept mentally reviewing our game plan, wondering if we had Carolina covered. I was gripped by the concern that we might have let something get by us.

There were a couple of reasons why I was uneasy. First, I knew from bitter experience that the regional final was the hardest game of the tournament to win, mentally and emotionally. It was a game of critical importance—you couldn't get to a Final Four unless you won it—and yet it was too easy to look past it. Our freshmen had been steady all year in big games, but this was new for them. How would they react?

Second, there was the matter of our opponent. Carolina was one of the few teams in the country that came close to matching our speed and athleticism. They had fought through a difficult regular season with a 27–6 record, but they were playing their best ball now, scoring eighty points or more nightly in NCAA tournament action. They were led by an All-American in Tracy Reid, a strong, elegant, and emotionally charged senior who came in averaging twenty-one points per game.

The Tar Heels had threats at virtually every spot. Chanel Wright, a 6-foot junior, had game both inside and outside and was red hot, averaging in the twenties in tournament play. Juana Brown was a physical, driving freshman and a vicious defender. Jessica Gaspar was a hard-nosed guard who could create plays.

Last but not least, they had a 6-foot freshman point guard named Nikki Teasley, a player whom most experts ranked with our own freshmen as among the best in the game. Teasley was the real deal, a big and deceptively quick athlete who was already a star, averaging thirteen points. She had been recruited by virtually every program of note, except us. I had just one conversation with her. I asked her how many schools she was looking at. She said, "You're one of fourteen." It was the last time we spoke.

Carolina's head coach, Sylvia Hatchell, was also someone to reckon with. She had guided the Tar Heels to a national championship in 1994, and I had no doubt she would come with a smart game plan. I knew her well; we had been in graduate school together at Tennessee in the mid-70s. Hatchell told the media that she had watched our Alabama game — twice. I knew there was only one thing to learn from the Alabama game: we could be slowed down by physical play. I suspected it would be a rough game.

But most of all, I was concerned that Chamique and Kellie would feel enormous responsibility to get the freshmen to a Final Four. They had championship rings, while the freshmen didn't. They might try to shoulder too much responsibility.

That's why, after practice, I asked Tree and Ace to meet with me. I often met with one or two of the Lady Vols individually on the day of a game, in order to plant an idea. Sometimes you just have a feeling that a player could be important on a particular night, and you want her to be that much more alert. On this night, I believed it could be Tree or Ace, or both.

Ace met me in the hotel suite. "If anyone feels pressure tonight, it will be Kellie," I said. "You've got to be ready to step in and help her out. You have to be a leader." Ace nodded like always.

Tree came in next. We watched some of the Rutgers game, and I told her, "Kellie and Chamique are going to feel pressure, but there's no pressure on you. You've come up big in big games, and you need to come up big again tonight. They need help. You have a chance to help get Kellie and Chamique to Kansas City."

After Tree left, I wondered what to do next. There was still an afternoon to kill. I was too hyper to sit around the hotel.

I decided to work out again.

I ran on a treadmill and rode a stationary bike for an hour. On the way back to the hotel, I passed a music store. I dodged inside and bought a stack of eight CDs, including Sarah McLachlan, Paula Cole, and Shawn Colvin. Now I was current.

Next, I lost my MasterCard.

Back at the hotel, I tore the room apart looking for it. Somehow I had lost the card in the two blocks between the music store and the hotel. Finally, a hotel clerk called. They'd found it in the parking lot. I realized how manic my behavior was. Mercifully, R.B. arrived from Knoxville, and we went downstairs for the team pregame dinner.

We gathered in a conference room, where waiters served the traditional meal: chicken, pasta, baked potatoes, fruit, bread, and ice cream sundaes for the staff. "Is this Bluebell ice cream?" Mickie asked, wearily, for what seemed like the thousandth time.

The coaches sat together. I was wordless with fatigue and preoccupied with the game. But Mickie was silly. Silly with lack of sleep, and silly with tension.

"S-o-u-l, *what does that spell?*" she sang.

Next, she announced she was out of clean underwear. She turned her attention to Tyler.

"You got any extra drawers I can borrow?" Mickie asked Tyler.

Tyler grinned.

"Tyler," I said, "Your Aunt Mickie's not right."

Mickie ignored me. "Go back, go back, go back to the woods," she chanted. "Your coach is ugly and your team is no good."

Tyler rolled his eyes.

"Are you gonna let me talk about your Momma that way?" she asked.

I left them giggling and decided to get some peace and quiet. I called our team masseuse, Connie Maxwell, and asked her to work me over. I lay on the massage table, thinking about the game, going over every possible scenario.

Afterwards, I scanned a sheaf of notes from Al Brown. Al never let me go into a game without providing me with some important last-minute observations about our opponent. He would sit in his hotel room evaluating film and exploring options right up until it was time for the pregame meal. That's how thorough he was.

Meanwhile, Mickie and Holly went back to their rooms to watch the afternoon's televised NCAA games. Holly's room adjoined Mickie's. She was too jittery to be alone. After a while, she knocked on Mickie's door. "Can I take a nap in here?" she asked.

On the TV screen, Connecticut was in the midst of getting upset by North Carolina State. As the game got tight, Holly and Mickie began coaching both teams. Semeka stuck her head in the door. "Y'all are too loud," she declared. She jumped on top of Mickie, crushing her. Mickie laughed, but she kept her eye on the TV. UConn eventually lost, 60–52.

The upset trend that had started with Harvard knocking out Stanford had become a fully-fledged groundswell. Texas Tech and Old Dominion had fallen, and now UConn was out, too. We were the only No.1 seed left in the tournament.

Mickie just hoped it didn't happen to us.

➤ ➤ ➤

CAROLINA came out running.

We were the running team. Didn't Carolina know that? Several teams had tried to run with us, and failed. A running game was to our advantage—or so I thought.

On the first play of the game, Teasley skipped a long pass to Reid for a fast break layup.

On the second play of the game, Holdsclaw shot an airball.

Uh-oh, I thought.

And that's the way it went for the next thirty-three minutes. Carolina beat us down the court on almost every possession. They whirled past us, while we looked like slow motion versions of ourselves. Later on, Tennessee fans would ask me if our team was tired that night, and I would have to say no. It was simply that Carolina made us look slow.

"If you just win by one point tonight, we'll take it," I had told the team in the locker room before tip-off.

But I had never anticipated this.

There were games in which an invisible hand seemed to be in front of the basket, swatting away your shots. You never knew when it might happen, or why. All you knew was that it seemed to happen most often in big games.

And this game was one of them.

Carolina ran and ran. On every possession, they burst through our traps like water. They kicked the ball out and skipped it up the court for easy layups. As it grew more apparent that Carolina was bent on giving us a game, you could see the Lady Vols tense up.

Suddenly, we stopped scoring.

We missed eight shots in a row. For five minutes, we went without a single point. Fortunately, Carolina slowed down too, temporarily. With 6:52 left in the half, we were tied at 21–21. But the trend wasn't good. Chamique was scoreless for the last 11:59 of the first half.

Somehow, we led by six at the intermission, 33–27. But there was nothing comforting about it. "They outran us," Catchings said later. "And it shook us."

It was stiflingly hot in Memorial Gymnasium. The coaching staff had all perspired through our jackets. I could see dark spots on the back of Mickie's green gabardine blazer. Sweat ran off Al's chin. I wanted to take off my own jacket, but I knew my silk blouse was wet through.

At halftime, I went into the coaches anteroom, and put on some more Dry Idea.

Then I returned to the locker room and addressed the team. "I don't know what your problem is, but you better get it together," I said angrily. "I cannot believe our lack of commitment to defense. You know that of all times, you have to bring your defense to the gym in postseason. We have to get some second and third shots. The ball isn't falling for us, so you have to work for second and third opportunities."

I paused. "Now, *look*," I said. "Whatever you do, don't let them go on a run to start the second half. Don't you let them come out and score."

➤ ➤ ➤

BUT THAT'S EXACTLY what Carolina did.

They ran off the first seven points of the second half, including a three-point play from Tracy Reid.

The Tar Heels had a 34–33 lead, and all of the momentum.

A slow dread moved over me. It felt like all of the blood in my body had stopped flowing in one direction, and suddenly started flowing in another.

In Memorial Gymnasium, the benches are on the opposite baselines rather than on the sidelines, which means the coaches work the game from underneath the baskets. I prowled our bench angrily as I watched the Tar Heels inch away—no, run away—from us, literally. Meanwhile, the pro-Tennessee crowd of 14,848 grew more and more frantic.

Tracy Reid got another fast break layup. Holdsclaw missed her umpteenth jumper.

Carolina increased the lead to seven.

Nothing was going in for us. The ball rolled around the rim, or ticked off the front iron, or clanged off the neck. I wondered if it had somehow changed shape, or if the backboard was suddenly made of a harder substance than glass.

Let me put it this way: we wouldn't have hit water if we had fallen out of a rowboat.

Meanwhile, the Tar Heels weren't missing anything. They sank 64 percent of their shots in the opening minutes of the half.

I had seen this sort of thing before, and it was the most helpless situation in the world. There was no coaching them out of it, no magical strategic adjustment, no speech I could deliver to make us suddenly shoot better.

No matter what she did, Holdsclaw couldn't will the ball into the basket. After a quick jumper to start the half, she was absolutely scoreless. Chamique clearly wasn't herself. She said later she felt submerged—she felt like she was playing in a lake.

Meanwhile, her counterpart, Reid, was racking up fourteen second-half points.

I thought about what to do. Chamique had won countless games for us over three years. I couldn't just tell her to stop shooting. I didn't know if she needed a hug, or a jolt. At first, I tried to encourage her. "You'll start hitting," I promised her. "You're okay." But she didn't start hitting. So the next time she came to bench, I tried to shake her up.

"You're going to jump-shoot us right out of this tournament," I said.

The rest of the Lady Vols were getting more and more anxious by the second as we realized Chamique wasn't going to save us. And neither were the other Meeks. They were all missing. Catchings was on her way to sinking just four of thirteen shots for the game. Semeka had gone just four for twelve in the first half.

Even Kellie Jolly was zero for three. Nobody could do anything. It was as though the rim had grown smaller before our very eyes. It looked to us like it had been put in a dryer—it must have been 100 percent cotton and we didn't know it. Shot after shot fell away harmlessly.

The problem was simple.

The game was an extremely physical one. There was excessive contact on and off the ball. Every move to the basket was met with a forearm shiver. As a result, our players altered their shots, more worried about the contact than getting the ball in the basket. The hurried, herky-jerkiness of the Lady Vols signaled a team playing in a state of barely controlled panic.

I turned to Al.

"Is the contact as bad as I think it is?" I asked.

He said, "It's brutal."

There was another problem, too. As the game got tighter, so did we. Our guards tried to place their passes instead of whipping them. Our shots ticked off the rim because we were trying to cozy the ball in the basket instead of shooting it. Even our press was soft: instead of attacking as we had all year, we were trying to contain the Tar Heels.

We weren't playing to win, I realized. We were playing not to lose.

Reid got another layup.

Holly couldn't take it any more. She got up from her chair and stalked away.

I wandered down to the end of the bench. Holly crouched on the floor, pale.

"What are you doing?" I asked, incredulously.

"I'm trying to change our luck," she said.

I glanced over at Kyra. She was rocking back and forth, tensely.

"Well, Kyra," I said. "You got any suggestions?"

Kyra looked stricken.

➤ ➤ ➤

ASSISTANT COACHES have the most thankless job in the business. They work long hours and make crucial contributions under pressure, they do it for considerably less pay than the head coach, and they get absolutely no credit. But Mickie DeMoss deserved praise for that night. I leaned as heavily as I ever have on our assistants. Down the stretch, each made crucial contributions that determined the outcome of the game. But most especially, Mickie did.

She never stopped coaching, never stopped looking for the play or word of encouragement that might a difference. The bench was in a state of pandemonium. Both bands were blaring. The crowd sustained a steady roar that seemed to envelope all of our senses. But Mickie drew on a clipboard, she shouted in players' ears, she signaled adjustments and changes, and she kept me constantly aware of the flow. She whirled through a dozen offensive suggestions, constantly seeking the option that might work, probing for something we might execute.

Semeka came to the bench for a breather and flopped down next to

Mickie. She sucked air in and out desperately. She bit into her towel. She turned to Mickie and said, "What else can we do? Tell us something to *do!*"

Mickie fought the urge to say, "I don't *know* what to do!"

Instead she said, calm as could be, "Semeka, there's plenty of time."

There were less than nine minutes remaining.

Semeka said, "I'm ready. I'm ready to go back in. Tell Pat."

Mickie said intently, "Calm down. You need to use this time to get your breath back. Relax, watch what's going on, and learn from it. You have time. This game isn't over."

But nothing was really working. Nothing.

Holdsclaw came to the bench. Her arms were covered by welts and claw marks, and she had a hip pointer from being thrown to the court and landing on her side.

"I can't hold onto the ball, it keeps slipping," she said, breathlessly.

"Stop making excuses," I said, harshly. "Make plays!"

Carolina went up by ten.

I fought my own rising panic. I glanced at the clock. Eight and a half minutes to go. And we were going scoreless for minutes at a time.

At this rate, we wouldn't catch up.

I couldn't believe it. Surely our season wasn't going to end like this. All of the work, all of the talent, the publicity, and the growth of the game, was shrinking down to one tough night.

The previous night, I had lain awake reviewing all of the possible situations we could be in. I had mentally rehearsed this very circumstance, trailing badly late in the game. I reminded myself that I was the one person who had to remain calm and clear. I forced back the cold feeling in the pit of my stomach and tried to think.

We cannot lose, I thought. *I have got to do something to help them.*

But what? I cast around in my mind. A few years ago, we had been in a similar situation. In 1996, we met Virginia in a disastrous NCAA regional final, when nothing went right, nothing would fall. We trailed the Cavaliers by seventeen points with fourteen minutes to go. But, somehow, we came back and won it, 52–46. I revisited that game. What had we done? We had remained poised and in command of our emotions, I remembered. We kept telling the team we had time.

I told myself, *We're in that situation now and you have to be poised to give them what they need. Poise, poise, poise. Under no circumstances can you panic. It's all about what they need.*

My body language could send a message to the team. I desperately wanted to take off my jacket. But I couldn't. I had sweated through my blouse, and I didn't want the team to see it.

Less than eight minutes remaining.

I strolled down the baseline.

I leaned against the goalpost, casually, and crossed my arms.

➤ ➤ ➤

Up in the stands, my sister Linda couldn't believe her eyes. Weeks earlier Linda had bought a stack of nonrefundable airline tickets for our entire family to go to Kansas City.

Linda stared downwards, appalled, as I leaned against the goalpost. I looked entirely too relaxed. Linda opened her mouth in shock. Then she yelled at me.

"Trisha, quit leaning against that dang pole and coach! Do you know how much money I've spent?"

Linda turned to our athletics director, Joan Cronan. "Joan, tell her to coach!" Linda said. "Doesn't she know how much money I've spent?"

But unbenownst to Linda or anyone else, Joan had made another sizable wager on the Lady Vols. Ordinarily, Joan wasn't the riverboat gambler type, but, just as in Nashville, there was a huge demand for tickets and hotel rooms in Kansas City for the Final Four. Joan was afraid if she didn't act fast she wouldn't be able to accommodate some of Tennessee's most prominent boosters. So Joan guaranteed a block of one hundred hotel rooms at $125 a night. Plus, she had bought one hundred extra tickets at $90 each.

While Linda heckled me, Joan did the math in her head.

She had $34,000 riding on the game in nonrefundable rooms and tickets. And no way to explain the deficit if we lost.

She felt like throwing up.

Joan thought to herself, "I've got a lot more riding on this game than you do."

> > >

TYLER SUMMITT, on the other hand, was fast asleep.

My son had gazed at the scoreboard with about nine minutes to go, and his eyes had filled with tears.

"Aren't we going to Kansas City?" he had asked R.B. tremulously.

"It looks pretty bad," R.B. had said, gently.

So Tyler had pulled out his little pillow, and had put his head down on R.B.'s knees. He was surrounded by 14,848 screaming fans, but he had fallen asleep instantly, stretched across his daddy's lap.

As Tyler dozed, R.B. felt a little bit better. When Tyler slept, it was a good sign. We had never lost a game that he had slept through.

R.B. cradled Tyler, unable to see the action on the floor. All around him the crowd was on its feet, blocking his view. Next to him the governor of Tennessee, Don Sundquist, stood with his cap turned backwards for good luck.

Meanwhile, Latina was fighting with a raucous North Carolina fan who was already celebrating.

"Let me tell you something," Latina said, furiously. "Tennessee is *going* to Kansas City!"

"I don't think so," the Tar Heel cackled.

"Oh yes we are!" Latina insisted.

R.B. sighed. He decided to stay in his seat and let Tyler sleep for good luck.

> > >

BACK IN BRISTOL, Connecticut, the ESPN control center crew was caught up in the game action. They weren't supposed to root. They were supposed to be impartial television journalists and technicians. But finally, a Tennessee-friendly staffer could no longer hide his emotions.

He dropped to his knees on the floor of the control room. "Please God," he announced, "if you let Tennessee win, I swear I'll join a seminary."

➤ ➤ ➤

ALL UP AND DOWN Farringdon Avenue in Cleveland, TV sets were tuned to the Tennessee game. Bertha Randall sat in her living room, surrounded by neighbors and friends.

"This is going to take a lot of prayer," Bertha announced. "A *whole* lot of prayer."

She started praying.

➤ ➤ ➤

THE TAR HEELS' Jessica Gaspar banked a wild jumper off the glass. It went in.

Carolina by twelve.

Kellie Jolly turned to me, with her arms out helplessly.

"What can I do?" she said, beseeching. "Tell me, what can I do?"

"If your teammates don't start running the floor," I said, "there isn't anything you can do. We're going to get beat."

The officials called a television time-out. I glanced upwards. The score was 61–49.

I looked at the clock. It read 7:19 to go.

I will probably remember that number for as long as I live.

With 7:19 to go, everything changed. My heartbeat slowed and my awareness narrowed to nothing else but our team. I tried to gather my thoughts. I wasn't prepared to lose, I decided. And therefore I refused to think about it.

Instead, I thought about our players. About how much I loved them. About how much I respected them. About how much they deserved to win the championship. They had created thousands of new fans. They had overcome personal obstacles. They had been the best team in the country for thirty-six games. And they had been the best team I had ever coached. Period.

So what are you going to do about it? I thought.

Somewhere, underneath the sweat and the pandemonium, and the brain-twisting task of orchestrating the closing minutes of such a frantically paced game, I suddenly realized that I was enjoying myself. Even in the midst of all that, I was happy.

I had always been obsessed with coaching in big games. It was one thing that had kept me in the sport when the pay wasn't enough. A game like this was a source of deep pride to me. I had worked for twenty-four years to see this team come into being. I had walked into gyms so empty you could hear your own footsteps echo, so empty you could hear the radio announcer at courtside. There were nights when I had driven to the gym just hoping there would be enough of a crowd that it wouldn't be embarrassing. So to stand on the floor of an arena before a crowd of nearly 15,000 in a state of bedlam, with players of the character and caliber of the Lady Vols staring back at me, made me catch my breath with happiness.

I've had people tell me that the crowd roar in Nashville that night was the loudest noise they had ever heard from a basketball crowd. But the strange thing was, at that moment I didn't *really* hear it. I was faintly aware of a deafening wall of sound, but that's all. Later someone asked me, "How could you hear with the band playing so close to you?"

I said, "Where was it?"

"Right next to your bench."

I never really heard it, or saw it.

They played "Rocky Top" over and over.

Gooooooood old ROCKY-Top, Rocky-Top Teennnnnnessseeeeeee.

As I stood there, in that moment, the game occupied my whole body and mind. On every level of consciousness, I was searching for a way to win.

I still wanted to take my jacket off.

We had made just four of twenty-one shots in the second half. Holdsclaw had missed twelve of her last thirteen.

She had been scoreless for sixteen agonizing minutes.

We were down to it. It was now or never. I huddled with Mickie, Holly, and Al. While the staff talked, the team was having their own conversation.

They were screaming at each other.

Kellie Jolly strode over to bench, in a state of rage and frustration. She picked up the small orange footstool that I always sat on during time-outs.

Kellie, our quiet leader, our composed point guard, lost it. She slammed the stool on the ground, nearly splintering it. She whammed it so hard on the ground that her blond braid stood up straight in the air. Then she sat down, faced the team—and let them have it.

"We've got to run the floor!" she howled. "Listen to me! We've got to go. We've got to go, and we've got to go now!"

The rest of the Lady Vols just sat there, toweling off. Their eyes were glazed over. Kyra stood over them and joined in with Kellie.

"Are we going to Kansas City?" Kyra demanded.

No one answered her.

"Are we going to Kansas City?" Kyra demanded again.

"Are we going to Kansas City?" Kyra yelled, furious. "Are we going to Kansas City? Somebody answer me! Tell me. You *tell* me we're going to Kansas City!"

Finally, Tree Geter slowly swung her gaze to Kyra.

"We're going to Kansas City," Tree said, calmly, with assurance.

Kyra said, "Okay, then. We're going."

I stepped into the circle of players. They looked at me, expectantly. It was time to send a message. A manager handed me my clipboard.

I threw it.

I slammed it down. It struck the orange bench and catapulted upwards.

"Am I coaching the wrong team?" I demanded, the veins standing up in my neck. "Do we need to change uniforms? Should I be over there? You're letting them beat you at your own game! This is not the team I've coached all season. *Where* is that team?"

They stared back at me.

"Listen to that crowd," I said. "They're doing everything they can. So what are *you* going to do?"

While I talked, Kyra frantically massaged Chamique's shoulders.

I said, more calmly, but still shouting, "Y'all are going to Kansas City! Do you understand me? You deserve to be there. You've been the best team in the country all year long. The game needs you there, and you're going to be there. So you go back out there, and you fight. *You scratch, you claw, you do whatever you have to do.* But you're going to win this game. We have time to do it. But it has to start *now*."

There was no strategy to discuss any more. A comeback was a question of intensity. Just before we broke from the huddle, Semeka got in Chamique's face.

"You can't hide on us," Semeka said. "You've been our go-to player all year. Don't hide on us now. You've got to make plays."

"I know, I know," Chamique said.

"You been saying that all night!" Semeka said. "Now do something!"

Meanwhile Tree Geter was staring off intently. Mickie couldn't tell if Tree was out of it, or if she was so intensely focused she just didn't hear anything.

Mickie said, "Tree? Are you with us?"

Tree nodded, wordlessly.

Tree told me later what she was thinking. It was a simple thought: *I'm not ready to go home yet.*

➤ ➤ ➤

WHEN WE RETURNED to the court after the time-out, Tennessee had possession under the basket. As our players took their places, it struck me once again that we had four pure freshmen in the lineup. Ace gathered them together. "We're not freshmen anymore," she thought. "We can't play like freshmen. Pat wouldn't have us out here otherwise."

The referee handed the ball to Ace on the baseline. She looked for an opening to inbounds it.

She found Tree and fired a pass. Tracy Reid lunged for a steal, but Tree grabbed the ball from the air, dodged Reid, and turned towards the basket.

Tree put the ball on the floor and drove straight to the hoop. It was as if she were trying to get to Kansas City in one bound.

Tree rose towards the rim. Carolina frantically shifted its defense to meet her. But it was too late. Tree put in the layup—and drew the foul.

The crowd exploded.

Tree screamed and pounded her fist against her chest. Ace embraced her.

Then Tree calmly stepped to the line and sank the free throw, for a three point play.

On the bench, Kyra forgot all about her knee and leaped in the air. "It is *on* now!" she hollered.

The band was going crazy.

Goooooood *old ROCKY TOP, Rocky-Top Teennnnnnessseeeeeee!*

Chamique hauled down a rebound, and was fouled by Juana Brown. Chamique went to the free throw line and sank two, to cut it to seven, 61–54.

Reid took the ball inside for Carolina. But Tree suddenly rose up and swatted the air in front of her. Reid altered her shot, and missed—and Tree came down with the rebound.

I glanced at the clock: 6:50 to go.

Catchings missed a three. It vibrated in the hoop, and then, tormentingly, popped out.

Story of the night, I thought, as the ball rolled off the rim.

Suddenly, there was Tree *again*. She surged upwards out of nowhere, seized the rebound, and gently put it back in the basket.

We had scored seven straight points in forty-eight seconds. Score: 61–56.

On the bench, Kyra turned to our trainer, Jenny.

"Oh, Jenny," she said, putting her hand to her chest. "I need some heart pills."

➤ ➤ ➤

IN COLUMBIA, South Carolina, Tree's mother, Joanne, shrieked in exultation. She stood up from her chair, and ran in a circle, then bolted out of her front door, and shrieked again into the night. She threw her hands in the air.

➤ ➤ ➤

ACE CLEMENT was in command.

She barreled down the baseline, and drew the defense to her. She whipped a sharp pass to Catchings alone under the basket.

We had scored eight of the last nine points to cut it to 62–58.

Fortunately, Carolina stopped finding Tracy Reid. She only touched the ball in the paint once in the final seven minutes. Meanwhile, we worked away at the lead. Holdsclaw grabbed a rebound and streaked up court. She was tripped from behind by Gaspar, and was awarded two free throws. She drained them.

Now it was a two point game. I checked the clock: 5:07.

We pressed.

Carolina inbounded the ball to Teasley, who tried to deal it off—but Catchings made a leaping interception of the pass. Catch wheeled, and slapped the ball to Ace, who faked a pass to the middle of the floor, and instead flicked the ball to Holdsclaw, who snuck behind the Carolina defense for a layup.

Tie game.

Randall and Holdsclaw chest-bumped, howling. The roar from the crowd was a gigantic wave. I couldn't make myself heard, so I just gestured.

Press again.

The roar gathered force. Ace screamed and pointed at her temple. "Focus," she screamed, clenching her fists. "Focus!"

Tracy Reid tried to inbound the ball from the sideline. Suddenly, Holdsclaw elevated and simply plucked the ball out of the air—our second steal in the space of twelve seconds.

Holdsclaw whirled and drove straight to the paint for a difficult touch jumper.

Tennessee was up by two, 64–62.

But only for a moment: Carolina's Chanel Wright hit a pull-up jumper, to tie it again at 64. I crouched down. If ever we needed a basket from a Meek, we needed it now.

Ace whisked the ball up court to Semeka, who saw a baseline path. It was her, alone, against three Carolina defenders. She never hesitated. She accelerated to the baseline, and pumped in a leaning bank shot to give us the lead again.

My mouth fell open. It was a huge reply, a critical score at a critical time. *Okay*, I thought, *now we're playing to win*.

We had outscored Carolina 17–3 in the space of four minutes.

But it wasn't over yet. We led by just a point, 68–67, with 2:48 to go. Time-out.

In the coaches' huddle, we had a serious discussion. I wanted to switch to a zone defense. For most of the night, we had been in our stock man-to-man scheme. But now I wanted to change, hoping to confuse Carolina. Mickie was opposed to the plan but I called it anyway.

Carolina hesitated—and turned the ball over. At the other end, Tree Geter retrieved yet another rebound for a put-back layup. "Before I knew it I saw these long arms come out of nowhere," Holdsclaw marveled afterwards.

Tennessee led by 72–67 with under a minute to go.

But if the zone defense was a good call for one possession, I stayed with it a beat too long. Chanel Wright hit a prayerful three-pointer with twenty-one seconds to go. Time-out. Score: 72–70, Tennessee.

Mickie leaned into my face and said, "We stayed in it too long, we need to go back to man." I hesitated. "Go back to man," Mickie insisted, almost angrily.

I signaled the change.

Next, Holly grabbed me. The sound in the arena by now was such a steady sustained roar that we had to scream to hear each other. Holly gripped me by the shoulders and put her mouth to my ear.

"Get Jolly in the game for free throws," she said.

I looked around. Holly was right—our best free throw shooter, Kellie, was still on the bench.

I nodded gratefully and made the substitution.

Catchings inbounded the ball to Kellie.

Carolina committed a desperation foul—against Kellie.

So Kellie Jolly went to the free throw line. Kellie, who had had an ineffectual game shooting, stood at the free throw line with two shots, and the game in her hands.

And she made both.

Five seconds to go. Carolina's Teasley had no choice but to hurl a desperate three—but it fell short, and the game was over.

The noise reached an unimaginable crescendo. Our players leaped around the court, in frantic jubilation. They chest-bumped, they folded each other in suffocating hugs.

Someone handed Tree a sign that said "Kansas City, 529 miles." She paraded around the court.

Up in the bleachers, R.B. shook Tyler. "Wake up," he said. "Let's go help your mom celebrate."

Down on the floor, I turned to the staff.

"Do you believe this?" I said. "We're going to Kansas City and we're going to win us a championship."

➤ ➤ ➤

We were emotionally spent. After the game, Chamique's arms were raw with welts and scratches, and her hands were so sore she could barely grip a soda can. Her right arm was heavily wrapped from her thumb to her forearm, and she had an ice pack on her hip. But she was radiant with relief. And she had been a hero in the end, hitting twelve of thirteen free throws down the stretch.

"We won ugly," I told the team. "But we survived and advanced. It counts and we'll take it. You never quit. And that's why you're going to the Final Four."

On our way out of the arena, I saw my parents. My father grabbed me and gave me a double clutch hug, nearly cracking my ribs.

"I about gave up," he said. "I believe that's the best coaching job you've ever done."

In the closing seconds, he admitted, he had impulsively hugged the lady in the seat next to him. I laughed.

"It took me forty-three years," I teased him, "but it only took her a forty-minute game."

Down the street from Memorial Gym, an old red neon sign kept a steady glow. It said, "Rotiers." It was a landmark restaurant with leatherette booths, formica tables, a grease-blackened grill, and photos of country western stars on the wall.

It was almost one in the morning, and the coaching staff was starved. We hadn't eaten since our ice cream sundaes the previous afternoon. We called over and the Rotiers kitchen agreed to stay open for us.

Inside, the bartender greeted us with cheeseburgers and heaping plates of onion rings. We slumped in a booth. On a television mounted in a corner, highlights of the game played on the late-night news. Bleary eyed, I watched a replay of Semeka Randall driving the baseline, to hit that gorgeous leaning bank shot again.

I wanted to hug her through the screen.

Semeka had hit four of seven critical shots in the second half to keep us alive, and wound up with twenty points. Tree Geter scored eleven points, seven of them in the last seven minutes, and grabbed eight rebounds. Catchings had four steals. Jolly had three steals. And Holdsclaw, on one of the worst shooting nights of her career, going twenty-two full minutes with only two points, still mustered a game high twenty-nine points and nine rebounds. They all deserved credit for a great comeback.

It's a forty-minute game, I thought. If it's a twenty-minute game, we win. If it's a thirty-three-minute game, *they* win. But it's a forty-minute game.

➤ ➤ ➤

I STAYED UP until 4 A.M. watching a replay of the game in my hotel suite. Then we rose at 7 A.M. to pack for the bus ride back to Knoxville. We were all exhausted. I figured I had slept a total of five hours in two days. And we would have just one day to repack and fly to Kansas City.

On the bus, we ate Egg McMuffins, swallowed from extra large cups of coffee, and made notes on legal pads. We were already working on our next game: we would meet Arkansas in the NCAA Final Four in Kansas City. In the other semifinal, Louisiana Tech would meet North Carolina State.

But much as we tried to look ahead, we couldn't help going back over the events of the previous night. Mickie was still drawing, trying to figure out something that might have worked.

"That was the longest game of my career," I said.

"We got to fix Catchings' three," Mickie said. "It's broke."

"I kept us in a zone too long," I worried.

In the back of the bus, our players dozed or watched a movie, *The Peacemaker*, on video. I hated to make them practice when we got home. But they were so sore that they needed to move around. It would be the best thing for them.

Tamika wandered up from the back of the bus, and leaned over Al's shoulder, playing with the collar of his shirt. She sat down next to him and took his hand, and touched his championship ring from the previous year.

"We're going to get us a ring, Al," she said.

Al examined Tamika's beat-up arms. "Two more games, if you take care of business," he said.

"I've got to get stronger," she said, urgently. "*We've* got to get stronger."

We pulled up to Thompson-Boling Arena in the early afternoon and gathered in the locker room, where we sprawled around on the floor, coaches included.

"How do y'all feel about what happened last night?" I asked them, hoarsely. My voice was gone.

"Tired," someone said.

We laughed.

"Well, I just want you to know that I am so proud for you," I said. "If you can do that, you can win a championship."

Then I told them something I knew from long experience about the Final Four. "Two teams will show up just happy to be there," I said. "Not us. Don't be one of the teams that's just happy to be there."

I paused. "Now what can we learn from last night?"

Silence.

"That everybody will play the game of their lives against you," I said. "There is a lot of good to take away from that game. You answered all the questions. What will happen if Holdsclaw has a bad night? Now we know. What will happen if Tennessee falls behind? You answered that, too. You found a way to win. You refused to lose."

I turned to Chamique and Kellie. I wanted them to speak to the team. They had reached their third straight Final Four, and they knew better than anyone in the room what it took to bring home a ring.

"I'm *accustomed* to winning championships," Chamique said. "I'm not just happy to be there."

Kellie said, "I'm not satisfied either. I want more."

We broke up the meeting and went out on the court. "We'll keep it short but intense," I promised them. They practiced hard. The only sign that they were exhausted was some arm weariness.

After practice, I gave them a day off. We would reconvene twenty-four hours later for a charter flight to Kansas City. I didn't want them looking at or thinking about a basketball in the meantime. I went over the schedule.

"If we win the first game—" I started to say.

Ace slapped me playfully.

"No *if*," she said. "We've worked too hard to say 'if.'"

With that, we all went home to do our laundry.

➤ ➤ ➤

BUT FIRST, I had a 4:30 meeting with Tyler's first-grade teacher. In the car, I blinked at my bloodshot eyes in the rearview mirror, and put on lipstick. I had to find a way to go from being a coach to a concerned, proper mother.

The meeting with Tyler's teacher was about fighting. Shortly before we had departed for Nashville, Tyler had gotten in a playground scuffle, typical kid stuff.

We had a pleasant talk, the three of us. Afterwards, as Tyler and I drove home, we discussed the problem.

"You don't start fights, right?" I said.

"Right," he said.

"Now, what do you do if someone pushes you first?" I said.

He looked at me.

"You push 'em back," I said firmly.

Q & A with Kellie Jolly (Junior guard)

What did Pat say to you before the national championship game?

She told me I needed to step it up. She pulled me over, and she said, "You're not being Kellie Jolly. Get that worried look off your face, and play like Kellie Jolly." She was pretty critical of me, actually. I was trying to focus, and probably overdoing it.

Did she yell at you?

No, it was the low thing, which is worse, actually, a lot worse. Under her breath she is telling you that you aren't performing up to your potential. She's questioning you. She said, "Are you going to respond?" And I said, "Yes, ma'am."

During the warm-up you told Chamique you were hot.

I know that at practice that day I couldn't hit anything. But I told Holly, "That's okay, I'll shoot good tonight." And I really felt that way.

How loose was the team?

Well, on the bus everyone usually listens to their own music. But Kyra put in "When We Were Kings." And I got cold chills. I love that song. Me and Kyra were back there just singing away. It was just another game. We were just going to go play another game. It just happened to be one for a national championship.

Did you realize that you were hitting from NBA range?

No, I did not. I didn't know how far out I was shooting—not until I watched the tape afterwards. And I was like, Oh—(laughs)—get out! What was I thinking of? If Pat had caught me missing those, I would have been sitting on the bench.

CHAPTER ELEVEN

K.J. and the Final Four

I wish I could put music in these pages. It was as though the last few days of the 1997–98 season were set to a score. It sounded like Puff Daddy and Kellie Jolly singing a hymn together.

I woke up on the morning of March 25 still fighting fatigue. I drank coffee, switched to Diet Coke, and then chased it with iced tea. I did laundry, studied some tape of Arkansas, dealt with the demand for game tickets from family and friends, and packed. We had two games, three banquets, and numerous press conferences to plan for. I ended up with three suitcases.

Early in the afternoon, R.B. drove Tyler and me to the airport for the team charter flight to Kansas City. R.B. would work again through the week at the bank and join us later. As I settled into my seat on the plane, I realized that my hands were trembling. Caffeine poisoning?

In the seat next to me, Tyler played with a small army of little men. Soldiers, spacemen, and aliens marched across my tray table. After a while, Tyler complained that he couldn't find two of them. I crawled on the floor of the plane, searching for them.

The hardest part of being a mother, I decided, was looking for all the little men.

The flight was uneventful. Semeka, bored, wandered up and

down the aisle. She stopped at Mickie's seat and tapped her on the shoulder.

"You don't stop to talk to me?" she asked, playfully.

"I'm too important," Mickie said.

"I see," Semeka said, downcast.

"Come here baby doll," Mickie said, holding out her arms.

Semeka brightened, and accepted a hug. Then she leaned over the aisle and poked me in the stomach, testing my abdominals.

We landed in Kansas City, loaded yet another bus, and drove to the Crowne Plaza Hotel, where we would spend the next few days. Signs and banners along the main boulevard welcomed the teams.

"There's a Final Four going on in this town," Mickie said.

At the hotel, I set up camp in a large hotel suite. Outside my door, I could hear our players giggling and tunes thumping. We were all staying on the same hallway. I could already tell it was going to be like a dormitory, only one with room service.

While our managers hooked up the VCRs, I loaded Diet Cokes into the refrigerator.

"Well, my face is breaking out," Holly announced, "so we're going to be all right."

It never varied. Holly's skin would break out from the stress. I was comforted by the announcement. One more superstition in place.

We had a standard drill for the Final Four. From here on in we would rarely leave the suite except to go to practice, a game, or an official function. In the center of the conference room we would use as head-quarters was a large easel with sheets of drawing paper, where we would form strategy in nightlong sessions. But our basic message to the Lady Vols was a simple one: there were no bad teams left.

We didn't want the team to think about that too hard—we wanted them relaxed that first night. We sent them off to shop and to have dinner. They wandered through a nearby shopping plaza, they milled around in The Gap, and lingered in a body and bath shop, smelling scents. They discovered a cosmetics store, and got makeovers.

Back at the hotel, the coaches were already fine tuning the game plan for our first opponent, Arkansas. We would have only the next day, a Thursday, to practice and prepare for the Razorbacks, who knew us well from SEC conference play. We clustered around the easel, drawing schemes.

We made no secret any more of the fact that we were desperate to see this team go undefeated.

"I'll do anything," I announced to our assistants. "I'll strip. I'll get a tattoo. I'll get a technical. I'll do whatever it takes to help them win a title."

➤ ➤ ➤

LATE THAT NIGHT, the phone rang in Chamique's hotel room, waking her up.

"I'm your number one fan," a man's voice said. "I'm down in the Crowne Court bar, and I'd like to meet you."

Chamique hung up and rolled over.

➤ ➤ ➤

OUR FIRST DAY IN KANSAS CITY was a long one of practice, strategy meetings, and press interviews, followed by an autograph session and a mandatory team banquet. While I did a television interview with ABC's *Good Morning America*, Tyler sat in a corner and patiently drew pictures.

He held up a sheet of paper with two stick figures on it.

"What's that?" someone asked him.

"That's Mommy yelling at the officials," he said.

After practice, the team was escorted to a main hallway of Kemper Arena for the autograph session. We weren't prepared for the mob that greeted us. Children swirled around our legs and pressed up against the autograph table; lines formed down the hallway, and out the door.

Our players scribbled their signatures faster and faster, until they reached an almost mechanical speed. While they tried to keep abreast of the demand, a guy worked his way through the crowd and sidled up to Tamika.

He handed her a card. Still scribbling, she glanced down at it.

He was an agent.

"Call me," he whispered to her.

Another guy cozied up to Chamique. He handed her a picture of himself.

Chamique started to discard the picture when she saw writing on the back. She held it up.

"I want to be your man," he had written.

➤ ➤ ➤

THAT NIGHT we went to a mandatory banquet welcoming the participants to the Final Four. On the team bus, the players rocked in the back to Puff Daddy. Al boarded the bus in an exquisite gray suit and a pair of silver shades. The team shrieked and fell about. "Ohhhhhhh, Al," they said. Then Mickie got on the bus. She danced down the aisle and dropped her jacket off her shoulder and spun in a circle. They screamed.

At the banquet, Robin Roberts of ESPN cornered Chamique.

"Okay, I want to know," Robin said. "Can Pat be as bad as that cover picture on *Sports Illustrated?*"

Chamique deadpanned, "Some days."

After the banquet, Tree Geter snuck on to the bus ahead of the rest of us. She sat in the driver's seat like a little kid, happily spinning the steering wheel and playing with the door controls.

Then she got a bright idea. Whenever someone made the mistake of walking in front of the windshield, she blasted the horn at them.

Semeka was the first to amble in front of the bus. Tree hit the horn. Semeka grabbed her ears, bolted into the bus, and slugged Tree in the arm. Then she went to the back and put in a CD, and started dancing. The rest of the team filed aboard and joined her. Music vibrated throughout the bus.

Still in the driver's seat, Tree eyed me as I crossed the street.

I was strolling by the front fender when an enormous blast hit me like a fist in the ear. I nearly jumped out of my skin. And then, I died laughing.

I climbed in the bus, still wailing with laughter.

"I'll bench your butt," I threatened her.

Suddenly, in the back of the bus, I saw my son.

My golden child. My prince, my boy.

His coat and tie were off, and his shirt was unbuttoned. He was pouring sweat and he was hip-hopping and windmilling his arms. The players were standing around him, clapping rhythmically and chanting, "Go Tyler, go Tyler."

He was jamming to Puff Daddy.

I've lost him, I thought resignedly.

As far as I could tell, this team was completely unconscious of the fact that we were at the Final Four. They thought it was just a dance party.

➢ ➢ ➢

THAT NIGHT, as I was preparing for bed, I felt like I was coming down with something. A flu was going around. I swallowed some homeo-pathic cold medicine, but it didn't agree with my stomach.

"Mama, are you going to throw up?" Tyler asked.

"I don't know," I said.

"Don't do it on me," he said.

➢ ➢ ➢

ON THE MORNING of the Arkansas game, I went to the lobby for my usual large styrofoam cup of coffee. There, I found Robert Geter loung-ing on a sofa. He had driven all the way to Kansas City from Columbia, an eighteen-hour trip. He was staying in a hotel across town, and he had barely seen his daughter since he had arrived. Typically, due to the hectic schedule, the most a Lady Vol parent could hope for during the Final Four was a quick breakfast or an early dinner—in fact, I could see Harvey Catchings waiting for Tamika across the lobby.

Tree was so focused on practice and meetings that she didn't have much time for visiting. But she told him on the phone, "Daddy, we're going to win this thing."

I chatted with Robert for a moment, and invited him upstairs. But he didn't want to bother Teresa, he said. He knew she had a lot to do to prepare.

He handed me spending money for Teresa.

"Just see that she gets this," he said.

➤ ➤ ➤

Semeka Randall body-slammed me.

It was early in the afternoon, and we were in the locker room getting ready for our final practice, when suddenly two muscular arms crept around me from behind, and locked like a vise. I felt myself rising slowly off the ground.

Now, I am almost six feet tall.

"Randall!" I said. "Put me down."

She kept lifting me, until I thought my ribs might crack. Then she flipped me around sideways, cradling me like a baby. "Randall!" I warned her.

She dropped me to the floor.

It was like falling in an elevator.

I lay on the ground in a state of disbelief. I had just been body-slammed by a pure freshman. I, Pat Summitt, veteran head coach and wife and mother of one, was pinned on the floor by an eighteen-year-old imitating Hulk Hogan.

Every player in the locker room gasped. Kellie said, low, "Pat's going to kill her."

But I couldn't kill her. I was too much in shock to move. Then I started laughing, helplessly.

At least I knew this team was relaxed.

➤ ➤ ➤

ALL EXCEPT for one player.

Kellie Jolly was uptight. Normally, Kellie had the most calm, open demeanor on the team. But ever since we had boarded the charter flight, Kellie had worn a frown. It wasn't a good sign. There was a difference between being focused and being tense. When Kellie was tense she tried to guide the ball around the court instead of letting the game flow. And when that happened we *all* got tense—witness the North Carolina game.

I needed to shake the anxiety out of her. When we got back to the hotel after practice, I pulled her off of the elevator, and we stood in the hallway talking.

"Get that worried look off your face," I said. "You've looked worried ever since we got here. What's wrong with you? You're not being Kellie Jolly."

As soon as I said it, she relaxed a little. But I knew what was eating at her. Kellie was assuming the burden of pressure for all of us. Deep down, Kellie was one of the most driven people on the team. I knew how badly she wanted a third championship.

Kellie had a secret. In her mind, she was pursuing a record. Kellie had told me as a freshman that she intended to win an unprecedented four straight national championships. If that sounded like a fantasy at the time, here she was with a legitimate shot at it. I remembered what she said to me on the sideline as we won her first title, in 1996. "One down," she said that night, "three to go."

I understood what was going through Kellie's mind. But I wanted her to relax.

"We're okay," I said. "We're right where we want to be. You need to go have some fun."

Kellie just stared up at me seriously, like always.

"Yes, ma'am," she said.

➤ ➤ ➤

THAT NIGHT, I rode to Kemper Arena in a police car. I had to be there early to do an interview with ESPN, so the police officer who was our official team escort offered to take me over. I climbed into his squad car.

The officer said, "Buckle up."

I said, "I do every time, officer, I swear."

The officer looked me over.

He said, "So is that what you're wearing to the game?"

I said, "Yeah. You want to swap outfits?"

He laughed and started the car. I pulled out my makeup bag.

I wrenched his rearview mirror towards me.

"Mind if I borrow this?" I said to the officer.

He grinned.

I started putting on eyeliner.

➤ ➤ ➤

BACK AT THE HOTEL, the Lady Vols wove through the throngs of supporters in the lobby and boarded the bus. As they drove to the arena, a manager punched in a videotape. It was part of our tournament pregame ritual to show the team a highlight tape cut to music.

On mounted TV screens throughout the bus, the team watched sequence after sequence of themselves in action. It was like seeing an MTV video with a basketball theme. The tune was "Catch Us If You Can."

As I awaited the team's arrival at the arena, I watched Louisiana Tech and N.C. State play in the first semifinal game. I sat in the back of the press room and made notes on my legal pad. Tech dominated State, 84–65, and they looked all-world doing it. I felt queasy.

I told myself, "You can't worry about them right now. Focus on Arkansas."

Our first task was to get by the Lady Razorbacks. We had beaten them handily in a regular season game at home in January, 88–58, but they had seriously elevated their game since then. Every single one of them was scoring well above her average in tournament play. They had a tough little point guard, Christy Smith, who, despite having split her lip open four times during the season, was now on a roll. She had played for seventy-nine straight minutes without committing a turnover. Their 6-feet-1 post player, Karyn Karlin, was throwing down twenty points a game.

There was a strained air in the pregame locker room. In some ways, a semifinal game was more pressured than the championship game. For all of our victories, a loss now to Arkansas would still mark the season as a failure.

I decided to take my own advice to Kellie Jolly, and loosen up. So I played a joke on Chamique.

I told our masseuse, Connie Maxwell, to swipe Chamique's video camera. All through the postseason, Chamique had taped everything. She was making a documentary, she claimed.

I teased my hair straight up from my head. It looked like I had been electrocuted. Connie turned the camera on me.

"Hey Chamique," I said, waving, "this is how I look right before the game when I get really nervous."

➤ ➤ ➤

WE CAME OUT COLD AND FLAT. It may have been the pressure, or it may have had something to do with the fact that the flu was going around. Before the game, I had a team doctor check everyone over. He stood out in the hallway, peering into ears, noses, and throats. Kellie was the most sick. She sat on the bench during the warmup, swigging a cold remedy.

The Lady Razorbacks stayed with us throughout the first half, thanks to their harassing defense. We were plagued by an inability to get easy shots in the paint, and we had nine turnovers, a fact that made me wince with distaste. And no one was hitting cleanly.

Arkansas was within eight of us with a few seconds left in the half, when Chamique kicked the ball out to Kellie, who squared up at the three point circle. Kellie buried the shot at the buzzer to jolt us out of the doldrums. We jogged into the locker room leading 39–28, finally feeling good about ourselves.

In the second half, it was as though that shot of Kellie's had freed something up in the Lady Vols. Only four seconds had elapsed when Holdsclaw hit a pull-up jumper to send us on a 13–1 scoring tear. Chamique's layup with 17:11 still to go gave us a twenty-three-point lead, and the Razorbacks never came within twenty again.

We were in the championship game. But in the locker room, there was only a brief moment of congratulations. We had just one day to prepare for La. Tech. "Take showers, eat, and go to bed," I said. "Sweet dreams."

Meanwhile, on ESPN, Theresa Grentz of Illinois and Geno Auriemma of Connecticut tried to summarize the versatility and athleticism of our Tennessee team, and to explain why we were the overwhelming favorites to win the title. I thought they summed it up as well as anyone.

Theresa said, "If you can get one player who shoots off the dribble, you've got yourself a gold mine. They've got three. If you can solve the Holdsclaw riddle, which most people can't, great. Then you've got to deal with the rest of them."

Geno said, "They're not like any team you play against, and you can't prepare for them. Their offense starts when they shoot the ball. When it comes off the rim, that's when they start playing. Their defense *is* the beginning of their offense. When they're on defense, and you think you're fine, that's when you're in trouble."

➤ ➤ ➤

ON OUR WAY to the team bus, Kellie stopped to talk to a tall, lean, straightbacked young man with close-cropped blond hair. He was Jon Harper, her boyfriend. While the rest of the team trouped past, Kellie put down her gear bag and stared into his eyes.

Kyra called out, "Coach! Kellie's not focusing."

➤ ➤ ➤

WHILE THE PLAYERS SLEPT, I sat in my hotel suite late at night, worrying myself sick about La. Tech. I flipped on the TV and pushed a tape in.

My family milled around the suite. My sister Linda wandered in and out, and so did assorted brothers, parents, nephews, and nieces. R.B. had arrived on the school plane with university president Dr. Joe Johnson, who regularly attended our games. R.B. ordered sandwiches while Tyler ran around with his cousins, shrieking. I barely noticed them. I talked to the air. A stranger would have thought I was crazy.

"Okay, everybody," I said, "what do you see here? Y'all watching the low post?"

I stared at the tape, hoping Tech would look human to me before I went to bed.

➤ ➤ ➤

WE HAD TWENTY-FOUR HOURS to scout Tech down to their shoe and shirt sizes. The coaching staff sat around the easel, taking turns drawing options on it. The suite was trashed with empty food cartons, fruit baskets, coffee cups, aluminum cans, and unread newspapers. There were stacks of videotapes and scouting reports everywhere.

A transcript of our strategy session would have been fairly unintelligible. You would have heard a lot of rustling and crunching noises, the sounds of Mickie, Holly, and Al eating Cajun-spiced pretzels. The conversation went something like this:

"Stack middle."

"Two man screen on the ball. Catchings on the step out."

"They slide behind deep . . ."

"They're going to sag *here*. . . ."

"That's right, that's right."

". . . and she flares."

"That's good."

"I need salt."

We huddled over the video machines and the easel until we were pale with lack of sun and lack of sleep. I wanted our team to know every twitch La. Tech made.

Al said, "We've got to get it in their heads that they have to run the floor from paint to paint, and I mean run."

Mickie said, "That number 35 hauls ass, let me tell you. Sorry. Is Tyler here?"

I said, "We've got to have legs. I want legs."

"I don't want La. Tech to get the three-pointer," Mickie said.

"Well, they're going to score, so get ready," I said.

"I don't want 'em to score," Holly said, bridling. "At all."

"That's right," Mickie said. "I want a shutout."

≻ ≻ ≻

IT WAS ALL a head game now.

We had played La. Tech before. We knew what they would do, and they knew what we would do: we would both run.

Tech posed, if anything, a more dangerous problem than they had early in the season. They had five different players averaging in double figures. Alisa Burras, their post, was racking up eighteen points and ten rebounds a game, and she was just the start of their offense. Tamicha

Jackson, their blazingly fast guard, was tearing up the opposition for fifteen points, and LaQuan Stallworth had doubled her average since we had last met, to sixteen points.

Player to player, we matched each other in quickness and athleticism. In fact, the edge might even go to the Lady Techsters. They could rattle off a lot of points in a short period—they had scored nineteen points off fast breaks in their semifinal victory over North Carolina State.

You never felt safe with a team like that. They could launch threes and fast breaks and be right back in the game.

The Lady Vols *had* to get off to a fast start. If we didn't run the floor, we were dead. North Carolina had proven that. By gosh, we had better know what was coming at us, I thought. There were no more surprises—at this point, the job was as much a matter of psychology as it was strategy, of preparing our players mentally and emotionally to finish what they started. I intended to knock any lingering overconfidence out of our team.

So I decided to make an impression on the Lady Vols.

Mickie and Holly spent hours splicing together a tape. It showed sequence after sequence of La. Tech romping up and down the floor as if they had wings. It was a brilliant bit of filmmaking. As we screened it, I could feel the mood of our team change, from cocksure to hesitant, to apprehensive.

The tape ended.

"Well, if that isn't a picture for you, I don't know what is," Holly announced.

I stared the team down. I was direct.

"If y'all run the floor like you did against North Carolina, you don't deserve to win," I said. "You can go home at your own expense. You'll have until October to rest your legs. You want this game, you'll find the energy to get your butt down the floor faster than them."

The team filed out of the suite quietly.

But I was still concerned. The Techsters would almost certainly try to put a chokehold on the Three Meeks. We couldn't afford a no-show from any of our players.

And Kellie Jolly was still not quite herself.

➤ ➤ ➤

EVERY ONCE IN A WHILE you meet yourself in a player. That's how it was with Kellie and me—we just knew each other right away. From the day I first recruited her out of Sparta, Tennessee, I recognized her. The small farming town in the Tennessee foothills. The quiet, hardworking father. The modest brick house, and the girl inside of it with too much ambition for her circumstances. When I stood on her doorstep, I could have been standing on my own.

Kellie and I didn't have to say much. We tended to communicate via looks and nods.

We had profoundly different temperaments, of course. Kellie was as placid as I was tumultuous. She had rarely raised her voice in three years, while mine was raised for the better part of nearly every day. But we thought alike. It seemed that no sooner did I have a notion than Kellie Jolly was already putting it in motion on the court.

"It doesn't matter how loud the gym is, I can hear Pat," Kellie said once. "I'm so tuned in to her voice. I may not hear anybody else, but I hear her."

As player, she didn't look like much at first glance. She was an upright 5-feet-10, straightbacked, with a tight blond braid and clear blue eyes. It was hard to describe what she brought to the team, or to quantify how valuable it was. You couldn't always pinpoint her contributions in the postgame statistics, but she was vital to us. Chamique Holdsclaw called her "our unsung hero."

With Kellie you always knew what you would get. I never questioned what mood she would show up in. Every day she came into the gym with the exact same attitude, ready to give you absolutely everything she had in her. We could count on her. As a result, everyone respected her.

Kellie didn't get caught up in jealousy or negative talk, and I never saw her bicker.

If you asked her what her role on the team was, she'd shrug and say, "I'm the glue."

Kellie had what I called pride of possession. She was realistic about who she was, she understood she was not as quick and explosive as some players, but she knew how to work around it. She understood that no one was born with all the goods. She understood that you had to work to get the ball in your hands, and take care of it when you had it. For instance, in seven different regular season games, Kellie went without a single turnover. She would go out on the floor against All-Americans every night, and play them to a standstill. And sometimes outplay them. When there was a loose ball, guess who got to it? Kellie Jolly.

I had come to feel about Kellie the way her own mother, Peggy, did. Peggy said, "If I asked the good Lord to make me a daughter, she's what I'd ask for."

Kellie's parents were warm-hearted regular people from Sparta, a town of about five thousand atop some hills smack in the middle of Tennessee. It was the seat of White County, one hundred miles from Nashville, one hundred miles from Knoxville, and eighty miles from Chattanooga. It was bluegrass and stock car country, and it was a hotbed of women's basketball.

Long before the game was nationally popular, it was the main cultural event in White County, sort of the way high school football is in Texas. It wasn't unusual for a big game in Sparta to sell out in advance, and for hundreds to line up outside the gym. Every season, four or five young women from Sparta won college scholarships.

Ken Jolly, Kellie's father, was an assistant principal at White County High School, as well as a teacher and basketball coach. Peggy Jolly was a former basketball player in her own right, who was at Tennessee Tech at the same time I was at Tennessee-Martin. (We actually played against each other.)

When Kellie was born, the first thing Ken did was buy her a bright red ball. She had only been home from the hospital a week when he stood over the crib, took his daughter's tiny, waving hands in his, and placed the ball in them.

The Jollys have old home movies of Kellie dribbling when she was just a toddler. Ken and Peggy would take her into the driveway of their house and teach her to bounce the ball. Soon, she was on to more sophisticated tricks. She would stand out in the driveway, dribbling behind her back, between her legs, on reverses, crossovers, right-handed, left-handed.

Ken had keys to the school gym, which was just a few blocks from their house. He would spend every weekend with Kellie in the gym, teaching her the game: how to square up and shoot; how to handle the ball without looking at it; he even put a pair of dark glasses on her while she dribbled, so she couldn't see her hands and feet.

When Kellie was eleven, she led a team of girls from Sparta all the way to an Amateur Athletic Union national championship. They traveled to Lousiana for the AAU tournament, and claimed the title for their age group when Kellie scored thirty-six points out of the team's forty-eight in the championship game.

Ken and Peggy began to notice there was something uncommonly serious about their daughter. When she was twelve, the Jollys took a family vacation in Florida. Kellie made Ken and Peggy buy a ball and drive around until they found an outdoor court. After she got done playing, she ran sprints on the beach. Ken and Peggy marveled at the odd sight of a twelve-year-old conditioning.

Even then, it was like there was a hard substance in Kellie. She seemed to have no sense of fear or pain. She was thin as a switch, and fragile looking outwardly, but she could stand anything. She would play on sprained ankles. It was easy enough to knock her down, but not to keep her down. She'd pop back up.

She spent three hours a day, five days a week in the gym, playing against boys. On weekends and in the summertime, she would pack sandwiches and stay there all day long, along with Ken and her brother Brent, who, although he was three years younger, was a growing prospect himself.

Kellie and Brent would play one-on-one—full court. Brent would warm up on one end, and Kellie would warm up on the other. Then they would go at it, driving at each other for ninety-four feet, pushing, shoving, posting each other up. Sometimes Kellie would drive her little brother into the backstop with a layup. Ken would referee until a fight broke out, and then have to separate them, just like the Catchings sisters.

You could tell there was something deeply determined in Kellie by the way she rode a horse. The Jollys owned a farm on the outskirts of town, a twenty-five-acre place where they kept some cattle and raised a little tobacco. First, Kellie started on a pony like any other child. But then they bought a huge quarterhorse named May Pine. Kellie insisted on learning to ride May. Ken and Peggy didn't think she was big enough to control that much horse, but Kellie would sneak off and teach herself.

One day Peggy looked up and Kellie was flying across the horizon on May Pine's back. It scared Peggy to death, the sight of the little braided girl jouncing on the back of that enormous horse.

Kellie behaved with the same fearlessness as a ballplayer. She might not look like she could do some things, but the fact is, she is capable of more than you realize.

Maybe to understand Kellie you had to see how she dealt with her injuries. Kellie had torn her anterior cruciate ligament—twice. The first time she did it was in high school, shortly before her senior year. She was playing in an intrasquad scrimmage, and had just hung forty-seven points on the board in four quarters. The team decided to scrimmage for a fifth quarter so the bench players could get some work. Kellie voluntarily returned to the floor, even though she had been playing full-out for over two hours. Then she went down holding her knee.

As soon as the injury was diagnosed, Kellie and her parents called me. They told me they didn't want me to feel obliged to offer her a scholarship any more, in light of the injury. I said, "Of course I want her." Kellie worked all year, rising at 6 A.M. to do her rehab, and then doing more after school. She would lie on the floor and walk up the wall with her feet, trying to regain her flexibility. She reported to Tennessee in perfect condition.

But Kellie blew her knee again in a pickup game at Tennessee, just before the start of her sophomore year, our 1996–97 season. She couldn't believe it, and neither could I. But, again, she took to rehab like a woman possessed. She was back on the floor in just two months to lead us into the NCAA tournament.

Then she tore her ankle ligaments in a second round game.

Lying there in pain, she didn't want our trainer to cut her sock off. "How will I get back in the game?" she said.

That injury should have been a season-ender. Instead, Kellie slept on a sofa in the locker room for two nights, with Jenny Moshak working on her ankle around the clock with a pressure boot, electronic stimulator, and ice bags. Kellie spent so much time on her back that when she finally stood, she got nauseated. But she was ready to play.

In the Midwest Regional final against Connecticut, Kellie was the difference. While we came into that game with ten losses, UConn came in undefeated and ranked No.1. We were clearly overmatched, and needed to find another offensive element. I told Kellie we desperately needed her to score. She answered with a career-high nineteen points, despite her bad ankle.

A few days later she took the floor again in the national championship game against Old Dominion—and had a career-high eleven assists.

After we won the title, Kellie required surgery to repair those ankle ligaments. She couldn't run full court, but, like always, she came back an even more skilled player. She used the time to work on other aspects of her game. She could handle the ball and shoot, and so she decided to get better at those things. Kellie knew she might not win a footrace, but she worked on hesitation, change of speed, and switching hands. And she shot three-pointers all summer long.

When she reported back to campus at the start of the season, everyone worried about whether Kellie would be able to keep up with

Chamique and the hotshot incoming freshmen. Even Chamique had doubts. "I wondered if Kellie could control us," she said. But true to form, Kellie quietly rose to the task.

She had become my liaison on the floor. With a point guard, as with your own child, you want them to learn to do things without you. You want to be able to trust them to make their own decisions. I trusted Kellie completely. She was effortless to coach. She was like an automobile you never had to service, but she ran like a beauty. That was because she understood something fundamental about the game that a lot of other point guards don't.

If another player is closer to the basket than you are, you give them the ball.

It is amazing how many players don't get that simple principle.

Interestingly enough, over the course of the season Kellie had become best friends with, of all people, Chamique Holdsclaw. They were an unlikely pair, the skinny All-American from Queens and the school-teacher's kid from Sparta, but their friendship was a direct result of their relationship on the floor. Kellie always knew how to find Chamique. When a game got tight, you could see Kellie dart her eyes at Chamique, and they would make a play. They had an innate knowledge of where the other was going and what she intended to do. We called it the "Jolly-Holdsclaw baseline connection."

If Kellie was the unsung player at Tennessee, it was because she was consumed with her devotion to team. She was so caught up in being the "glue" and in helping to create an All-American in Holdsclaw that she forgot about herself.

But I hadn't forgotten about her.

➤ ➤ ➤

AS THE GAME APPROACHED, the press coverage grew more intense. We made the front page of the *New York Times*. *USA Today* ran a story debating whether we were the best women's college team ever. There was a seemingly endless series of press conferences, luncheons, and banquets, to attend: the WBCA coaches banquet, the NCAA banquet, the Basketball Writers Association luncheon. And everywhere we went, the press asked our players the same question: did they feel pressure to win a championship ring? Did the weight of Tennessee's five previous titles bother them?

Finally, Semeka Randall answered the question for all of us. She sat on the arena floor, surrounded by reporters, and she laid her hands on the table in front of her.

"Look at my fingers," she said. "Do you see any rings? No. You don't. I want a ring."

> > >

ON THE BUS back to the hotel after practice on the day before the championship game, a Knoxville-born actor named David Keith rode with us. David, who had starred in *An Officer and a Gentleman*, was a longtime Lady Vols fan.

On the bus, I introduced him around. "David, this is Ace Clement," I said.

"We've already met," Ace said.

"Of course you have," I said.

In the lobby of the hotel, Ace paused to talk with David. Chamique held the elevator door open, determined to make Ace come upstairs. Ace was Chamique's roommate for the week and they were becoming good friends, bonded by their Glamour Girls routine. "Ace," Chamique insisted, "Come here, I need you."

Ace jogged to the elevator and got in. As soon as the doors closed, the other players fell upon her. "*Cha-ching, cha-ching,*" they chanted, making cash register noises.

Chamique said, "Ace is working on a new career. A film career."

"That's not nice," Ace said. "That's not nice at all."

"The rest of us are going to have to work for our money," Chamique continued, to rising wails from the others. "We'll just be limping along, and Ace will be living large."

➤ ➤ ➤

A WHILE LATER, I heard a high-pitched shrieking and whooping. I opened my door and peered down the hallway.

Ace stood there, holding her hands over the eyes of one of our team managers, a young man named Drew.

"What's going on?" Drew said, blindly.

Chamique Holdsclaw darted out of her room in nothing but her underwear and socks. She jumped up and down in front of him, wind-milling her arms.

Our players were hanging out of their doors, screaming with laughter. "What's going on?" Drew said again, oblivious, his eyes still covered. Smiling, I shut my door.

➤ ➤ ➤

THE SUITE was empty except for Tyler and me. We sat quietly work-ing together. I squinted at the TV screen and made notes.

Tyler drew pictures on the easel.

Tyler said, out of the blue, "Mama, I love them."

I looked at him.

"I do too, honey," I said. "I love them so much."

➤ ➤ ➤

WE WERE OVERBANQUETED.

It seemed like every night there was an official function to attend, with the same iced tea, boneless chicken, and limp vegetables. But now it was Saturday, the night before the championship, and we had one last dinner to attend.

Tamika and Chamique had both made All-American. Kodak hosted a semiformal affair for the ten players who made the team, a large elaborate dinner in one of the nicer downtown hotels. The whole team helped Tamika and Chamique get ready. They argued cheerfully over what they should wear and how to do their hair and makeup. Ace put red lipstick on them, and I could hear the shrieks of hilarity all up and down the hallway. "A white girl doing up two black girls!" I could hear Semeka cackling.

A small Tennessee party accompanied Chamique and Tamika to the banquet, including Kellie. She went simply because Chamique asked her to. Kellie had planned to have an early supper with her parents, but Chamique moaned that she wanted Kellie with her. So at the last minute Ace dressed Kellie in one of her outfits, and we all trouped off to the banquet in a bus.

Tamika beamed like a child on the dais. Down below her, Harvey and Wanda Catchings took turns pointing their Instamatic cameras at her, taking pictures.

At one point, Harvey and Wanda turned to each other. Harvey said, "Congratulations." Wanda said, "Congratulations to you, too."

After the banquet, the bus ride back to hotel was, for once, a quiet one. We sat in the dark, thinking about the next day's game. Mickie pronounced herself already exhausted, and she still had a night of work ahead of her. She was in charge of putting together film of Louisiana Tech, and would be up half the night.

"I am far from the peaceful shore," Mickie said. "Far, far from the peaceful shore."

It was a line from Mickie's favorite hymn, "Love Lifted Me."

She tried to remember the rest of the words, casting about for phrases, reciting them aloud. Kellie joined in—she knew the words by heart. She began to sing, low. Mickie joined her, and then so did the rest of us. It was a sweet moment, murmuring a hymn in the dark:

I was sinking deep in sin, far from the peaceful shore
Very deeply stained within, sinking to rise no more
When the master of the sea heard my despairing cry

From the waters he lifted me
Now safe am I
Love lifted me.

> > >

THAT NIGHT, I had another nightmare. I dreamed that I was getting into a car with our players, when a large, menacing hand came out of no-where and wrenched the car door open. A large, frightening figure moved in front of me. I tried to close the car door again, but the large hand stopped me. Someone yelled. A policeman in the distance shouted, and pointed a gun.

I woke up.

It was 5 A.M. I lay next to R.B., thinking about the game and about the things I wanted to get across to the team. What would I say to them if we panicked? What would I say if we trailed? What would I say if we had a lead, what would I say if we fell behind?

I fought my old control-freak urge to play a slowed-down game. Lying there in the dark, part of me was afraid Tech could outrun us. I debated whether to revert to that old methodical half court game.

Stop it, I thought. *Knock it off.* We hadn't come all this way to slow down now. It was just the anxiety talking.

By 7 A.M., I was on my third cup of coffee. Semeka wandered into the suite, and flopped on the sofa. I sat down next to her, and we talked. Bertha had finally arrived, but she hadn't been around much. "She doesn't want to hang with me," Semeka said. Bertha, who was staying at a nearby hotel, was determined not to bother Semeka. She wanted Semeka to get plenty of rest.

"She's just trying to stay out of your way," I said.

Bertha had phoned Semeka at the hotel the previous night.

"What are you doing up?" she demanded.

"Ma, it's only eight o'clock," Semeka said.

"It's time for you to go to bed," Bertha said.

Semeka asked me if I had seen ESPN. La. Tech's Monica Maxwell had announced on the air that Tennessee was going down.

"She says they're going to beat us," Semeka said.

"That's wrong," I said.

After breakfast, the team gathered in the suite for our last team meeting. We went over some strategic points, but mainly we talked once again about running the full court.

"Forty minutes," I said. "You only have to run for forty more minutes. And then, Tree Geter, you won't have me yelling at you for I don't know how long."

"Where's Geter?" Holly blared. "Geter, don't you make me come after you."

"Only reason you'll come after me is to give me a high five," Tree said.

The meeting broke up and the players filed out.

But as the other players left, I held Tamika back for one of my so-called film sessions. Tamika was in a shooting slump—she had scored just two points in the second half against Arkansas. I wanted to reassure her that she still had plenty of offense. Her problem, I pointed out as we watched film, was that she was quick-shooting, and trying too hard to live up to her All-American billing. She was pressing the trigger too fast.

Tamika nodded as she watched the film. Confidence was the key to her game. She had to feel in her bones that she was the best player on the floor. As we talked, I almost felt as though I was trying to hypnotize her.

"They can't guard you," I said. "They can't hold you for forty minutes. No one in the country can. You hear me? They can't guard you."

➤ ➤ ➤

AT PRACTICE, we walked through what we intended to do that night. Mickie methodically led the team through various offensive and defensive sets, every option and response. It was like blocking out a stage play.

As Mickie finished speaking, Semeka snuck up behind her. She picked Mickie up, just like she did me.

"Semeka, put me down," Mickie said, calmly.

Instead, Semeka hoisted Mickie on her shoulders and began spinning around. The rest of the players joined in, tossing Mickie around as if she were a beanbag. Everyone in the gym stopped to watch. "Dang, they sure are loose," someone said.

Everyone except for Kellie.

I called Kellie over to the sideline. She stared up at me, her blue eyes as frank and open as always.

"You need to step it up," I said, almost snarling. "You've got to be aggressive and offensive-minded tonight. You could be the one player Tech overlooks. Someone is going to be open. You got me?"

Kellie just nodded, and said, "Yes, ma'am." She retrieved a basketball to practice her shot.

But Kellie was awful in shooting practice. She couldn't hit a thing. Every shot glanced off of the rim. She shook her head, and wandered over to Holly.

"I can't hit the side of a barn," she said.

Holly drifted over to me. "I'm worried about Kellie," she said.

Great, I thought.

➤ ➤ ➤

WE BOARDED THE BUS for our last ride. As soon as the players were settled, we punched in the highlight video. Puff Daddy pounded out of the speakers, accompanying spectacular action sequences from the season. The Lady Vols watched themselves spinning, driving, and punching the air to the pounding, warlike baseline of the music. *Whatchyou wanna do? Be ballers? Shot callers, brawlers?*

After the highlight film ended, Kyra pulled a compact disc from her bag. She turned to Kellie. "I've got a surprise for you," she said.

A few soft introductory notes drifted from the speakers. It was the title song to *When We Were Kings*, the prizewinning documentary about

Muhammad Ali's fight against George Foreman in Zaire. We had heard the song once before—it was the theme to our highlight film from the previous year's bus ride to the national championship game, and the team had fallen in love with it. But most of us had forgotten about it. Kyra had remembered, and had the presence of mind to bring it with her.

How can I describe the feeling that came over us as the song floated down the aisle of the bus? A steady rhythmic drum beat underneath the gospel-like melody. It was a soaring anthem, lifted by the voices of Brian McKnight and Diane King.

Kellie rose in her seat, and so did the rest of us. You could feel the tension drain out of the bus. It was replaced by peace of mind, followed by sheer joy as the song reached a crescendo. I twisted in my seat to look to the back of the bus. All of the players were singing along.

And when the long night has been fought and won, we'll stand in the sun. . . . I saw a dozen pairs of raised hands. All of them pushing upwards.

They were raising the roof.

The song continued to play as we pulled in front of the arena. The players collected their belongings and filed off the bus as the music drifted out of the speakers.

I sat in my front seat, watching their faces carefully as they disembarked.

They were singing; our team got off the bus to play for the national championship . . . and they were *singing*.

I had an overwhelming sense of confidence. And something else, too. Pure affection, for every one of them.

➤ ➤ ➤

IN THE LOCKER ROOM, I wrote my usual neat instructions on the blackboard. But from the corner of my eye, I tried to gauge their state of mind. To go into a championship game undefeated with a 38–0 record was something new for me, for all us. How would they react? Would they be tense? What would the air in the locker room be?

I called them into a circle. I had meditated all day on what kind of speech to give, how to prepare them to play. But now, looking straight into their eyes, I realized they didn't need a speech. They knew all of the answers for themselves. It was what you strived for, as a teacher. My job was done.

Randall bounced both of her legs. Usually, she bounced her right leg all through my pregame talk. Tonight, she bounced both.

They were all smiling.

Just don't screw them up, I thought.

"I want you to know something," I said quietly. "I've been doing this for twenty-four years. I've been to fifteen Final Fours. And I have never felt so confident of anything in my life. I've never been so sure of a team as I am of this one. Never. It's the last game. Just forty more minutes. That's all. This is your title. So just go on and get it."

And that's all I said.

> > >

On the floor for the pregame warmup, Kellie announced to Chamique, "I'm hot." Chamique looked at her strangely. But Kellie picked up a ball and shot it. It rippled through the net. She grabbed another ball, and launched it. Again, the net waved as the ball fell through.

Kellie turned to Niya Butts. "I got my shot back," she said.

Kellie moved farther out and tried one from the three point circle. More net.

"I'm telling you, I'm hot," she said to Chamique.

She launched another three pointer. The net fluttered crisply. Kellie returned to the bench and lifted an eyebrow at Niya.

"This could be ugly," Kellie said, smiling broadly.

> > >

I t was time for the introductions, and the tip-off. The players took their places. Tech won the jump, and Burras immediately broke to the basket for a layup.

Terrific, I thought. Exactly what we didn't want.

But on the other end, Kellie surveyed the La. Tech defense, took two quick dribbles, and then unexpectedly accelerated. She drove all the way to the La. Tech basket, dove into a crowd, and went up for a double-clutch layup.

It fell in. Our bench hurled themselves upwards from their chairs as one, screaming.

And that's how it began.

For the next twelve minutes, Tennessee played some of the most glorious basketball I had ever seen. As a coach you allow yourself certain wild imaginings, you picture in your mind how the game *might* be played, if you had the athletes who could carry it out.

That night, it was for real. There were times when the ball didn't even touch the floor.

With 15:48 to go in the first half, Kellie called out to Holdsclaw. "Meek," she said, "Give me the ball." Chamique did a double take. Kellie never asked for the ball. Chamique smiled, and dealt it to her.

Kellie buried a three, for a 15–6 lead.

Kellie slugged the air. Chamique said, "I don't mind switching roles with you, as long as you knock it down."

But Kellie's shot seemed to give Holdsclaw a magical rhythm: she hit six points in a row, with an off-balance leaner, a little jumper from the lane, and one on the fast break, for a 21–8 margin.

The acrobatics were just starting. Randall and Holdsclaw combined to race the ball up the court, and Catchings leaped up for a one-handed put-back of the rebound, a Meek-to-Meek-to-Meek play.

Holdsclaw lunged for a steal and flipped the ball to Catchings, who hurled it to Clement, who swung it to Jolly, who zipped it to Holdsclaw, for a layup. The ball never even bounced. Now the score was 27–10.

On the press, Kellie stole an inbounds pass under Tech's basket and slapped it to Holdsclaw, who spun and dished an underhanded pass to Clement for a showtime layup.

At the other end, Geter blocked a shot by Burras and tipped the ball to Holdsclaw, who slung it to Clement for another no-dribble fast break.

Randall's turn. She skipped into the paint, all by herself against three Tech defenders. She switched hands, spun, and finger-rolled the ball into the basket to make it 40–17.

Finally, we got a little sloppy. We gave up two straight turnovers, allowing Tech to cut it to twenty in a matter of seconds, 47–27. I took a time out to snap at the Lady Vols, just on general principles.

Again, it was Kellie who responded. As soon as we hit the floor after the time-out, she set up for a three, edging her toe out. Only this time, she was two full paces back from the line. She launched it. It knifed into the basket, with 3:10 to go in the half.

We went to the locker room with a 55–32 lead.

Our fifty-five first-half points was an NCAA record, and we had shot 62 percent from the floor. But I realized that the pace probably couldn't continue.

At halftime, I took off my suit jacket to write on the board. As I slipped out of my blue blazer, down to a sleeveless black shell, the players started whooping. I turned around, amazed. They were giggling and pointing at my arms. I had been working out so hard in the last few weeks that I showed the first signs of biceps. They whistled at me.

It was halftime of the national championship, and they were teasing me.

I wanted to laugh, but I couldn't.

"Y'all be serious," I said. "This is the national championship."

The whistles and whoops died down.

"Now, you can't let them get back in it, like you did North Carolina," I said. That quieted them down.

"Don't you let them come out and start the second half by scoring ten in a row," I said.

But that's what happened. Tech scored the first seven to open the half, cutting it to 55–39. I was livid.

I called time-out immediately. They gathered around. I just looked at them.

"Are you going to let them back in it?" I snarled. "Is that what you're going to do? Or are you going to play some defense?"

Tamika thought, *Wonderful. We're going to get yelled at in this game, too.*

We pressed.

Catchings threw a pass the length of the court to Clement for an uncontested layup. Holdsclaw hit a long jumper.

Catchings got a steal and went coast to coast for a finger roll. It was 63–39.

But Tech worked away at us. With 11:50 to go, they cut it to eighteen. The scoreboard read 72–54, and I was concerned. That may sound silly, but I knew how dangerous Tech was offensively. They could turn it into a single digit game in no time at all.

But Kellie took over one more time. She started to drive the lane, and the defense sagged. Kellie took a neat step back, and sent up another three. It trembled once and settled into the basket, 75–54.

Holdsclaw brought the ball up on the next possession. Kellie called for it again, this time right in front of our bench. Holdsclaw no longer questioned Kellie. She flipped it straight over to her. Kellie squared up for another three.

I started to yell, "No!"

Kellie was six or seven feet *behind* the three point circle. But in her mind, Kellie saw something different from the rest of us. She thought the Tech defense was playing low under the basket, leaving the three point circle unprotected. It was a delusion. She had no idea where she really was. She simply saw the basket, and to her, it looked closer than it actually was. Kellie launched the shot.

The ball barely rustled the net as it fell in.

No one could believe it—the shot must have been a 25-footer. Mickie stood on the sideline with her arms out in disbelief. The score was 78–54.

But there was still reason for concern. We got casual with our lead, turned the ball over again, and threw up some bad shots. That allowed Tech to climb to within seventeen with 8:04 to go, 79–62. Holdsclaw had lost focus and given up two turnovers. I called time-out, furious.

"You're the junior and the leader," I said. "It's your responsibility not to turn the ball over. *Sit down!*"

I benched her. Chamique took a seat, her eyebrows raised, and smothered a giggle. After a few minutes, I relented and sent her back in. You had to give great offensive players freedom—and at the pace we played it was easy to quick shoot. Chamique just needed a reminder to be more careful with the ball.

In the final two minutes of the game, I began substituting, shuttling our supporting cast onto the floor: Brynae Laxton, Misty Greene, Niya Butts, and Laurie Milligan had spent the majority of the season playing valuable roles on our team. I was as proud of their patient, selfless contributions as I was of any of our players on the front line.

Lastly, I was especially eager to get Kyra in—she had come so far, so fast, that she was cleared by our medical staff to play in the closing seconds. As long as she didn't do anything foolish.

As the substitutions ran in and out, Kellie came to the bench. She gave leaping high fives to Holly and Mickie and then hurled herself into my arms. I hugged her close. "Awesome," I shouted. "Absolutely awesome."

Kellie said in my ear, "Three down. One to go."

Finally, I let Kellie go. She jitterbugged down the sideline, thrilled. Next, I pulled Chamique from the game.

Chamique turned her departure into a three-act play. As she came to the sideline, she grabbed Kellie in a euphoric hug. They held three fingers in the air. Then Chamique turned to me.

And dissed me.

As I held out my arms for a hug, she waved her hand at me and turned away, as if to say "No."

Two could play that game. I grinned, and leveled her with a stare. "Okay, fine," I said. "But you'll pay."

Chamique wheeled and grabbed me in a hug. I hugged her back, laughing. "Are you mad at me?" I said.

"Nah," she said, "I'm just messing with you."

Finally, the last seconds ran out, and our players sprinted onto the court. It was official. We were undefeated, and national champions. For the record, the final score was 93–75.

≻ ≻ ≻

HERE IS WHAT our players did that night. Their thirty-nine victories were an all-time record, the most wins ever recorded in a collegiate season without a loss by any team, men's or women's. Tamika Catchings burst out of her postseason shooting slump to become the game's leading scorer with twenty-seven points, and broke Chamique's freshman scoring record. Holdsclaw had twenty-five points, ten rebounds, and six assists, a virtuoso performance.

Kellie had twenty points, a career high, and three steals.

Tree Geter had seven points and four blocked shots. Semeka Randall had ten points, eight rebounds, and two steals, Ace Clement got six points. LaShonda Stephens didn't have any points, but put a body on Burras all night. Niya Butts contributed a key layup, Brynae Laxton a rebound, and Laurie Milligan went into NCAA record books as the first player to appear in four consecutive Final Four championship games.

And Kyra Elzy, despite my strict instructions not to risk her knee, was so overjoyed to be on a basketball court that she actually led a fast break. She threw up a jumper as Jenny and I screamed from the bench, "Kyra, no!" It missed.

We barely had time for the accomplishment to sink in, with all of the postgame ceremony. It was a blur of TV interviews, speeches, trophy presentations, and net cutting.

Finally, we reached the locker room. I wanted to say so much, but there wasn't time. I knew from experience that events would overtake us as soon as we stepped out into the world. There would be receptions, press conferences, and morning-after interviews to do. It might be days before we were all together alone again, with no strangers.

I gathered the team around. My throat closed with emotion.

"That was some of the best basketball ever played," I said. "I am so proud for you, and so happy for you. You are the most exciting team I've ever seen. And you have no idea what you've done for this game. You didn't slip in the back door, either. You marched in the front. You deserved it. You're 39–0, an NCAA record. That's history. You've made history. And it all belongs to this team."

The phone rang. It was Vice President Al Gore, calling to say congratulations. I spoke to him for a moment, and then put Chamique on the phone.

"I bet you're getting tired of seeing me at the White House," she teased him.

But when I hung up, a remarkable thing happened. I realized the room was virtually silent. You would never have known that we had just won a championship, much less staked a claim as the greatest women's college basketball team ever. Our players sat in front of their lockers, subdued. Semeka practically hung her head. Even Kellie had a downcast expression. No one spoke. They just looked at me.

"What's wrong with you all?" I said.

"We're sad," Semeka said, softly.

"Why?" I asked, incredulous.

Semeka gazed up at me with those moist brown eyes.

"Because it's over," she answered.

Q & A with Mickie DeMoss (Assistant coach)

Why do you think this team commanded so much affection from the coaches?

Because they weren't afraid to ask for it. My opinion is that if you couldn't be affectionate with those freshmen, you had a heart of stone. They're such warm people, and they demand that from the people around them. It kind of opened the door for the rest of the players. And then I think Pat realized, it's okay. You can have this relationship and still coach them and maintain respect and authority. Pat had been affectionate with some players in the past. But on this team, everyone hugged. It became a ripple effect. That was what you did on this team. You hugged.

CHAPTER TWELVE

Aftermath: Raise the Roof

IT WASN'T A TEAM. It was a tent revival.

What the Lady Vols really wanted to do after winning the national championship was just keep on playing, a season without end. But in our business the final score tells all. Without some form of completion we would never know what we had accomplished. Endings are how we measure things.

But the deeper truth is that while a season ends, life goes on. In a way, the 1997–98 season was just an illusion, a neat framework with an all-too-easy answer. The reality of it was a lot more subjective and complicated, and a lot less convenient. The curtain didn't just fall.

Several interesting things happened in the aftermath of our title.

➤ ➤ ➤

CHAMIQUE FINALLY SETTLED the question of whether she would turn pro. In the postgame press conference, she announced she would return to Tennessee to seek an unprecedented fourth straight title. "I will be back at Tennessee," she said. "It's firm, and it's final."

Kellie Jolly couldn't contain herself and burst into applause.

Next, Chamique was asked if she thought this was the best women's basketball team ever.

"You know what?" she said. "I think next year's team will be the best ever."

Chamique spent the spring and summer playing for the USA national team, the only collegian on a squad of WNBA and ABL players that brought home a gold medal from the World Championships. She continues her remarkable streak of winning campaigns. She has yet to play on a team that didn't claim a championship.

In August, Chamique was named as one of *Esquire* magazine's Women We Love. In the story, Michael Jordan declared, "She is, without a doubt, the most exciting women's basketball player ever."

➤ ➤ ➤

I NEVER DID REALLY SLEEP. My last restful moment came on the bus after the game. Chamique slid into the seat next to me and we rode back to the hotel together, replaying the events of the night.

"Coach, we were up by twenty points when you yelled at me," she teased me.

I shot back, "That's because I refused to let y'all lose that game."

The team hollered and swayed with laughter.

At the hotel, we had a huge celebration in the dining room for the Tennessee contingent. Afterwards, the coaching staff, our families, and a few friends came to my hotel suite. I was especially grateful that Lex and Mary Margaret Carter were there. Meanwhile down the hall, the players gathered in a room with some of their peers for their own celebration. You could hear the thumping music and shrieks.

I changed into baggy blue jeans and clutched a bottle of Dom Perignon champagne. As I moved around the suite filling glasses, Mickie and Holly and Al declared, boastfully, "*We* coached the first fifteen minutes of that game."

We stayed up until 4 A.M. watching the game over and over. Even on third and fourth viewing, I couldn't help but admire the standard of play.

Championship games had a tendency to be ugly, tension-ridden affairs, and almost never lived up to the importance of the occasion. But the Lady Vols had brought their best game, on the biggest night. They fashioned their own personal statement on the subject of whether they were the best team ever, and I was so proud of them for it I couldn't find adequate words.

At 7 A.M., I rose to appear on *Good Morning America* again along with the Three Meeks. Then we had to pack and fly home on a charter, because several thousand people were waiting to throw us a parade and a rally. I was so tired I barely remember the flight.

In Knoxville that evening, our players rode in open cars through the streets, packed four-deep with fans. The parade ended at Thompson-Boling Arena, where Semeka and Ace addressed a crowd of over six thousand. Semeka said into a microphone, "I don't know what to say, and there's no music so I can't dance."

The university band started up a rap rhythm. Ace and Semeka hip-hopped, to roars.

"Are we talented, or *what?*" Semeka shouted.

Finally, I fell into bed at about 10 P.M. I was so comatose I didn't know what day of the week it was. I think it was a Monday, but don't count on it.

I had only been asleep for a little while when I woke up to a reminder that a winning season is just a suspension of reality.

Tyler shook R.B. and me at 3 A.M.. "I have an earache," he said.

We were up the rest of the night.

➤ ➤ ➤

KELLIE JOLLY was named to the NCAA All-Tournament team for her twenty-point performance in the championship game. It was the second straight year she had been so honored. I couldn't help remarking on the fact that Kellie had never won an individual award, never made All-American, and yet twice now she had delivered career highs for us in consecutive title games.

In the spring, Kellie became engaged to be married to Jon Harper. She returned home to Sparta for the summer, serving as a substitute teacher at her old high school, White County.

> > >

CHAMIQUE had a baby named after her.

One afternoon in the late spring she was wandering through a Knoxville mall, when a woman pushing a stroller stopped her.

"Oh my gosh, you're Chamique Holdsclaw," she said. "You have to see my baby. I named her after you."

Meek couldn't believe it. There was a Baby Chamique on this earth. But what she really couldn't comprehend was that the person speaking to her was a white woman. Chamique peered in the stroller, and saw a tiny little girl staring back at her. "A white baby named Chamique," she marveled, telling me the story, in her wispy voice. She's still not over it.

> > >

ACE CLEMENT's father continued to write to her, and Kyra Elzy's father continued to call. It would be nice to think that they would reconcile. Of course, there are two sides to every story. If single motherhood has its burdens and heartaches, there is no doubt in my mind that disenfranchised fatherhood has its own frustrations and anguish.

> > >

IN JUNE, Tamika Catchings received a different kind of award. She was honored for achievement by the National League for the Deaf and Hard of Hearing.

I accompanied her to the Waldorf-Astoria Hotel in New York City for yet another banquet. Tamika stood at a microphone before several hundred people in the hotel's Grand Ballroom, and gave a speech that moved everyone to tears. Why, I thought, was this team always making me cry?

As she spoke, I finally understood the extent of her isolation.

"It seemed like I always had to make a choice," Tamika said. "I could wear a hearing aid, and be made fun of because I had a hearing problem. Or I could not wear one, and be made fun of because I missed what was said, or because of the way I talked, or because of the way I looked at people, trying so hard to read their lips. I was self-conscious, and it was pretty lonesome at times. But I've finally learned to accept myself for who I am."

➤ ➤ ➤

KYRA ELZY'S stalker was arrested on the Tennessee campus in May.

He showed up one day as Kyra, LaShonda, and Niya walked to lunch after their morning classes. He saw them from across the street, waved, and, incredibly, jogged towards them as if they were old friends. He was carrying a knapsack, just like any other undergraduate.

"Don't I look like a student?" he asked.

The players kept their cool, continuing towards the Gibbs Hall cafeteria, as he tried to make conversation.

"Where you going?" he asked.

"To lunch," Kyra said. "You can't eat with us. It's students only."

When they arrived at Gibbs Hall, Kyra quickly disappeared into the building. "I come all this way to see her, and then she treats me this way," he complained to Niya. Finally, he left, announcing that he would eat at the Thompson-Boling Arena cafeteria, which was open to outsiders as well as to students and faculty. Meanwhile Kyra called Mickie, who summoned the police. They found him eating in Thompson-Boling cafeteria.

The university prosecuted him for stalking and criminal trespassing. I went with Kyra and Sheryl to the court as he was sentenced to two years' probation, and barred from attending Lady Vols games. We hope we have seen the last of him.

≻ ≻ ≻

SOME FINAL NUMBERS you won't find in a box score:

In the academic semester following our championship run, the Lady Vols turned in one of the best classroom performances I had ever seen in our program. Over half of the team had a 3.0 grade point average or better, and the rest were close.

Brynae Laxton, our reserve post player and a perpetual A-student, reluctantly decided to leave the team in order to apply to medical school.

Laurie Milligan graduated in August with a degree in marketing.

Season ticket sales for the Lady Vols almost doubled in the wake of our sixth title. An anonymous donor gave a $50,000 gift to the program.

At one point, we were receiving two hundred pieces of mail a day. It became impossible to return all of our phone calls. A lot of the mail and calls were from coaches.

They wanted to talk about our press defense.

≻ ≻ ≻

WHEN YOU PLAY at such an ambitious tempo, when you win thirty-nine straight games, and beat your opponents by an average of thirty points, what motivates you? I still don't fully understand the answer to that question. All I know is that the 1997–98 Lady Vols were unprecedented in my experience. In attempting to analyze their success, I can only point out that, despite their varied backgrounds, they shared certain characteristics. They shared the determination to make something good out of any misfortune. They shared a revulsion towards peer pressure, towards that insidious coercion that is called "fitting in." They didn't want to fit in, they wanted to experience that difference called excellence. And they shared an inexhaustible work ethic.

The Meeks and Company played to their own lofty standards and no one else's, and for the moment, their standard is the one to measure by. There will be other great teams, and other undefeated teams. But I say this in perfect honesty, and hopefully without bragging: until a team comes along that is as committed to each other as ours was, no one will match us. People will sit around and say, "Yeah, that's a great team, but are they as great as that '98 Tennessee team?"

Of course, we have made life difficult for ourselves. Now that we set the standard, how do we live up to it?

I'll tell you how. With Holdsclaw, Jolly, Elzy, Catchings, Randall, Clement, Geter, Stephens, Butts, and Greene. Along with a couple of incoming recruits, Michelle Snow and Shalon Pillow. And I'll let you in on a secret. Last time I saw her, Catchings was working on a dunk.

As for me personally, in the aftermath of the title, some people suggested I needed a bigger arena. There was even some talk of putting me up for governor. What those people don't understand is, I already have important work—redefining what young women are capable of and how they compete.

➤ ➤ ➤

THE 1997-98 LADY VOLS were young women who were raised to keep score, who had developed their games on asphalt tarmac, playing shoulder to shoulder with boys. That didn't mean they were hard. In some ways, they were the most sensitive, emotional team I've coached. They simply refused to be bound by conventions.

And that's what I loved most about them. They understood better than any other team that what we try to teach at Tennessee is about far more than basketball. It's about life skills, and life stories, it's about trading in old, narrow definitions of femininity for a more complete one. It's about exploring all of the possibilities in yourself.

Let's face it. Women aren't becoming firefighters, pro athletes, and space shuttle astronauts these days just because political activists waved signs. Somewhere along the line, a woman had to prove she could pull a 250-pound man from a burning building.

But this team taught *me*, too. If I had spent most of my career testing the limits of young women, I finally met a team that would test *my* limits.

They demanded that I be flexible enough and secure enough to change. They demonstrated how much fun it could be to lose control. They challenged me every day to coach up to their talents, to be more creative, and to explore their seemingly open-ended capacity for winning.

The Lady Vols played as if they had no internal or physical boundaries. There was something beautifully unself-conscious about them, a spiritual-emotional element that was hard to describe. Most of us have inner barriers, invisible obstacles made up of fear or insecurity; we think far too much about what we *can't* do.

I suspect that what allowed them to play that way was that they were in good company. Individually, they had as many fears, insecurities, and frailties as you or I do. Some of them were the progeny of welfare mothers or absent fathers, others experienced ostracism, loneliness, disability, divorce, or some other obstacle. But together, they created something complete and perfect.

So to me, the 39–0 record, the "Three-Peat," the trophies, the banners, the rings, and all of the other final measurements, were merely the tangible rewards and hardware of a larger achievement. It was the way that we won, the unfetteredness with which we played, that was the lingering accomplishment in my mind. Throughout the season, I had a curious sensation of something rising. I felt that I had watched our team literally raise the roof. It became almost a mission on the part of the Lady Vols to set a new standard for themselves, and for the sport. As Ace Clement said, "We wanted to make people true believers in the women's game." And they did.

Of course, the hardware was nice too.

CHAPTER THIRTEEN

The Last Lesson

THERE WAS JUST ONE THING left to teach them: how to lose. It's so much easier to teach players how to handle winning than it is to teach them how to handle losing. Just as with your own children, you wish for your players' unbroken happiness and you want to shield them from every unpleasant reality. The truth is such a thing is not only impossible but it's probably not even good for them.

What happened next was only life. We lost. We lost three games in 1998–99 and failed to win that fourth straight championship. Instead, Purdue, led by All-American Stephanie White-McCarty and coached by my friend Carolyn Peck, won the NCAA title.

I've often said that what our players do at Tennessee between the ages of eighteen and twenty-one should not be the pinnacle of their entire lives. However, I do think that the habits and lessons they learn here shape them for their futures. Our players are forced to ask themselves a crucial question: *Who is it you intend to be?* Hopefully, a part of the answer is "a winner." But it is equally important that the answer include being a team player, and a gracious loser.

So, in its own way, Tennessee's 1998–99 season was as valuable an experience as the one that came before. It just wasn't as joyous. In the end, maybe we had to lose a fourth title to really appreciate winning three straight. It restored our balance. Despite Chamique's comment after the '98 championship that our next team would be the best one ever, our expectations were unrealistic. The fact was, after 39–0, there was only one way for us to go: down. We couldn't improve on a perfect record. Furthermore, we all had trouble keeping our heads on straight. We were showered with attention and praise, and it was only human nature to hear it, to believe it, and to give in to it. In the meantime, our opponents were more motivated and better prepared than ever.

As with any Tennessee season, we had our share of victories, laughs, tantrums, and setbacks.

We began the season with two pieces of bad news. Kyra Elzy did not recover from her torn ACL injury as we had hoped. After her initial rapid recovery, her knee began to swell, and finally, she required more surgery. By then it was clear she would not be able to play in the '98–99 season. Also, LaShonda Stephen's knees continued to deteriorate, and when she returned for fall practices, she had difficulty keeping up. One afternoon she came to me and said she wanted to quit the team. She didn't think her knees could physically handle the daily grind of practice. Though I discussed an option with her—that she continue to play in a limited role—she stuck by her decision. LaShonda remained on scholarship and traveled with us when her class schedule permitted, but we missed her presence on the court.

That meant our frontcourt was made up of Tree Geter and two pure freshmen, the 6-feet-5 Michelle Snow of Pensacola, Florida, and 6-feet-3 Shalon Pillow of Addyston, Ohio. With arms outstretched, Snow measured a full 7-feet-10, and she could dunk. She was also a kid at heart, who quickly became Tyler's new favorite. Shalon was a soft-spoken and endlessly agreeable young lady, who nodded at everything I said to her but who could suddenly turn into a forceful player on the court. With the addition of those two, we had the potential to be deeper than the previous year's team—and we indeed had a chance to repeat, if we played with the same commitment and intensity.

But in practices, I could see right away that we weren't quite the team we had been. I told our staff, "Maybe our standards are too high." It didn't seem to me that we were playing with the passion and togetherness that we had in '97–98. "We're different," I said. "There's something missing. It's not the same."

Our wake-up call came when we lost to eventual-champion Purdue in just the second game of the season. We got exactly what we deserved. I told the team it was coming. I warned them. "You're going to get your butts beat," I said.

In the pregame dressing room, I asked our trainer, Jenny Moshak, if she thought they were ready. She said, "Yeah." But Mickie DeMoss just shook her head. "I don't have a good feeling," she said. I didn't either.

Purdue had great guards in White-McCarty, Katie Douglas, and Ukari Figgs, they had a sellout crowd panting for an upset, and they had poise. On our side of the court, the Lady Vols looked like five individuals instead of a team. We played a lot of one-on-one basketball, and we took a lot of quick shots. On the defensive end, we got beat one-on-one and had no help from teammates. It was Purdue from the beginning, and clearly it wasn't a fluke. In a game that would become a microcosm of the entire season, we were beaten by the Boilermakers, 78–68.

Flying home that night, I could hear a couple of the players laughing, including the distinct giggle of Holdsclaw. I knew Chamique well enough by then to know that that whoop-whoop giggle was her way of handling stress—to laugh it off—but I was in no mood to hear it. I marched to the back of the plane and confronted her. "I cannot imagine that anything is funny to you at this point," I said. "I don't want to hear another word."

But deep down, as frustrating as it was, I also felt that the loss was the best thing that could happen to us. There is nothing harder to do than to *repeat* success, because you have a tendency to expect things to come to you. The Lady Vols had fallen into thinking that more victories would just happen, when the truth was that we had a long year in front of us. We had a brutal schedule with virtually all of our biggest games on the road. After the loss to Purdue, I finally had the team's attention.

From then on we began a 24-game winning streak and at times

played a brand of basketball that made me think we were indeed better than we had ever been. Some people remained critical of us because we didn't dominate the way we had in '98, but I had to credit the opposition. They were prepared to handle us. On November 30, we pulled off a terrific victory on the road when we beat No.2 Louisiana Tech, 92–73.

We fought through setbacks, including a serious one just before Christmas, when Tree Geter limped off the court in a 100–77 victory over UCLA. At first we feared she had torn her ACL. As it turned out, she had hyperextended her knee and torn some cartilage. She hyperextended it twice more in the next couple of months (after the season was over she underwent surgery). The first injury occurred just when she was coming into her own on the court, and she wouldn't be quite the same for the rest of the season.

Nevertheless, we kept clawing out wins. We went to Connecticut and beat the top-ranked but injury-riddled Huskies, who in '99 had stolen our reputation as the most aggressive running and pressing team in the country, 92–81. A few days later we went to No.4 Georgia, an eventual women's Final Four team, and dominated, 102–69. On a road trip to Auburn, Randall jumped me in my room, trying to body slam me again. This time, her weight was too far forward, and I flipped her over on the floor. That was just an example of the contest of wills between Miss Randall and me all season.

In the final game of the regular season, we fell short of our goal of going undefeated in the Southeastern Conference when we lost to Louisiana State, 72–69. We reverted to the form we had shown at the start of the season against Purdue, appearing motivated as individuals but not as a team. But we responded well to the loss, tearing through the SEC Tournament, beating Florida, Alabama, and Georgia in order to win the title. By season's end, we had three All Americans. Holdsclaw, Catchings, and Randall were all named Kodak selections, the first time three players from the same team made it. But we would have traded that for a championship.

I had the team over for our traditional home-cooked meal as the NCAA tournament brackets were announced on TV. We learned we would meet Appalachian State in the first round of the NCAA tournament. The next day, Ace Clement came into my office. She had a question. "If I have zero turnovers, can I paint your fingernails?" she said.

I said, "Any color you want."

Against Appy State, Ace had just one turnover, and we won, 113–54. But what should have been a celebratory night turned sour when the thing I most dreaded, injury, struck us yet again. With just a few minutes left in the game, Randall fell to the floor on a rebound, and rolled her ankle. She writhed around in terrible pain and had to be taken off in a wheelchair. She had torn two ligaments and was possibly out for the rest of the season.

Next, we faced Boston College. While Semeka slept in the locker room, undergoing round-the-clock treatment, Ace prepared to start in her stead against the Eagles. Everyone would have to do her part. But deep down there was something I wanted from Chamique Holdsclaw before she graduated: I wanted to see her dominate a game one more time. Against the Eagles, I got my wish. With Semeka Randall watching the game from a wheelchair next to the bench, Chamique shouldered the scoring responsibility and put on a bravura performance with 39 points. She knocked down fallaways, leaners, and double-clutches. It was her career-high, and we defeated the Eagles, 89–62.

It marked the last time Chamique Holdsclaw and Kellie Jolly would play a home game in Thompson-Boling Arena. With a few minutes to go, I substituted for each of them. As they came off the floor, each of them stopped at the jump circle, kneeled down, and kissed the floor. I tried not to show how moved I was. There was too much important basketball left to play in the season. We were bound for Greensboro and the NCAA East Regionals.

➤ ➤ ➤

MEANWHILE, Jenny Moshak was working miracles on Semeka Randall. I felt we needed Semeka if we were to get by our next opponent, Virginia Tech, who we would meet in the East semifinals. Within a couple of days, Semeka was walking around, and by tip-off we had an okay from our team doctor, Bill Youmans, to let her play sparingly off the bench. We kidded Jenny that she was a faith-healer. With Semeka giving us valuable minutes in relief, we defeated Virginia Tech, 89–62.

In the other regional semi, Duke beat Old Dominion to become our opponent in the next round. We had beaten Duke earlier in the season, 74–60, but the Blue Devils had come on strong in the second half and were playing with attitude. This time around it would be a lot more difficult to get through them and into the Final Four.

Looking back on it, we seemed loose externally, but none of us had a good feeling in the pits of our stomachs. The morning of the game, Semeka came to my suite to use the whirlpool in the bathroom for her throbbing ankle. After awhile, she came back out, limping.

"How is it?" I asked her.

"It's good," Semeka said.

"You wouldn't tell me if it hurt anyway, would you?" I said

Semeka just laughed and hobbled out.

At the pregame shootaround that afternoon, Tamika Catchings kept her sweatshirt on. She had been fighting the flu for over a week, and she still had chills. Then, at our pregame meal that evening, Catchings suddenly bolted from the buffet line, with tears in her eyes. She didn't feel well. A trainer took a plate to her room, but she wouldn't eat.

In the locker room that night, however, everybody seemed to have recovered. The Lady Vols looked genuinely confident and ready to play. While they knew they would have to battle Duke, in the end they thought they were "destined." It was a dangerous assumption.

The Blue Devils came out playing great, and we came out playing as badly as we had all year. I could tell it was going to be one of those nights. In the first half, Duke hit a stunning 60 percent of its shots. It seemed like everything the Blue Devils put up, fell in. Our defense had no influence on them—much like our Purdue loss. Meanwhile, everything we put up, fell out. We shot a miserable 31.4 percent. Given that disparity, we probably should have been blown out, instead of trailing by 35–24 at the half.

But in the second half, the Blue Devils continued to play together and refused to give up easy baskets. We still couldn't make our shots drop, and no one had a tougher time than the Meeks. Holdsclaw was in the process of going 2 of 18, Catchings 5 of 14, and Randall 8 of 17. Worse, we were missing our free throws, too. That's when I knew it was bad. One after another, the free throws ticked off the front of the rim or clanged off the neck. For the game we made just 8 of 18 from the foul line.

We fought our hearts out in the second half, but we kept making small costly mistakes and couldn't catch a single break. We would close to within a point or two, and miss a free throw. Snow was called for a walk, Jolly was whistled for a charge, Holdsclaw threw the ball away. We never led.

Finally, it became apparent that there would be no repeat of the North Carolina game. We were going to lose. There would be no four straight titles, and the Holdsclaw–Jolly era was about to come to an end. The fact that it was Kellie and Chamique's last games as Lady Vols made the loss so difficult to face.

No coach enjoys the task of instructing players in how to accept failure and handle pain. It is the worst part of the job. With less than a minute to go, Chamique fouled out and came to the Tennessee bench for the last time. As she left the court, she dropped her face into her hands, sobbing. She walked into my arms and buried her face in my shoulder. "Coach Summitt, I was awful," she cried. "Can I please go to the dressing room?" She had nothing to be ashamed of. I couldn't help thinking of all her great performances of the last four years, of the hundred-odd occasions on which she had taken over games. "No, Meek," I said. "You handled winning three championships, and you handled it well. Tonight you've got to handle losing, and you're going to handle it well. We're all here to help you. Sit down there by Mickie."

She turned to the bench and sat by Mickie and put her face in a towel. Next, Kellie committed her fifth foul. For a moment, Kellie didn't realize that she had just played her last possession. Then she put her hands to her face and burst into tears and came to the bench. I hugged her. "I'm sorry," she said. "I just can't believe it." I comforted her as best as I could, and then she sat down next to Chamique. I kneeled down in front of them, and we sat there together, our heads down, staring at the floor, until the game was over.

In the stands, Tyler was sobbing inconsolably in the lap of his nanny, LaTina Dunn Haynes. To a small boy who has known little but celebrations (in four of his eight years on this planet, we had won championships) the game was a traumatic experience. "I'm never going to see Chamique again," he cried. LaTina tried to calm him down and assured him that he would see Chamique within the next ten minutes. When the buzzer sounded, she brought him back to the locker room area. He threw himself into the arms of Chamique and Kellie.

Next door, the Duke team arrived in their locker room. We could hear them shrieking and howling in elation. The noise seemed like it was right outside the door, and it cut into our players. They sprawled around the dressing room, distraught, and for the next several minutes apologized to each other. No one pointed fingers. But they were inconsolable. Ace sat on the cold white tile of the bathroom, her eyes vivid red, weeping. Catchings sat on top of a massage table, staring into space. Randall hunched in a corner, her head buried in her arms.

I thought about what to say. I was grateful to them for so much. We had achieved extravagant success, we had learned how much we are all capable of, and we had done these things together. The Lady Vols had played under a crushing weight of pressure and expectations for an awfully long time, and in the end it had taken a toll on their nervous systems. But they had only lost just three games in two years, and I was deeply proud of them for that.

"Let's get our heads up, you've got nothing to be ashamed of," I said. "You're going to learn volumes from this, more than from all those wins. So let's go to the press room and handle it. And give Duke all the credit in the world. They were ready."

Finally, they calmed down enough to file out of the dressing room and on to the team bus. As the last players were leaving, I sat down in a chair, and, finally, I cried, too.

> > >

I KNOW SOME PEOPLE around the country felt we had nothing to cry about, that we had won more games than any team had a right to. I know, too, that some people were tired of Tennessee winning championships and were glad they wouldn't have to hear Rocky Top one more time. They were ready for a new title holder. But what you have to understand is that we lost more than a game that night. We lost Kellie and Chamique. The dream state of the last year was really over, and two of the greatest players and friends we had would be moving on.

That's why I say that losing Number Four helped us to stop and realize how incredible winning Three was. I don't think we ever *had* stopped to enjoy it. We moved so hard and so fast that we didn't savor it. But now we would have time to think about it. Too much time.

I don't believe a word was spoken by any of us on the flight that night back to Knoxville. We finally landed at about 3 A.M. and by the time we got our luggage and cars, it was almost morning. But when I got home, I put a videotape of the game into the VCR. I sat down and watched, gritting my teeth.

The next day, I stayed in my pajamas until 4 o'clock. Maybe it's difficult for me to teach teams how to handle losing because it's not a subject that I handle all that gracefully myself.

When I lose, I've been known to take to my bed.

In 1994, the Lady Vols lost to Louisiana Tech in the first round of the regionals. Afterward, I went to bed. Literally. I crawled underneath the covers and didn't raise my head for two days. I might have brushed my teeth. I don't remember. I was so depressed I didn't realize that it was raining outside, hard, and that the river in back of our house was beginning to rise. A massive storm had hit Knoxville, and there were flash floods all over town. My husband watched the water, worried, as it covered our dock. Then it reached a small gazebo at the foot of our property. Next, it covered the gazebo roof and started to work its way up the hillside. Finally, he came into the bedroom.

"Pat, you've got to get up," he said. "The river's flooding."

I raised my head from the pillow, irritated.

"Well what do you expect *me* to do about it?" I said.

With that, I pulled the covers back over my head.

So that's how I cope with losing.

But late in the afternoon after the Duke loss, I finally roused myself. I took a walk outside and played some ball with Tyler. Then I sat down in a chair and called our players, one by one. This was my message to them: If there was one thing I knew after twenty-five years of coaching, it was that you can't have wins without losses. Nothing improves a team, or a person, more than losing. It forces self-examination, it reveals flaws, and, if you choose to learn from it, it inspires something better.

There are certain inevitabilities in life. You will grow older. You will be forced to compromise in ways you never imagined and confront problems you thought you were immune from. You will find a job, and perhaps lose it. You will have to nurse an ailing parent, fight with your mate, shoulder unwanted responsibilities, and cope with unfairness. You can allow that to demoralize you. Or you can let it shape you into a deeper, stronger person.

> > >

LIFE WENT ON, of course. Some of us went to the women's Final Four in San Jose as spectators. Kellie and Chamique played in a WBCA all-star game for collegiate seniors, which was held during the Final Four before a host of scouts from the WNBA. Kellie badly wanted a chance at playing in the pros, but the ABL had just folded, which meant all of the pro talent from that league would be up for grabs and there would be fewer jobs available for the college seniors. Still, Kellie put on a great performance in the all-star game, caught the eye of the scouts, and earned herself a potential career option.

Chamique won the Sullivan Award, the most prestigious award in the country for collegiate athletes. She was the first female basketball player ever to do so. She also won the Naismith Award for player of the year, and a pair of ESPYs. She prepared herself to be drafted by the WNBA and courted offers from the shoe companies.

Then came draft day. Chamique was the No.1 pick of the Washington Mystics. Her grandmother thought it was the best possible thing for her, and I tended to agree although others didn't. Everybody in the sport was dying to see Chamique play in her hometown, New York. But June felt that in New York, Chamique would be pressured by expectations and pulled in too many directions by friends and family. In Washington, she would be able to start her career more quietly.

We listened to the draft in our office via an Internet feed, hoping to hear Kellie's name called. Three rounds went by and none of the fourteen teams selected her. The fourth and final round started. Still, her name wasn't called. I sat at my desk, listening, and clenched my teeth. I felt sick. Just three teams remained. Then, we heard her name. She was selected in the fourth round by the Cleveland Rockers. Kellie would get a chance to play pro ball. The office erupted into screams of exultation.

And then they graduated. Kellie and Chamique received their diplomas in Thompson-Boling, which had been transformed from a basketball arena into an amphitheater. I snuck down the stairs and stood in the very back of the arena, along with our assistant coaches, and we watched proudly as Kellie and Chamique walked across the stage in the procession. Kellie said, "I bet you were proud to see us sitting in the second row." I laughed. It was a team rule that our players had to sit in the first three rows of their classes. Kellie and Chamique had followed the rules to the end.

The very next day, Kellie married Jon Harper. The whole team drove over to Sparta for the wedding, and Chamique was a bridesmaid. It was a beautiful late spring day, and an emotional one, but I didn't realize just how emotional until it was all over. Finally, Chamique got ready to leave. She had an all-night drive ahead of her to make it to Washington, D.C., by morning, in time for her first practice as a professional.

She said, "Okay, ya'll. I've got to go to Washington now."

It hit me. I had given them each letters on graduation day, and we had shared a lot of talks since our last game. There had been so many types of endings: last home games, final team meetings, draft day, graduation day, and a wedding day. But this was the final departure.

They are with you for four long years. You teach them, shout at them, urge them on, hear their deepest confidences, feed them from your own kitchen, and turn your small son over to them. And then you let them go? How?

I don't know. Truthfully, I'm not sure I ever do let our players go. Like I say, loss is not something I'm especially good at.

They'll never get rid of me.

ACKNOWLEDGMENTS

John Sterling of Broadway Books, Bob Barnett of Williams & Connolly, and Esther Newberg of ICM actually believed us when we told them there might be a book here. What's more, they refrained from laughing when we said we could meet the deadline. John, especially, saw the possibility of an undefeated season back in December. The word "thanks" is hardly an adequate return for their support and clairvoyance.

Luke Dempsey of Broadway personally shepherded the manuscript to publication, and provided humor under duress.

Debby Jennings and Katie Wynn of the Tennessee women's athletics department saved the book from numerous grievous errors, and counseled us wisely.

University of Tennessee president Dr. Joe Johnson and his UT administration, including women's athletics director Joan Cronan, generously supported the project, as did the editors at Condé Nast's *Women's Sports and Fitness*.